THE BANKS

The Ongoing Battle for Control of Canada's Richest Business

Les Whittington

Stoddart

Published in 1999 by Stoddart Publishing Co. Limited
34 Lesmill Road, Toronto, Canada M3B 2T6

Distributed by:
General Distribution Services Ltd.
325 Humber College Blvd., Toronto, Canada M9W 7C3
Tel. (416) 213-1919 Fax (416) 213-1917
Email customer.service@ccmailgw.genpub.com

03 02 01 00 99 1 2 3 4 5

Canadian Cataloguing in Publication Data

Whittington, Les
The banks: the ongoing battle for control of Canada's richest business

Includes index.
ISBN 0-7737-3169-5

1. Bank mergers – Canada. 2. Banks and banking – Canada. I. Title.

HG2704.W45 1999 332.1'0971 C98-933086-9

Jacket Design: Angel Guerra
Text Design: Tannice Goddard
Computer layout: Mary Bowness

Printed and bound in Canada

Stoddart Publishing gratefully acknowledges the Canada Council for the Arts and the Ontario Arts Council for their support of its publishing program.

To Matthew and Margot

CONTENTS

Acknowledgements

I would like to thank the editors of the *Toronto Star* for their cooperation and assistance on this project. I covered financial services for the *Star* throughout the merger affair, and many of the interviews that contributed to this book were done for the newspaper. Thanks also should go to the hundreds of politicians, government officials, advocacy-group leaders, bank customers, and members of the financial-services industry who graciously took the time to help out with this project. If the book works, it is their voices and their knowledge that have, to a great extent, made it work. I wish also to thank Janice Weaver, my editor, for her excellent contribution, and my friend and collaborator Larry Hoffman, of Authors' Marketing Services Ltd., without whom this book might still be just an idea. I should also thank everyone in the *Toronto Star*'s Ottawa bureau, and especially Darlene Newman, for putting up with me during my frequent and not always convenient (or announced) visits to the *Star*'s office in the capital during the course of this story. And special thanks go to my wife, Jane Armstrong, for her help – as both a journalist and a partner – in the preparation of this book.

One

Barking With the Big Dogs

It was five days before Christmas, but there was still little snow as John Cleghorn walked alone up the canyon of office towers on the now-darkened corridor of Bay Street. The 6-foot-2 Cleghorn, in his usual business suit and wire-rimmed glasses, had been chairman of the Royal Bank of Canada, the country's largest, for three years. Now, as he strolled along the sidewalk past the art-deco steel doors of the old Toronto Stock Exchange and the sleek glass façade of the Commerce Court building across the street, the pragmatic, unassuming fifty-six-year-old banker contemplated perhaps the single most dramatic corporate gesture in Canadian history.

A block and a half north of the Royal's gold-tinted skyscraper loomed the headquarters of the Bank of Montreal. The sixty-eight-storey white monolith stood well above the other half-dozen bank buildings whose brash, self-aggrandizing silhouettes had come to dominate the skyline of modern Toronto. On the highest floor, in a blue-carpeted hall where guests could look out past the gold draperies to the CN Tower and the twinkling lights of the city below, hundreds of Bank of Montreal employees chatted and laughed around the punch-bowl at the annual Christmas fête, thrown for everyone in the company by Bank of Montreal chairman Matthew Barrett. Suave, glib, and handsome, Barrett, with his swept-back silver hair and mustache, was as romantic and adventurous as Cleghorn, an accountant and former football lineman, was plodding.

These men, who ran two of the country's largest and most powerful financial institutions, could hardly have been less alike. Cleghorn, in a characteristic gesture, had sold off the Royal's Challenger jet years earlier and was in the habit of driving himself around in his Chrysler LHS sedan or taking the subway to work. The frugal Royal chairman had also moved his office to less ostentatious quarters. Barrett, by contrast, seemed to revel in the trappings of making it big. A native of Ireland, and the son of a dance-band leader, Barrett had started with his current employer as a lowly clerk trainee in London at age eighteen. By the time he was forty-five, he had captured the top job, making him one of the youngest senior bankers in the world. Now he travelled in a chauffeured limousine or executive jet and was a fixture on Toronto's society scene.

While Cleghorn's idea of a great time was a weekend at the cottage in Quebec's Eastern Townships with Pattie, his wife of thirty-four years, Barrett's personal affairs had taken a sharp and controversial turn only a few months earlier. A year after divorcing his wife, he was married to Anne-Marie Sten, a one-time Sunshine Girl and jet-setter, who dazzled Toronto with her see-through evening gowns. It was widely believed that Sten had given Barrett a somewhat changed perspective on life. "When I cash my stock options, you won't be seeing us around here any more," announced Barrett, with his new wife looking on, to the surprised diners at a literary gathering some months after their marriage.

Both bank chairmen earned salaries beyond the imagining of average Canadians. By 1997, Cleghorn was pulling in $3.2 million in annual compensation, but even this was eclipsed by Barrett's take. As the best paid of the country's Big Six bank chairmen, Barrett made $4.2 million that year. In 1998, he made $4.5 million. As for professional prowess, Cleghorn had climbed the ranks of the Royal's executive team with steady, unswerving success and enjoyed widespread respect as a shrewd, if traditional, manager. Barrett, on the other hand, had chiselled out a mercurial reputation as the free-thinking visionary of Canada's financial-services industry – a shatterer of icons who had attracted national attention by using a Bob Dylan song to promote mbanx, his company's experimental electronic-banking division.

Despite their differences, Cleghorn and Barrett were about to be plunged into a shared undertaking that would bind them together in an all-out public struggle for the next twelve months. For as he headed up Bay Street that December evening, the Royal chairman was on his way to invite Barrett to join with him in what would be by far the biggest, and most controversial, corporate merger proposal ever contemplated in Canada – a $40-billion deal meant to create the second-largest bank in North America by asset size. The story of Cleghorn's lonely stroll to the Bank of Montreal that day was appealing in its spontaneity and directness, and was before long to achieve the status of legend.

A little more than a month later, Cleghorn would recount how, with the financial world caught up in an unprecedented merger frenzy that December, he had gathered together his senior managers to discuss possible corporate strategies. After that meeting, Cleghorn recalled, "I said to myself, 'What's to lose if I go and see Matt?' " Later that day, December 19, he telephoned Barrett and, with typical Cleghorn understatement, said he needed a few minutes of the other man's time to talk about Symcor, the two banks' shared back-office document-processing operation. At about 5 p.m., Cleghorn arrived at the Bank of Montreal. As he got out of the elevator on the sixty-eighth floor, he was immediately immersed in the party going on in the large adjoining rooms. Later, Bank of Montreal employees would joke that some had kidded Cleghorn, saying, "Hey, John, couldn't you afford a Christmas party of your own?"

While the employees partied, the two men talked privately in a nearby office. Around Bay Street, what happened next is referred to as the egg-nog agreement. But Cleghorn says there were no drinks and no toasts: "I don't think I even got anything, maybe I got a coffee or something." As Cleghorn recalls the conversation, the subject was broached in a straightforward fashion: "I asked him, 'How would you like to build a globally competitive, Canadian-based financial institution on a merger of equals?' " Barrett would later say it took him a "nano-second" to say yes. The two chairmen talked for twenty minutes in all and agreed to think about it over the holidays and talk again. Then they emerged, making idle chit-chat about the latest movies and so on. It was, by any standards, a stunning moment: the birth of a bold corporate stroke that would soon stun the financial markets, prompt a year-long national debate that touched Canadians of every stripe, and change forever the banks' cosy relations with the people running the country in Ottawa. But was it as spontaneous as it looked? Hardly. Like many later aspects of the drama that unfolded in the months after Barrett and Cleghorn's Christmas chat, the origin of the deal was far different from what it appeared to be to outside observers.

The notion of merging big banks into even bigger financial institutions landed on Canadians like a bombshell when, in January 1998, the Royal and the Bank of Montreal announced their desire to amalgamate. But while this development itself was shocking, the theory behind it was nothing new to the financial community. Although it had been little noticed by Canadians, the country's bankers had, since the mid-1990s, been tentatively speculating about mergers in public. And, for years behind the scenes, they had been busily sizing up possible partners in Canada and the United States. As early as the late 1980s, according to banking legend, Cleghorn, Toronto Dominion Bank chairman Charles Baillie, and Bank of Nova Scotia boss Peter Godsoe were sitting around musing about who would survive if foreign financial institutions were allowed to buy Canadian banks. Only a few of the Canadian operations would last in those circumstances, they had agreed.

Around the same time, Cleghorn said he and Barrett had attended a bankers' convention where they wound up playing doubles tennis against Americans who referred to their Royal and Bank of Montreal opponents as "Team Canada." Cleghorn said that he and Barrett discussed, during the conference, the possibility of sharing back-room banking operations as a cost-saving measure.

But certainly there is no doubt that in December 1997, Barrett and Cleghorn shared the view that mergers were inevitable. As opposed in style and experience as the two men were, they did agree on the challenges faced by today's Canadian financial institutions in a world of immense, rapid change. And as far as Cleghorn was concerned, initiating a merger to create a global banking powerhouse was nothing less than the logical outcome of his entire professional career. Before joining the Royal Bank in 1974, he worked for Citibank, one of the largest in the United States, and its Canadian affiliate, Mercantile Bank. There he drew assignments from New York to Vancouver to Asia and honed the idea that "you're only going to be strong if you're a global player." Not surprisingly, then, the Royal, like many of its competitors, had been discussing possible mergers at the senior management level since 1996. In fact, under Cleghorn's leadership, the bank had for years been quietly looking at the possibility of creating a mega-bank by buying up an American financial player. Deterred by the high prices of U.S. properties, however, the Royal had switched to scouting possible Canadian merger partners, an exercise that had spewed out the Bank of Montreal as the most suitable of the lot. But in the meantime, Cleghorn had turned his attention to expanding the Royal Bank's insurance holdings. Only six months before his overture to the Bank of Montreal, Cleghorn had tried to buy the London Insurance Group, offering $2.5 billion for the insurance franchise that included the venerable London Life. The attempt to flesh out the Royal's insurance capabilities by buying a ready-made sales force ultimately failed when the bank was outbid by Great-West Life Assurance, but it demonstrated Cleghorn's commitment to expanding through acquisitions.

For his part, Barrett was perhaps the best-known proponent of the idea that only through mergers would Canadian banks survive and prosper. Like the Royal, the Bank of Montreal had spent a lot of time and effort trying to pick a possible partner. In fact, it appears that it was Barrett, as much as Cleghorn or anyone else, who led the way in creating the merger fever that transfixed Canada for most of 1998. Certainly Barrett was a key player in the merger discussions in 1996 and 1997.

One of Barrett's overtures was to Canadian Imperial Bank of Commerce chairman Al Flood. Barrett approached his CIBC counterpart in the spring of 1997 about a possible consolidation when both men were attending a meeting in Geneva. The two chairmen met again shortly thereafter to discuss the idea, but Flood told Barrett that "it was too early" to bring about a major bank merger in Canada, and that it was "not politically feasible" yet. In this period, Barrett also talked about a possible consolidation with Bank of Nova Scotia chairman Peter Godsoe to no avail. But Cleghorn is adamant that he and Barrett never discussed a possible corporate merger until December 19, 1997. "Matt and I never had a discussion, period. That's a fact," the Royal chairman said in an interview.

Whatever the origins of the hoped-for amalgamation, Barrett and

was completed. CIBC officials, however, were adamant that such a tacit understanding did indeed exist, and that the Royal and the Bank of Montreal, by pre-empting the process, had created enormous complications for any banks seeking future amalgamations.

Meanwhile, the merger news, at first dismissed as a wild rumour, rumbled through Toronto like an earth tremor. By the time the Royal and the Bank of Montreal convened a news conference at 10 a.m. on January 23, the thick snow that had been falling earlier had given way to a layer of fog, and the two banks' office towers were eerily hidden in thick, grey mist. In a long, oddly formal ballroom in the Royal York Hotel, more than a hundred shocked, bedraggled reporters milled around eating croissants and muffins and drinking coffee from the spread that had been laid out on tables along the back of the room. The press conference that followed was infused with the electric urgency of once-in-a-lifetime events. Cleghorn and Barrett, sitting side-by-side at the front of the room, tried out their explanations for the bombshell that everyone knew would reverberate through Canada's once-sleepy banking industry for years to come. First and foremost, they said, the merger would give the new combined bank (which they had not named) the size and clout to stand up to competition from increasingly massive foreign financial institutions. "We don't plan to be the corner hardware store, waiting for Home Depot to arrive to put us out of business," quipped Barrett in what became the signature remark that day.

The Bank of Montreal chairman handled reporters' questions with the flair of a balloon sculptor captivating a children's party. "It's not five-minute rice to put two big organizations together," he said at one point, explaining that it would take three to five years for the merged companies to achieve the promised 10 percent cost savings from the deal. The two men pledged that the organizations' combined ninety-two thousand employees would be spared the kind of job slashing long associated with bank consolidations in the United States. And they maintained that as the two merged banks became more efficient, customers would see the results in the form of lower banking costs and better service. This claim, of course, was to be greeted with scepticism by the millions of consumers already fed up with the existing service charges and sometimes outrageously bad treatment from this industry.

Cleghorn, for his part, droned on and on in his earnest, rambling manner. In answer to one question about the banks' desire to get bigger, he intoned, "Size matters because it allows us to make necessary investments in technology and to achieve the kind of scale that will make it possible to offer our customers better service and better value." Neither of the chairmen seemed to twig to the irony of two men telling the world that size matters. But the sexual innuendo provoked a national smirk, particularly among women, who were prone to view the entire merger as an exercise in macho corporate one-upmanship.

Not surprisingly, given the immensity of the announcement, the fund of reporters' questions was inexhaustible. Tape recorders ran out of tape long before the press conference was over. Afterwards, photographers crowded around Cleghorn and Barrett. With their strobe lights blazing, the agitated camera people snapped pictures of the two men posing for deal-sealing handshakes. And then, as the pair prepared to leave, reporters besieged them for information on their early morning chat with Paul Martin. But there wasn't much to say. By then, the finance minister, steaming about the way it had all unfolded, had issued a bluntly worded statement that said the government would not even consider approving the merger anytime soon. A decision, Martin said, would await the completion of the study of the financial-services industry that was already under way, and after that, full public and parliamentary consultation. "One might say," the angry-looking finance minister had remarked tersely, "that their actions were somewhat premature."

Two

Upping the Ante

The blockbuster announcement landed on a public whose deeply ingrained dislike of big banks was rivalled only by its hatred of Ottawa politicians. And the merger news came only a few weeks after the annual open season on bankers that accompanies the release of their year-end profit numbers. The previous year, Canadians had just learned, the Big Six enjoyed another record annual performance. With the stock market then roaring ahead, the banks were raking in untold millions through the brokerage houses they had been allowed to buy up in the past decade. Total profits for 1997 by the Big Six – the Royal, the Bank of Montreal, the Canadian Imperial Bank of Commerce, the Bank of Nova Scotia, Toronto Dominion, and the National Bank – hit $7.5 billion (fully 43 percent higher than the $5.2 billion in profits recorded only two years before). The Royal and the Bank of Montreal between them accounted for nearly $3 billion of those 1997 profits. And the press was full of stories about million-dollar bonuses, shortages of Porsches brought on by free-spending brokers, and thousand-dollar, wine-drenched lunches at Bay Street's tony restaurants.

In terms of gross earnings, anyone could see that the banks and their brokerages were among the most profitable corporations in Canada. Understandably, then, Cleghorn and Barrett's explanation that they had to join forces to survive encountered widespread scepticism. It came from the customer still getting 0.5 percent annual interest on a savings account, from rival bank chairmen, from small business people, from Canadian nationalists, from the political Left, and from seasoned economic analysts. Many saw it as a simple power grab. "The banks are symbolic of everything that's wrong in our society," Rosa Dehmel, a Torontonian whose husband worked at the Bank of Montreal, told a *Globe and Mail* reporter. "It's greed gone mad. The loot the banks make is outrageous." Others saw the proposed merger as an outgrowth of Cleghorn's and Barrett's grandiose dreams of global mega-banking. "Consolidation is often aggrandizement of empire," Peter Nicholson, a former banker now at BCE Inc., Canada's largest telecommunications conglomerate, observed in the *Financial Post.* He said there was no proof that size automatically equals success in the financial-services business. But it might be true, he allowed, that in the high-stakes game of global stock underwriting, you need to be very large if you want to "bark with the big dogs."

John Kenneth Galbraith, the economist who wrote so memorably about the causes of the Great Depression of the 1930s, warned that the proposed bank deals were a sign of impending economic disaster. "This is always something that happens in the last stages of a boom," he said in an interview. "One of the past consequences of this has been the first step toward a major recession." In the long run, he said, the current wave of corporate consolidations in North America is likely to weaken both the U.S. and the Canadian economies.

However the proposed Royal–BMO merger stacked up, it was undeniable that the deal, the first of its kind between two Canadian banks in almost forty years, signalled a new era in the Canadian financial-services business. Banking, for all its button-down tradition and stodginess, was in the midst of an upheaval all over the world. Pressured by stunning technological change, uncertain revenue growth in a largely mature business, and aggressive competition for credit-card users and mutual-fund buyers from new financial players, banks had been pairing off in Europe, Asia, and the United States in unprecedented numbers. By 1998, the total value of financial-services mergers in recent years was being counted in the trillions of dollars. In the U.S., a decade of consolidation had reduced the number of banks there to nine thousand from fourteen thousand. And the size of the new players was gigantic. After months of multi-billion-dollar deals joining American conglomerates, New York–based Citicorp and the insurance giant Travelers Group inked the largest corporate marriage to that date. The planned consolidation, valued at $70 billion (U.S.) in stock, would establish a single company with more than 100 million customers in 100 countries.

And financial companies were not the only ones charging onto the world stage to land ever bigger mergers or acquisitions. Americans had also seen a spate of huge consolidations in the telecommunications industry. But there was still shock in May 1998 when Daimler-Benz of Germany, maker of Mercedes cars, announced it was merging with Chrysler for $39 billion (U.S.).

The deals were emblematic of the coming of age of the world-straddling mega-corporation. "What we're seeing now is really the formation of global enterprises," commented Jay Myers, chief economist at the Alliance of Manufacturers and Exporters Canada. "It's unprecedented," chimed in Toronto historian Michael Bliss. He viewed the round of consolidations as a natural outgrowth of the gradual shift to a world-based economy. "Just as you now have, in effect, economic activity almost without barriers on a world basis, so now the mergers are becoming global in scope."

In Canada, the proposed Royal–BMO merger alerted the country to the immensity of the changes under way in an industry that affects almost everyone on a personal level as well as exerting enormous influence on business conditions and the smooth functioning of the economy. The Royal–BMO deal also marked another intense phase in the continuing struggle for survival and dominance in financial services – a battle that had been gathering force for decades and was certain to continue no matter what happened with the banks' mega-deals.

Unlike what had happened in the United States, where government policy resulted in the creation of a mosaic of thousands of local and regional banks, in Canada government policy had led to the establishment of a small number of banking institutions with the wherewithal to dominate the industry. For many years, Canadian governments have nourished this oligopoly by protecting banks from competition. Up until the 1950s, financial services were strictly segregated into four areas, usually described as "the four pillars." These were banking, insurance, stock brokerage, and trust-company activities. And each of the four businesses was barred from the others' areas.

As a result, when Ottawa began in recent decades to dismantle some of the regulatory structures governing financial services, the banks had already been given the chance to build up a position of great strength. They enjoyed both market dominance and financial resources unrivalled in Canada's private sector. They were therefore extremely well-situated to take advantage of revisions to the federal Bank Act, which went a long way to eliminating the "four pillars" concept.

As this unfolded, all of the larger trust companies, with the exception of Canada Trust, were absorbed by the banks. Smaller chartered banks such as Continental, Mercantile, and the Bank of British Columbia were compelled to sell their operations to more powerful competitors. And at the same time, the big banks bought up most of the independently owned brokerage houses, a move that made the major banks the beneficiaries of the stunning profits generated by the death-defying bull market experienced through much of the 1990s. While the banks did force down prices – to the benefit of the consumer – as they expanded into other lines of business, they also reduced customer choice.

In the 1990s, with more and more of these regulatory boundaries being chipped away, Canadians were witnessing a vast restructuring of financial services. The real question was not whether this realignment would continue, but how it would evolve and which companies would come out on top. In its annual study of the industry in the spring of 1998, Dominion Bond Rating Service, the respected rating agency, declared: "DBRS believes that consolidation among Canadian banks and other financial services firms is inevitable. As global financial services consolidation continues, it is inconceivable that Canada, as an open and trade-dependent country, will remain an island isolated from events occurring in the major financial centres of the world."

The winds of change had been picking up speed in Canada for years. The summer before the Barrett–Cleghorn deal was born, the Bank of Nova Scotia had won Ottawa's permission to take over National Trust from former Ontario lieutenant-governor Hal Jackman for $1.25 billion. And long before talk of bank mergers registered on the national radar screen, the insurance industry, once the symbol of prudence and permanence, was experiencing a period of rapid consolidation and realignment. Here, too, the driving forces were historic shifts in business conditions and intensified competition. With the greying of the Canadian population, customers were turning away from traditional insurance products in favour of mutual funds and other investment vehicles. Armed with an array of aggressively marketed products and services, banks, mutual-fund dealers, and direct marketers were capturing large chunks of the insurance industry's traditional business. This, coupled with high industry cost structures and too many companies chasing too few clients, created optimal conditions for a series of mergers and acquisitions among insurers.

By 1998, no one could say with certainty what the financial-services landscape would look like in five years, let alone ten. But there was every likelihood that Canadians would see more consolidations, buy-outs, and strategic innovations in the industry. Companies could not stand still. They would be forced, one way or another, to adjust to the runaway change that new technologies and shifting customer needs had thrust upon them. Looking ahead, the leaders of the financial-services firms knew that success would increasingly depend on their ability to provide a full range of sophisticated, well-priced products. The goal, as Herbert Allison of New York–based Merrill Lynch & Co. explained after his huge investment house bought the last independently owned Canadian brokerage, is "building stronger client relationships everywhere we do business [worldwide]." Put another way, this means going all out to capture a client's business from cradle to grave, including his savings, investments, credit cards, mortgage, retirement savings, and so on. And the competition will be intense. Forget about the august façades, the formalities, and the conservative atmosphere of banking – from now on, it will be just another dog-eat-dog retail business, asserted Richard Kovacevich, one of the most dynamic figures in U.S. business. "Financial services are a bunch of commodity products," he argued. Energetic and hard-driving, the chairman of Norwest Corp. was so busy that he had to be interviewed in a bouncing taxi on the way to La Guardia Airport in New York. "Even if you can differentiate your product, it takes about a week for someone else to copy you, just as it does with clothes, toothpaste, or food." Norwest, which had recently purchased Eaton's credit-card business, already had a foothold in Canada and was soon to have more: Kovacevich ended up running Wells Fargo & Co., the giant

San Francisco–based financial institution, after another mega-merger.

Mindful of the fiercely competitive dynamic now at work in the industry, many believed the Canadian banks, with their size, deep pockets, political influence, and other advantages, were on the verge of expanding their lucrative empires even further. With bankers clamouring for new powers that would allow them to hawk insurance in their branches, insurance companies were no doubt facing new risks. Would they suffer the fate of most of the trust companies and investment houses, and be gobbled up by the banks? Or would insurance giants end up merging with major banks, as was the case with Citicorp and Travelers Insurance in the United States? Or would life-insurance companies find other alliances that would allow them to keep pace with the new behemoths in a sector whose new shape had yet to be imagined?

In the wings lurked other mammoth corporations. These ranged from GE Capital, the financial arm of one of the world's largest companies, to software giants like Microsoft, who were only too aware that financial services was ultimately just an information business. At the final curtain, the winners would be those who managed to survive and expand their control over the richest business in Canada. To them would go a financial bonanza born of profits from the sale of everything from mutual funds to car leases to annuities and mortgages.

How big was the jackpot? Through banks, trust companies, insurers, and brokerages, the industry directly accounts for 5 percent of Canada's entire economic output. In 1997, it held $1.4 trillion in Canadian assets and its revenues reached $155 billion. After-tax Canadian profits totalled $11 billion. As a group, financial-services companies paid a higher proportion of federal taxes than other industries. In 1996, the latest year for which figures were available, taxes from financial services made up nearly one-fifth of all federal corporate taxes collected. In dollar terms, the 1996 total, when taxes paid to other levels of government were added in, was $8.4 billion.

Also on the line were the jobs of one million people employed directly or indirectly in financial services. They were holders of some of the most advanced and well-paid positions in the country. As of late 1997, the average weekly salary in the sector was $801, which is 33 percent above the similar industrial rate of $602.

The outcome of the contest to see which corporate giants end up holding the most levers of this prodigious money machine will be felt in every household. Consumers, stockholders, homeowners, and business people will all have to adjust in some way. Because the stakes are so high, the events surrounding the proposed bank mergers turned into an all-out struggle. It was a saga fought out across the country – both in private and in public – by well-heeled lobbyists, MPs, armies of public-relations people, pollsters, and powerbrokers of every description. Before it was over, the banks had invested tens of millions of dollars and countless hours in the pro-merger campaign. The ferocity of the effort was no surprise, since the personal fortunes and the careers of some of the country's richest, most successful executives were on the line. Many believed men like Cleghorn and Barrett might find themselves searching for other opportunities if the project sputtered out.

But much more than corporate and personal ambition was being played out here. Also entangled in this struggle for business supremacy were conflicting visions of the future of the country and how best to preserve its economic vitality. In a world increasingly dominated by global corporations with little national identity and even less accountability, could Canada's financial institutions, in many ways the economic lifeblood of the country, be kept Canadian? Or would they inevitably fall under the control of foreigners as mega-mergers swept the globe? When questioned about this possibility before a committee of Liberal MPs probing the planned mergers in June 1998, Barrett, in remarks somehow missed by the media covering the parliamentary committee, said, "My answer may surprise you. I don't think it matters – for the consumer of a product – I don't think it matters who owns it. I really don't." Pointing out that he believes in free markets, Barrett added: "For the consumer of financial services, it would probably be better, or at least as good, and probably wouldn't be worse" if Canada's major banks were owned by foreigners. He went on to say, "Now you come to a different public-policy issue for Canada as a whole: Would the head-office jobs [be] more or less likely [to] drift out of Canada into New York? The answer is New York." Pressed to say if that outcome would bother him personally, Barrett hesitated, then finally said no.

It quickly became evident in the months after the two banks dropped their bombshell that getting Canadians to accept mergers that would reduce the already thin ranks of major banks even further would be a monumentally tough sell. As disgruntled Canadian consumers never tired of pointing out, they were already faced with an oligopoly. Only six major banks controlled the vast majority of the nation's banking assets, and for those consumers who wanted to do most of their financial business with one company, signing up at the Royal, TD, CIBC, the Bank of Nova Scotia, the Bank of Montreal, or the National Bank seemed the only realistic alternative. Discontentment over the concentration in banking was rampant even before any talk of mergers. A senior banker told me that public animosity was even deeper than the banks themselves realized. This revelation emerged from secret opinion polling commissioned in 1997 by the Canadian Bankers Association, which was trying to develop a public-relations strategy for improving the banks' image in what was to be a $20-million national publicity campaign. But one senior banker reported that public attitudes towards the banks turned out to be so much worse than expected, that the CBA's strategists had to scrap their plan to develop a communications campaign that would directly address Canadians' concerns about these financial institutions. Talking about the banks' good points was a non-starter, the CBA discovered. Instead, the association decided on an innocuous consumer-education campaign focused on personal finance. Similarly, bankers quietly admitted that the main stumbling block when it came to convincing Canadians of the potential benefits of bank mergers was that the public just did not believe anything the banks said about preserving jobs, lowering service charges, or other issues.

By the spring of 1998, the national flare-up of concern and impassioned debate over the proposed Royal–BMO deal was beginning to fade a bit. But the country was in for another shock. The men who ran the other major banks were secretly plotting their counter-moves. Peter Godsoe, the chairman of Scotiabank, met not long after the Royal–BMO announcement with his counterpart at Toronto Dominion Bank, Charles Baillie. Back in the winter, when the Royal and the Bank of Montreal had declared that they must get bigger to survive, one of the dissenting voices was that of Baillie, who ran the country's fifth-largest bank. Donning a white Stetson at TD's annual meeting in Calgary, Baillie told four hundred shareholders that contrary to the Royal and the Bank of Montreal, his bank saw greater bank size not as a plus but as a liability. "It's going to be more than a year before there will be a ruling [by Ottawa on the Royal–BMO deal], and we see that as a tremendous opportunity for our bank," the tall, professorial Baillie said. "We outperformed all the banks last year, including Bank of Montreal and the Royal. If we can outperform the Royal when we're half [its] size, just think what we can do when we are a quarter of [its] size," he joked. But by then he was already taking part in behind-the-scenes discussions that might have lead to a merger for TD. Baillie and Godsoe appear to have been very close to a deal, but it seems to have fallen apart because neither could agree on who would be the chairman of the combined bank. Scotia-bank denied discussions went that far, but the story has assumed legendary proportions in the financial community. "The joke," said one bank executive, "was that Charlie Baillie would leave his meetings with Godsoe and get in a taxi and go see Al Flood, [the chairman] at CIBC."

It was, in any case, Baillie and Flood who quietly reached a deal of their own three months after the Royal–BMO revelation. The announcement came on Friday, April 17. The $43.3-billion pact between TD and CIBC would create a new bank with ten million customers and assets of $460 billion. In Canada it would be second in size only to the proposed new Royal–BMO combination. Rejecting the word "Toronto" as too local, Baillie and Flood decided the new bank would retain the name CIBC, but would adopt TD's familiar green colour scheme. "On January 23, the competitive landscape changed," Baillie explained at a news conference in a gloomily lit hall in Toronto's SkyDome Hotel. His January 23 reference was to the Royal–BMO announcement, which Baillie said had forced him to re-examine the merger concept out of fear of being left out in the cold. "Our options could be severely limited as other potential partners may have filled in their dance cards," he told reporters.

The second merger plan, which if approved would have meant two superbanks controlling 70 percent of Canada's entire banking assets, brought a renewed chorus of alarm from consumer groups, small business advocates, and political leaders. But Paul Martin reminded Canadians that neither merger would be approved by Ottawa without a full investigation by regulators and extensive public consultation. Prime Minister Jean Chrétien, once a member of the board of TD Bank, expressed his reservations as well. "I think it's very important that Canadian consumers have a choice between different financial institutions," he said during a break in a diplomatic mission to South America. "If not, they will find themselves prisoners of one or two or three organizations. We will see if there is not some other solution. That will take time."

Those left reeling by the announcement of another merger

included executives at the Royal and the Bank of Montreal. They guessed correctly that the TD–CIBC announcement, whether planned this way or not, would make it much tougher for Martin to approve any mergers. And if Ottawa gave the go-ahead to one consolidation, it would likely have to approve both. Either way, by jumping on the merger bandwagon, TD and CIBC appeared to have eliminated the possibility of a new Royal–BMO mega-bank towering above the rest of the pack.

Questions about what Baillie and Flood were up to deepened when, a couple of months later, the TD chairman began saying publicly that bank mergers were not, in fact, in the best interests of consumers and business borrowers. Indeed, the two bankers said earnestly, they had arrived at their deal only because they were forced into it by the Royal and the Bank of Montreal.

For all the unknowns, there was general agreement that the sudden turn of events in the previously predictable, conservative realm of banking had forced Paul Martin into a corner. The millionaire shipping magnate's masterful performance in the Chrétien Cabinet had established him as one of the most accomplished finance ministers of modern times. And now, with Chrétien seemingly near retirement, Martin had a shot at becoming prime minister, the one job he coveted and the one job that had eluded his father, the long-time Liberal standard-bearer and Cabinet minister Paul Martin, Sr. But to reach that pinnacle, the younger Martin had to win his party's leadership when Chrétien finally decided to step down. Martin's ambition made him hostage to a group of people sometimes viewed as non-players on Parliament Hill: the Liberal back-bench MPs. Martin would need their support if he was ever to win a leadership race. And many of these MPs, particularly those from Ontario, were engaged in a personal crusade against the banks, which they regularly characterized as fat, arrogant, and overweening bureaucracies with little regard for the average consumer, small business person, or farmer. In the political equation, the back-benchers' disdain for and suspicion of the big banks took on important significance. At the same time, Martin would not want to bear responsibility for a decision that might one day be seen as the financial equivalent of the scrapping of the Avro Arrow. But would he risk his political dream to help out a few bankers? Where was the upside? Who outside Bay Street would applaud a decision to allow the mergers?

The crunch Martin faced on the merger issue raised other vexing questions. Chief among them was how to open up the financial-services sector to increased competition to improve the options and service available to customers. And how could the government ensure that banks remained Canadian-controlled? Takeovers by foreign conglomerates did not pose a threat because the federal government had no intention of scrapping existing laws that barred non-Canadians from controlling banks. But technology and the easing of banking restrictions were nonetheless making it easier for foreign companies to offer financial services in Canada. And TD, CIBC, the Royal, and the Bank of Montreal argued that these big foreign corporations were creaming off the best lines of business. Eventually, the pro-merger Canadian banks said, this would weaken their operations to the point where they would cease to be a major force in the sector or where the government would have to allow them to enter into alliances with foreign companies to stay healthy.

If that happened, it would mean that prized head-office jobs and tax revenues might end up being transferred to some U.S. cities, these bankers warned. "It was not long ago that Philadelphia and Los Angeles were major financial centres – today they are not," remarked Baillie in a speech to a business audience. He explained how those cities' bank headquarters had been siphoned off to New York City and upstart Charlotte, North Carolina. "The potential for a parallel development in Canada is real – with one important difference,"

Baillie continued. "If Toronto were to decline, another Canadian city would not be the beneficiary. It would be New York or Charlotte. And make no mistake, the gravitational pull of New York is formidable."

Many others dismissed this argument as exaggerated fear-mongering. "I do not believe [that] Canadian banks face a crisis or that foreign competition is about to overrun us," Bank of Nova Scotia chairman Peter Godsoe told a Senate committee. "Canada's domestic banking industry is safe, healthy and strong, competitive, and enjoying record profits."

As the year wore on, the war for the hearts and minds of Canadians mounted. By summer, bank mergers were a constant hum in the background of public life. Hearings, debates, town-hall meetings, media discussions, and noisy demonstrations were being staged ies, polls, petitions, letters to the editor, task-force analyses, pamphlets, tracts, Web sites, commentary, and multi-million-dollar advertising than it had seen on any one issue other than Quebec separatism in years. Some compared it with the 1988 free-trade debate, although it appeared both more immediate (in that almost everyone had a personal stake in banking) and more diffuse (in that, unlike free trade, it lacked the focus automatically conferred on the main issue of a national election campaign).

But the more Canadians learned about it, the more alarmed they became over the prospect of even bigger banks – to the point where the Bank of Montreal's Barrett remarked in a speech in Vancouver: "I hope that I have convinced you that this merger is not a caprice, a whim, not a sinister plot from an Oliver Stone film." The airwaves sizzled with accusations and rejoinders on job losses, branch closings, and bank service fees. The debate pitted rich against poor, city against rural, the political Right against the Left, big business against small business, labour against corporations, nationalists against globalists, banks against insurance companies, politicians against businessmen, and Eastern Canada (as in Bay Street) against the West. It was by turns high-minded and absurd. Stung by Godsoe's very successful anti-merger campaign, Barrett likened the Scotiabank chairman to a flat-earther who believed Elvis is alive. Barrett was himself skewered by actor Mary Walsh of *This Hour Has 22 Minutes*, who confronted him for a cheeky TV interview in her Marg Mega Warrior breastplate outfit, and by *Frank* magazine, which ran a doctored cover photograph of Barrett, Martin, and Cleghorn in bed together. And while the bankers planning the mergers publicly stood together to promote their schemes to the government and the public, there was continual tension and back-stabbing behind the scenes. Not only were people at CIBC and TD secretly taking shots at the Royal and the Bank of Montreal, and vice-versa, but the Royal–BMO team also had to struggle to overcome some much-questioned early strategic decisions.

The whole subject began to take on the bitter currents of high-stakes politics after the report, in November 1998, of a task force of Liberal members of Parliament headed by Toronto MP Tony Ianno. Despite its title, *A Balance of Interests*, the report excoriated the big banks over their treatment of Canadians and said the companies had utterly failed to make their case for mergers. Ianno and company urged Martin to turn the banks down flat. In one memorable statement, Ianno blared at reporters: "Banking is not a right. It is a privilege. We will dictate how this country is governed – not the bank chairmen." In response, TD's Baillie suggested that Ianno was talking like a tyrant. "The only countries in which operating a business is considered to be a privilege – and not a right – are, in fact, totalitarian," the TD chairman shot back.

All this left some Canadians, notably a group of women entrepreneurs, shaking their heads in dismay. "We're fed up with the narrowness of the bank merger debate thus far," declared Barbara Mowat, a small-business owner in Abbotsford, B.C. Saying the discussions were being dominated by politicians and special interests, Mowat and a group of like-minded women decided in November to put on their own public forums on the issue.

By the time 1998 began to wind down, the top bankers had spent many months occupying the unaccustomed and uncomfortable position of centre stage in a national controversy. With the tide of public opinion now running against them, they became almost desperate with frustration and worry. How did this happen? How did these men, the giants of Canada's most straight-laced, conservative industry, arrive at such an untenable juncture? What follows is the story of the long year of public agonizing whose outcome shaped the future of Canada's most lucrative, and perhaps most vital, business.

THREE

BRAVE NEW WORLD

Like many of the trends that have shaped the twentieth century in North America, the high-tech upheaval now unfolding in the financial-services industry can be traced to California. There, in the western coastal state that in the post-war years came to stand for all that was glittering, new, and full of promise, the Bank of America, in 1959, offered consumers their first chance to carry "plastic." This early BankAmericard experiment, in what was in time to become the so-called cashless society, did not go unnoticed, of course, by business people north of the border. But it would take another nine years before Canada's bankers, a deeply conservative group who looked with disdain on consumers' desires, began issuing the first blue, white, and gold Chargex cards to one million valued customers in Montreal, Toronto, and Vancouver. Nonetheless, despite the reluctance of Canadian financial institutions to discard the traditional cash-box approach to their business, the shift to new ways of banking would before long pick up a momentum that has proven unstoppable to this day.

Thanks to an aggressive marketing campaign across Canada in the late 1960s, the slogan "Will That Be Cash or Chargex?" was soon part of the national culture. In just one year, the Royal Bank recorded $50 million in credit-card transactions. And within ten years, as the Baby Boomers came into their own in the new consumer society, credit cards had altered forever the way Canadians did their shopping. While this was happening, bankers in the United States, Japan, Britain, and elsewhere were busy devising the next step: the combination of the personal bank card with the computer. Following up on experiments that stretched back to 1957, Walter Wriston, the visionary chairman of New York–based Citibank, spurred his organization to deploy computerized consumer-banking machines. Some five hundred of them, called CATs, for customer-activated terminals, were unveiled in New York City in the late 1960s. Again, it took some years for Canadian banks to join the rush to what became known as automated-teller machines (ATMs). By 1972, however, the Royal Bank was experimenting with cash-dispensing "bankette" machines in Toronto. It introduced the new contraptions with an advertising blurb that promised "Tomorrow morning at 9 a.m., the Royal Bank will open and never close again." Although it was not until the 1980s that ATMs became common in Canada, the slogan was more accurate than its creators might have suspected. The age of electronic banking had arrived, and there would be no looking back. By the 1990s, Canadians were using sixty million credit cards – or almost three cards for every adult. Transactions were approaching 900 million a year, with a net retail volume of $67 billion.

Today, this revolution that began with the credit card is rushing forward with more speed and fury than ever. Only thirty years after charge cards arrived in Canada, consumers are on the verge of an entirely new type of banking that, for some, will make the once novel and futuristic-seeming ATM machines appear like dusty museum pieces. In only a few years, Canadians will see an explosion in consumer options as credit cards and Internet-based electronic commerce come together in a transformation likely to change banking in ways as yet unimagined. "The next ten years will no doubt bring more changes to the way we bank than we have seen in the previous century," declared Virve Tremblay, director of communications at the Toronto-based high-tech supplier NCR Corporation. C. Rudy Puryear, writing in *Outlook*, a magazine about change published by Andersen Consulting, compared the coming transition from the Industrial Age to the advanced Information Age with a similar upheaval two centuries ago, when the arrival of steam-driven machines put an end to the craftsman's way of life. Addressing business readers, Puryear wrote: "The threats to economic survival [today] are just as real. Every business assumption you've made will be challenged. Every competitive advantage you've enjoyed soon may be obsolete."

Much of this upheaval will focus on the so-called smart card. To understand its potential capabilities, you should imagine dumping out your wallet or purse on the table and then replacing its contents with a single piece of plastic. While little different in appearance from a credit card, the smart card is immensely more powerful. Each card will carry a computer chip that can handle five hundred times more information than the old magnetic stripe card. This makes it a very portable data-storage device with the capability to manage information, authenticate the user, and handle coded information.

What does this mean in practice? Well, let's look at a morning not too many years from now. You get up, dress, and prepare to go to work. But before leaving, you remember you're out of spending money. So you go to your personal computer, which is equipped with the new smart-card reader hardware and with software that hooks you up to your bank through your Internet browser. Through the computer, you download two hundred dollars onto your smart card, money you can spend for your daily purchases of newspapers, lunch, cosmetics, and so forth at stores equipped with special card readers. Then you head for work, hopping on a bus, where you swipe the smart card through a transit-fare reader that deducts the cost of your journey. Later that morning, you have a doctor's appointment. When you arrive at the doctor's reception desk, you hand over the same smart card, which contains your medical history and information on your medical-insurance coverage.

On the way home from work, you stop at the grocery store for a few items. As you check out at the cashier, you decide you'd like sixty dollars in actual cash. So you ask the clerk to ring in an extra sixty dollars under the store's cash-back plan. The sixty dollars is deducted from your smart card along with the cost of your groceries, and you walk out with your purchases and your cash. Later that evening, you decide to update your bank accounts. Once again, you turn on your personal computer, where, using the Web and software designed for your bank, you go over your recent transactions, justify the accounts, and move a few hundred dollars from one account to another. While you're at it, you decide to pay some bills. With a software program offered by your bank, you have dispensed with bills that come in the mail. Instead, they arrive electronically through your bank, and you then look them up on your computer and pay them. Before you log off, you decide to book a flight for an upcoming holiday in Acapulco. On the Internet, you find the appropriate site and purchase your airline ticket. The ticket information is downloaded to your smart card and, along with your frequent-flier miles, stored until you arrive at the airport ticket counter for boarding.

Like all recent high-tech developments, however, the innovations depicted above are emerging in fits and starts. Parts of this vision are already in place, while others may take some years to materialize. By late 1998, for instance, credit-card companies – despite experiments around the world that ate up billions of dollars in investment – had failed to tap into significant consumer interest in the cash-loadable aspects of smart cards. Partly this was because of the ease of use of debit cards, popular with both consumers and the merchants who must purchase the equipment to handle electronic transactions. "Smart cards are a technology chasing a business case," Richard Speer, the chief executive of financial consultants Speer & Associates, told the *New York Times*. In Canada, the major banks struck out after investing heavily in the development of the Mondex smart-card system. Experiments had been mounted in Vancouver and in the Ontario cities of Toronto, Barrie, and Guelph (where the municipality even equipped six hundred parking meters to handle the cards).

Some say this was only a temporary setback in this new electronic-shopping option. In any case, smart-card technology had far greater implications than making it easier for consumers to buy newspapers or access parking meters. The cards were already in wide use in Europe, with one billion in circulation, and they were the subject of experiments all over the world. The Chinese government, for instance, was supporting various smart-card programs, in particular a business-registration plan that issued six hundred thousand cards in its early stages. Spain was set to send out forty million social-security smart cards in 1998, and Malaysia was considering issuing multipurpose smart cards equipped to carry ID, medical records, and a full range of electronic financial transactions. Meanwhile, computer manufacturers were producing smart-card readers for use on home PCs, and Toronto-based Northern Telecom had given new meaning to the phrase "dialling for dollars" by coming up with a telephone that, for about four hundred dollars, would allow you to download cash to your smart card by phone.

As they assessed the setbacks suffered by the new cash-loadable cards in Canada in 1998, proponents could remind themselves of the evolution of direct payment, or debit, cards. Despite a lukewarm early response, Canadians had in time taken to them with a vengeance. In fact, although the cards had been available since the early 1990s, it was only in 1996 that consumers were able to start using them on a widespread basis to pay directly for purchases of groceries, hardware, and other items. In that year, the cards accounted for 73 million transactions in Canada, worth $3.8 billion. Four years later, annual transactions were expected to hit one billion, with a value of more than $30 billion. Total debit-card transactions in Canada are now said by bankers to equal all similar transactions in the United States, which has ten times our population. "It's huge, beyond anyone's expectations," Bank of Montreal spokesman Joe Barbera declared. In the last few years, debit cards have supplanted cheques as a preferred payment method for Canadians. Whether it's convenience or the security of knowing you cannot plunge into debt with a debit card, this form of payment has proven extremely popular here. "Canadians generally love plastic," says Jim Kenney, a bustling, dark-haired marketing expert at Toronto-based Interac, which runs Canada's direct-payment network. Of Canadians, he adds: "They're very big users of credit cards, they're very big users of ATMs, they're already comfortable with the technology."

By the late 1990s, the high-tech revolution was well-advanced. In a little more than fifteen years, for instance, the cost of a microprocessor capable of handling one million instructions per second had dropped from about a thousand dollars to $1.30. By 2006 or so, the cost may be in the range of one-hundredth of a cent. The microprocessor, Bank of Montreal chairman Matthew Barrett pointed out, is at the heart of a revolution that "is now penetrating every aspect of our lives. The family car, for instance, has become a mobile information centre with ten times the computing power of the Apollo spacecraft that took man to the moon and back." As of 1998, Statistics Canada was reporting that the proportion of Canadian households with home computers had reached 36 percent, three times higher than a decade earlier. Some 37 percent of the population were telling pollsters they had used the Internet in the previous three months, and 28 percent said they had access to it in their home. At the same time, Canadian customers could use any one of fourteen thousand bank-operated ATMs in Canada, plus another five thousand run by non-bank businesses. Only Japan was said to offer greater ATM access on a per capita basis. Telephone banking, through which consumers can pay bills, check account balances, and transfer funds between accounts, was also blossoming. In 1995, only one percent of bank transactions were done by telephone. Within three years, this had grown to an estimated 10 percent. As well, the opportunity for customers to bank from home via their PCs was growing rapidly.

"Fifteen years ago, 90 percent of routine banking transactions were conducted in branches; ten years ago, 50 percent were conducted through branches and 50 percent through automated-teller machines," Royal Bank chairman John Cleghorn told the House of Commons finance committee in a meeting under the high ceilings and chandeliers of a conference room on Parliament Hill. "Today, less than 15 percent of transactions are done through our branch network, with more than 85 percent being done electronically, through ATMs or telephone banking." He was taking part in hearings on the contents of a landmark study of the future of financial services. The work, referred to as the MacKay report, after task force chairman Harold MacKay, was delivered to the federal government in September 1998.

Not surprisingly, as electronic banking was exploding in popularity, consumers were witnessing a proliferation of technology offering new ways to access financial services. One of the most fascinating of these experiments was the stand-alone electronic bank. The best known of these was the electronic-banking division of the Bank of Montreal, launched in 1996 with an advertising campaign worth more than $10 million. Called mbanx, the operation offered twenty-four-hour banking, 365 days of the year, through the Internet, by fax, or by telephone. It was on track to sign up its one hundred and fifty thousandth customer about two years after its inception. In another widely watched experiment in 1997, Vancouver City Savings Credit Union sought to capitalize on its reputation for straightforward and respectful customer relations by launching a branchless bank – the Citizens Bank of Canada. Of course, all of the big banks, along with a number of mutual-fund and trust companies, now offer banking by personal computer or the Internet.

Computer banking was not only convenient, Canadians found, but also opened up new choices. You no longer had to walk or drive to a financial institution to deal with a local provider. Now you could pore over the Net to compare services and costs for loans, insurance, credit cards, bank accounts, and mutual funds offered by companies all over the world.

Indeed, it seems impossible to exaggerate the implications of this rapidly evolving technological era. To get an idea of the scope and power of the burgeoning electronic-based global Web, consider the international foreign-exchange market. From $207 billion a day in transactions in 1986, the global foreign-exchange market grew in a decade to more than $1.3 trillion daily. The respected Paris-based Organization for Economic Co-operation and Development (OECD) estimated that Net-based electronic commerce, now called simply e-commerce, would explode to $1 trillion worldwide by 2005 from $26 billion a year in 1998. Suffice to say that, as we look out into the future, very little about banking seems immune to change as a result of the potent combination of new bank products and the Internet.

"What is a bank? That's a really interesting question," muses Libby Gilman, a Toronto lawyer who specializes in financial services. "In many respects, banking is information management, and who is capable of managing information?" she asked in her office overlooking

Bay Street. The answer to her question was obvious: a wide variety of people.

In a paper released in early 1998, IBM outlined the potential impact on banks of Internet commerce (what it calls the network economy) in much blunter terms. "The world's banking and financial services industry is undergoing a revolution as profound as any since the banking system began almost 1,000 years ago," IBM's analysts predicted. "Network technology is democratizing financial markets and precipitating a global contest for customer relationships and brands. . . . It will no longer be feasible to maintain competitive boundaries between industries, financial-service providers, or geographies. Few of the touchstones of the industry's past history will apply."

The paper points out that the number of Internet hosts, which had been about one million in 1992, had reached more than seven million by 1998. This expanding network is fundamentally altering business conditions, and Canada's banks will not be spared, IBM says. "In Canada, the 'Big Six' banks enjoy the huge advantage of a superb distribution system. The Canadian Imperial Bank of Commerce (CIBC), for example, has almost 1,400 branches serving its 6 million customers. But by embracing technology, banks have let the 'genie out of the bottle.' Technology is making the branch system – the banks' biggest advantage – irrelevant. If more customers start buying financial products from the comfort of their homes, a powerful competitor such as ING Direct [the Dutch-based multinational financial conglomerate] benefits because it does not own the bricks and mortar of a branch network and can therefore deliver the same products at a lower cost.

"Technology is a double-edged sword. It has robbed newspaper companies and television networks of the franchises they once enjoyed. It has weakened governments by taking away their ability to control the flow of information. Banks should not expect immunity from unpredictable transformations brought about by technology."

In 1998, experts predicted that by the year 2001, the number of people who will be accustomed to tapping into and using global communications networks will grow from some 100 million to one billion. "A decade from now," Microsoft chairman Bill Gates told *American Banker* magazine in early 1998, "many bank customers will have used computers all their lives. If you ask college students, I bet that almost all of them would want to use the Web for a variety of activities, including their banking. These kids are the closest to what I call 'the Web lifestyle.' They'll use electronic mail, pay bills on-line, file taxes electronically, check the Web for sports, news, weather, investing tips, movie listings, gifts, even order pizza – it will be totally taken for granted, like the telephone, fax machine, or TV today." However, Gates was not among those who argued that banks will be left behind in this new high-tech universe. With their key role in the payments system and in consumer lending via credit cards and mortgages, banks are in a strong position to adapt and thrive, Gates maintained.

Behind the profound reshaping of financial services envisioned by Gates and others is the reduction in costs that new technologies have brought about in communications and information-processing – activities that are fundamental to financial services. E-mail over the Internet is now not only the fastest way to send information, it is also the cheapest (at one-third of one percent of what you pay to send a fax or enlist an overnight courier). "Processing information is right at the core of financial services, and its unit costs have plummeted dramatically," says Bank of Montreal's Barrett. "A consultant told me once that if the car industry had been affected in the same degree, a Lexus would now cost two dollars, travel at the speed of sound, and go for six hundred miles on a gallon of gas."

Electronic transactions also mean much cheaper operating costs for banks. In 1997, a transaction that cost a bank one dollar in a branch cost only 33.8 cents at an ATM, 27.5 cents over the phone, 21.7 cents on a personal computer, and 0.9 cents over the Internet.

When measured against the cost of building and maintaining branches and paying human beings to act as tellers, the electronic operations were an obvious money-maker. No wonder Canada's banks did everything possible to encourage customers to shift to ATMs and telephone banking – including cutting in-branch service to the point where actually getting to see a teller often required a long, painful wait inside the ropes bankers threw up to keep the lines of impatient customers in order.

Some of the trials and tribulations of the consumer may, if anything, get worse as technology evolves. Take, for example, the latest product California-based Chordiant Software proudly displayed at a high-tech fair in New York in late 1998. It was a software program for banks that pulls up a complete profile of a consumer who phones in on the bank's help line. It rates the customer's profitability and assigns the caller a place in the phone waiting list depending on how much money the bank makes off that particular customer. The software also determines what sort of ad the customer hears while waiting for someone to answer the help line.

As for proposed bank mergers, Duff Conacher, the bank gadfly who chairs the Ottawa-based Canadian Community Reinvestment Coalition, said the consolidations would only exacerbate the decline in personal service at banks. "What it will do is push the banks' agenda farther down people's throats," he said. He described the agenda as "You better learn how to push those buttons or you're not going to be able to bank in Canada."

By the late 1990s, it was clear that the very efficiencies that wrought all these changes were posing a stiff challenge for Canada's big financial institutions. The cost of staying abreast of new technological innovation is huge. The MacKay report pointed out that in 1996, the three largest banks in the United States spent \$5 billion (U.S.) on technology, whereas the three biggest in Canada spent only \$1.6 billion

(U.S.). To take another example, Toronto Dominion Bank chairman Charles Baillie notes that in 1997, his bank spent $7 million on technology in its credit-card business. By contrast, MBNA, the mammoth American credit-card distributor, spent $150 million. This mismatch in funding capability may keep Canada's financial institutions from moving to the leading edge of high-tech development, according to the MacKay task force report. Financial-services companies, added the CIBC in an information paper, must learn to compete in the same marketplace as technology companies like Microsoft, Hewlett-Packard, IBM, and Sun Microsystems. "Hewlett-Packard, for example, spends over $3 billion (U.S.) a year on research and development and generates 75 percent of its worldwide revenue from products and services that didn't exist 24 months ago," wrote CIBC. "Similarly, Microsoft spends $2.6 billion annually on research and development." The Royal Bank was also concerned about this challenge. Referring to Royal Bank chairman John Cleghorn, one Royal executive said, in mid-1998, "It's coming up to the worst time of the year for John, when he has to draw up the budget and leave a lot of great high-tech ideas on the cutting-room floor."

In addition, full-service banks have the added cost of maintaining the traditional branches much loved by some customers. The Bank of Montreal's Barrett told MPs studying the MacKay report that this was a prime cause of the decline in profitability of Canadian banks relative to U.S. banks. "Our industry has increasing difficulty in funding the massive investment required by new technologies, compounded by the continuing high costs of maintaining our traditional bricks-and-mortar branch distribution network alongside the new channels," he testified before the Commons finance committee.

Conversely, new entrants into the market, such as ING Direct with its branchless telephone banking, can set up with far less investment and overhead than established players. Some estimates placed the cost of opening an Internet bank in the mid-1990s at between one million and two million dollars (U.S.), about the cost of opening a single branch. This has handed tremendous advantages to so-called non-banks, a category that includes discount brokers, credit-card specialists, software companies, and huge leasings conglomerates. Discussing the trend towards internationally based commerce, Lowell Bryan, a respected analyst with the international consulting firm McKinsey & Co., remarked, "I'm not prophesizing that it will be banks which will lead the globalization of personal financial services. Rather, I believe it will be non-bank financial institutions which will lead the process and, more specifically, American non-bank financial companies."

Among those companies mentioned by Bryan were Fidelity Investments, a mutual-fund company; Charles Schwab Corp., a discount brokerage; Merrill Lynch, a brokerage; MBNA, credit-card distributors; and GE Capital, the financial-services operation owned by General Electric. Speaking of these and other non-banks, Bryan added, "Since they have funded themselves in the capital markets, rather than with deposits, they have avoided state and federal bank regulations and have used innovation to overcome local banks' physical distribution advantages through a wide variety of direct channels based upon using the mail and the telephone in addition to branches."

In addition, the banks face a potentially damaging assault on another front: big Internet players such as Microsoft. These companies are endeavouring to place themselves between the banks and their customers by providing Web sites where consumers can screen financial services and products, Cleghorn explains. These companies, which Barrett labelled "stealth competitors," could, if successful, reduce the role of Canadian financial institutions to that of providers of commodities.

Coupled with shifts in customer preference and increasing global competition, the new trends in technology posed an apparent threat to the continued health of traditional, full-service banks, even those whose profits were so big in the 1996–97 period as to make them seem invulnerable. In the face of these developments, Canada's banks were forced to re-evaluate their businesses from top to bottom. Out of this came a remarkable, far-reaching change in the way bankers viewed their business, as well as a flood of new services, new delivery vehicles, and new products. A day rarely went by when one of the major banks was not unveiling some new entry in the increasingly heated competition for consumers' allegiance, whether it was a financial-services bus that travelled from town to town; a microwave bank with touch-screen technology built into the oven door; mini-banks in post offices; or electronic kiosks located in supermarkets, parking lots, hardware stores, or even in the middle of the hectic, noisy Calgary Stampede grounds. In a speech to Bank of Montreal customers in Calgary in mid-1998, Barrett tried to give his audience an inkling of how profoundly the business was evolving. "Teachers often give schoolchildren a well-known word – cat, tree, or house – and ask them to draw a picture of it. What would happen if Canadians were all asked to take pen in hand and draw a picture of a bank? I strongly suspect we would have a lot of pictures of a two-storey brick or stone building, probably with pillars in front. If the picture were at all realistic, the bank would have a forbidding air, it would face another bank exactly like it across the street, and there would be no parking whatsoever for either of them.

"This is significant. Architecture is a language, and the traditional bank branch is an eloquent sentence in that language. It says, 'Safety first.' It says, 'We've always been here and intend to stay.' It says, 'We expect you to come to us.' And all too often it seems to say, 'In here, it's our way or the highway.' While safety and permanence will remain cherished objectives, much of that old picture is being erased by technology and increased competition," he asserted. "In 2004, where you do business with us will be entirely up to you. And wherever you choose to do it, we will do business your way – the way that suits your business and your circumstances. We are entering a world of unparalleled access to financial services. A world where banking can be done anywhere, anytime, and anyhow." He added, "Five years from now, we will be doing things that are barely imaginable today."

Despite the banks' enormous profits, some observers were convinced that the demands, risks, and above all, the costs of staying on top of new technological developments, constituted a strong argument for mergers. MacKay, who recommended that the federal government scrap the long-standing prohibition against mergers among major banks if the public interest was not jeopardized, told the government and Canadians that the need to adapt to the new world of commerce was urgent. "No country is immune to change," he declared. "The real issue is how well we manage it to our own benefit." And lest there be any doubt about how serious an issue new technology is for Canada's banks, the usually subdued MacKay used a Commons committee hearing to pass on to surprised MPs a remark attributed to an unknown software magnet. In today's world, he declared, "banks are roadkill on the information highway."

FOUR

THE EMPIRE BUILDERS

Dressed in his elegant dark blue suit and blue-and-white polka-dot tie, Matthew Barrett smiled with satisfaction as he strode through the corridors of a downtown Toronto hotel. The Bank of Montreal chairman had spent the previous half-hour captivating a business luncheon audience with a lengthy, complex speech on the purported economic advantages to Canada of bank mergers. As he and his media people turned the corner to wait for an elevator, a bulky, animated woman jumped in front of the banker. In his years at the bank, Barrett had come across plenty of irate, noisy customers. But he wasn't ready for the feisty woman in the red breastplate who accosted him with a microphone and a sidekick holding a video camera on his shoulder. "Size has always been important to me, but not necessarily at banks, if you know what I mean," the woman bellowed. Barrett said nothing. He only stared at her with a half-grin on his face while the other people waiting for the elevator tittered and shuffled their feet. Barrett was being ambushed by comedian Mary Walsh of *This Hour Has 22 Minutes.* Calling herself Marg Mega Warrior, Walsh is famous for dressing up like the TV character Xena the Warrior Princess, to harangue the rich and famous with irreverent interviews.

She held her microphone in Barrett's face and blared, "I have been a loyal customer of the Bank of Montreal for over thirty years now. I've loyally put up with it all. I've paid those 17 to 20 percent interests on my MasterCard and I've steadfastly stood in those endless lines in the peak bank hours, when the one teller who hasn't been downsized is bitterly powdering her nose in the other room. But my loyalty is coming to an end, my darling, because, like you say in your ad, 'The Times They Are a-Changin'.' Oh, Matt, don't make me go down to the main branch and haul out my little bit of savings and take it home and put it under the mattress, okay?" As she finished, Barrett, laughing by now, muttered, "All right. No, no, no." With that, the banker headed into the elevator as Marg and her cameraman dove in after him. Even the loquacious Barrett, when confronted by Marg Mega Warrior, had seemed momentarily speechless. But it turned out there was a good reason for this. When he sat down in a room upstairs for an interview, he was still chuckling about the incident as he lit up a Craven A. Since he was not a regular viewer of *This Hour,* he said, throwing his arms wide in consternation, "I had absolutely no idea who she was."

As Walsh and the other comedians on *This Hour* knew instinctively, the men who run Canada's banks hover just below the surface of the national consciousness – one-dimensional, easily despised figures who spur thoughts of fat cats, foreclosures, and farmers being kicked off their land. The proposed mergers placed the country's bank chairmen squarely in the national spotlight, a development that served to remind Canadians of everything they disliked about big banks and their obscenely well-paid bosses. And in all this, no one seemed to attract the attention of the public like Barrett, with his glib tongue, perfectly tailored suits, gambler's looks, and dazzling younger wife.

In fact, it might be argued that whatever the outcome of the high-stakes merger bids, however much money might be lost and how many careers ruined, the low point for Barrett and the Bank of Montreal actually came deep in the quiet days of summer in 1998. On July 13, the *Globe and Mail* published an article about Barrett that began on the front page and took up most of an entire inside page. Ostensibly a profile looking at Barrett's public role promoting the mergers, the story was really a frothy rehash of cheap shots and salacious gossip about Barrett and his wife, former model Anne-Marie Sten. It featured a wedding photograph of them with Sten in a see-through dress, outside the cathedral where they were married, as well as reprinted covers of *Frank* magazine, the Ottawa rag which was so fixated with the Bank of Montreal chairman that it was running a "Marriage Mileage" meter with an odometer-like dial that counted the days Barrett and Sten stayed hitched. One of the reprinted *Frank* covers showed Sten wearing a fur bikini in a seductive 1970s Sunshine Girl spread from the *Toronto Sun*. The *Globe* article dwelt on *Frank*'s nasty jibes about Barrett's second marriage, repeating, for example, one of the Ottawa magazine's cover headlines: "Can a Banker Change Wives? You Betcha." (This was a take-off on the "Can a Bank Change?" slogan Barrett used in BMO advertising.)

It was such a departure for the staid *Globe and Mail* and such a questionable piece of journalism that senior Toronto editors and writers were still shaking their heads about it months later. At the time, Barrett's would-be merger partner, John Cleghorn, uncharacteristically exploded in outrage. He is said to have denounced the article in a blistering conversation with *Globe* publisher Roger Parkinson. Cleghorn threatened to pull the Royal's advertising from the *Globe*, saying that if he wanted to read the kind of trash contained in the Barrett profile, he would buy *Frank*, but he had no intention of helping the *Globe* sink to that level. Parkinson later revealed that he had indeed heard complaints from the banks about the article. "The general concern was [over] the pictures used from the covers of *Frank* magazine," he said in an interview. Parkinson said he went to see Cleghorn "and talked about our philosophy and editorial policy at the *Globe and Mail*." He maintained that the story itself was a legitimate one, but added, "If I had it to do over again, I would edit it differently."

Barrett himself was by all accounts deeply stung by the *Globe*'s attention to his personal life and by the insulting references to Sten and her reputation as a jet-setter whose former companions included Saudi Arabian arms dealer Adnan Khashoggi. It had been the same with an earlier article full of snide allusions to Sten's sexual appeal in *Toronto Life* magazine. After that piece appeared, *Toronto Life* editor John Macfarlane, no stranger to Barrett, ended up printing an apology. In the *Globe*'s case, Editor-in-Chief William Thorsell said he "scribbled a note" to Barrett afterwards. The note, as Thorsell recalled it, acknowledged "the fact that they were upset about it, but [pointed out that] these things happen in the media."

Of course, Barrett stands for everything that many Canadians love to hate. A millionaire accustomed to travelling in a chauffeured limo, attending the best parties, eating in the top restaurants, and jetting around the world in a private Challenger, he exudes privilege, power, and some would say, Bay Street smugness. He also has a remarkable ability to reel off memorable one-liners. Asked at the press conference announcing the mergers how rival banks would react to the proposed Royal–BMO amalgamation, he never hesitated. "There are memorial services right now," he told a room full of reporters. Later, extemporizing at a literary gathering, he explained how his relationship with his rival chairman at the Royal Bank had changed since the two decided to join forces. "I used to call him that son-of-a-bitch Cleghorn," Barrett said. "Now I call him that son-of-a-bitch John." At hearings in front of the House of Commons finance committee, Barrett was confronted by the late Shaughnessy Cohen, a Liberal MP from Windsor, about the banks' desire to be allowed to lease autos through their branch network. Cohen said that, as a parliamentarian from Windsor, she was a "great friend" of Chrysler, Ford, and General Motors, the U.S.-owned Big Three automakers. If she had to choose between helping the banks or the car companies, Cohen implied, she'd side with the Big Three every time. "I like Americans, too, I really do," Barrett replied.

If Barrett felt at home jousting verbally with elected members, it was only to be expected. For beneath his slick appearance and corporate élan, Barrett considered himself a man of ideas and a public persona of no little importance. His mentor, said to have "created" Barrett, was Dick O'Hagan, the Bank of Montreal's pre-eminent image doctor in the 1980s and 1990s and the press secretary to former prime ministers Pierre Trudeau and Lester Pearson. It is not surprising, then, that Barrett is said by those who know him to have thought seriously about running for office in Canada. While Barrett's glibness did not endear him to everyone – some members of Parliament and the media were particularly put off by what they considered a too polished, too self-centred performance – the bank chairman could reduce a normally restive rubber-chicken luncheon audience to a hushed, transfixed sea of listeners hanging on his every word. He'd even done it with a business group in Toronto – while talking, of all things, about productivity. It was a topic that in the hands of most executives-turned-orators would have had heads bobbing in the audience before the coffee could be passed round. But unlike many executives, Barrett actually takes an acute interest in the content and concepts woven into his speeches and likes to stretch his audience's grasp of a subject. "He's a big idea man," his speech writer, the lion-maned Orde Morton, explained. If anything, Barrett's speeches suffer from the chairman's desire to cram too many ideas into each one.

It is ironic that Barrett, as a supposed fat-cat banker with tens of millions of dollars worth of stock options, is disliked by so many

Canadians, because if there is a twentieth-century Canadian dream, Barrett seems to be living it. In the decades after the Second World War, modern Canada was shaped and energized to an inordinate extent by its immigrants, men and women who often came to this country with little more to live on than their wits, and not only survived but prospered, making Canada richer both economically and culturally in the bargain. One of them was Matthew W. Barrett, born in County Kerry, Ireland, in 1944, the son of a touring Celtic musician and a dance-band leader whose livelihood went up in smoke when music tastes changed. The big-band era expired, Barrett says, "replaced by rock-and-roll, by four unskilled kids – the Beatles." It was a lesson Barrett never forgot. "You can be very good in your professional life, like my father, and the next minute [be] struggling for survival," he told an interviewer years later.

With his high-school education, Barrett got his start at the lowest rung on the ladder, as a trainee at a Bank of Montreal branch in London, then transferred to company headquarters in Montreal to work as a teller in 1967. From there, he worked his way up through the bank's extensive bureaucracy with legendary success until he was spotted as possible leadership material by former Bank of Montreal chairman Bill Mulholland, a Harvard MBA who sent Barrett off to his alma mater's three-month advanced-management program in 1981. That experience contributed to Barrett's awareness that those at the top must think beyond the numbers and the day-to-day analysis. "You've got to try to be a Wayne Gretzky, to be aware of the whole game," Barrett once said. "I'm not striving for functional mediocrity," he quipped another time.

Certainly, Barrett has a prodigious appetite for ideas. He reads one hundred books a year, by his count, and travels the world for sessions with thinkers and business leaders. He is also a great believer in education. "Knowledge is a wonderfully democratic thing," he says. "You can level the playing field, liberate people, inspire them with knowledge." At the Bank of Montreal, he has led the way on employee training and in trying to improve employment equity within the corporation for women, aboriginals, and minorities. In everything he does, Barrett's commitment to come to grips with change, rather than dodge it, seems to shine through. It's clear he felt that Canadians' doubts about his plan to join up with the Royal Bank reflected a head-in-the-sand attitude. "We are living in 1998, but often still thinking in 1988 or 1958," he once griped. At the bank, if there is a knock against Barrett's managerial style, it is that he fails to spend enough time with the bank's rank-and-file employees.

By 1990, at age forty-five, Barrett was chairman of the bank's board, one of the youngest heads of a major bank in the world. By then, his quest for visionary solutions was not just a nice idea. He was beginning to define the concept of edge in this country's business circles. With imagination and guts, he pushed his organization into electronic banking through mbanx (with its strange black-and-white commercials featuring the Bob Dylan song "The Times They Are a-Changin'") and an expansion into the United States market that was one of the main attractions for the suitors at the Royal. He also broke new ground in China, which Barrett correctly identified as the economic giant of the coming century. And he began talking about the need for banks to grow bigger through mergers years before the current wave of bank consolidations registered in the minds of most Canadian business observers.

That was one reason some Bank of Montreal executives dismissed the notion that Barrett's decision to link up with the Royal Bank was somehow connected to his wedding to his second wife. Whether true or not, the theory that his new life with the gorgeous Sten had taken a bit of the edge off Barrett's corporate ambition, and therefore made him more amenable to ceding corporate leadership to someone like Cleghorn, had a fierce attraction on Bay Street. "Although Barrett's core beliefs in the bank, his professional approach to his business, haven't changed, his personal life has been revolutionized," says an associate. "Here's a guy who used to take home work from the office, work till three o'clock in the morning, the only life he had was the bank. Now it's very hard to get him to look at anything very long after hours, apparently. He really is enjoying his new marriage, having some time to himself. He is a romantic at heart, one of those guys who's decided enough is enough." At the new, proposed bank, Barrett was to be co-chairman and head of the executive committee reporting to Cleghorn. Some said Barrett's willingness to take the number-two job was testimony to how much he believed in the importance of the merger. But, although bank officials disputed it, many believed the merger was to be Barrett's way of easing into retirement. It was said on the party circuit at the time that Sten made no secret of her desire to whisk her new husband out of the demanding corporate world. "Have you seen his new wife?" asked one banker who had heard such musings. "How much money can you spend? Barrett walks away with thirty million bucks [roughly the value of his stock options in early 1998] and he's got a young wife. It takes a few years to get this [the merger] through, and then he retires at fifty-five. That's not a bad life."

If there was one executive in Canada whose personal image seemed out of synch with Barrett's, it was Royal chairman John Cleghorn. The first thought that popped into the heads of many people assessing the would-be partners at the top of the new, combined bank was that they qualified as the oddest couple of all time. While the Bank of Montreal boss was a self-made millionaire who exuded style, lived the good life, and had chosen a glamour girl as his second wife, Cleghorn was a plodder, a hard-driving accountant who drove his own Chrysler LHS, lived for weekends at the cottage, and counted his wife of thirty-four years as his closest adviser. If Barrett came across as a riverboat gambler, his counterpart at the Royal was the Boy Scout, peering intently over his wire-rimmed glasses to deliver sincere, never-ending explanations peppered with guy talk. "Bulking up" was a phrase he used at one point to describe the plan to invest a merged bank with $453 billion in assets.

A centre on the McGill University football team that won the national championship in 1960, Cleghorn is a hard-driving, down-to-earth executive who, until the proposed merger, was best known for his no-frills approach to running one of Canada's biggest companies. His sedate, grey-carpeted office on the eighth floor of the Royal Bank tower is a far cry from the palatial penthouse suites occupied by many a chief executive officer. In keeping with his reputation as the economy-class chairman, he scrapped the Royal's chauffeured limousines for his own car or the subway, cut back on subsidized loans for bank executives, and sold off the company's Challenger jet. On most flights, he can be found in the economy seats where, he says, he gets a chance to talk with the kind of people who make up most of the bank's customers. "He's a guy who sometimes takes the subway to work," said an executive who works closely with banks in Toronto. "I can't imagine Matt [Barrett] taking the subway to work."

The everyman image, beguiling and unexpected as it is for a bank chairman, has become something of a stock-in-trade for Cleghorn. Seldom do you see an article about him that is not adorned with sumptuous photographs of Cleghorn and Pattie tending the flowers at their twenty-hectare spread in the Eastern Townships of Quebec; Cleghorn and his dogs beside an idyllic stream; Cleghorn in jeans and boots with his weed-whacker – you get the idea. But it works because it is the real John Cleghorn, a Bachelor of Commerce grad who, when referred to as a robber baron by a provocative TV interviewer, could only stare back, appalled. "Actually," he replied, "I'm an accountant."

When it comes to banking, Cleghorn is enthusiastic to a fault. Showing off the Royal's vast new $50-million trading floor, with its hundreds of traders and investment dealers, he is like a kid in a toy emporium. "This is a powerhouse, world-class," he brags. Without this kind of commercial prowess, no bank will survive in today's fiercely competitive global market, he contends. His humour, while running to the Kiwanis luncheon brand of laughs, seems omnipresent. On the week Cleghorn announced his merger plans with Barrett, the Royal boss relished telling everyone how he once lost his own bank card while using a Bank of Montreal automated-teller machine. Then there's the old standby about how Cleghorn had to show Finance Minister Paul Martin, a fellow cottager in Quebec, how to use an ATM card. (Although they know each other, Cleghorn and Martin are not close friends. Both belong to the Knowlton Golf Club, but they have never played together. Cleghorn said this is because he doesn't like to lose. "Paul is an excellent golfer – I'm pathetic," he told *Report on Business* magazine. "He got a hole-in-one last year. He gives me enough abuse, I don't need that on the golf course.")

Cleghorn and his wife live in Rosedale, Toronto's oasis of peace and quiet and lush beauty for the rich, but their real love is the country and their cottage. If you get Pattie talking about mergers, she bubbles over with frustration at the highly sceptical reception the idea got from members of Parliament and the public. It's Cleghorn who has to keep intruding in his good-natured way to remind her that in Canada mergers are not a given, that it's up to the banks to prove their case to the public, and so on. While Cleghorn may seem easy-going, few who know him mistake the depths of his steamroller-like drive. No one had high hopes, for example, for a McGill University fundraising campaign Cleghorn spearheaded in the early 1990s, especially given the troubled political outlook and spotty economic climate in Quebec. But by 1996, Cleghorn helped bring in $205 million, making it one of the most successful campaigns ever for a Canadian school. In judging the man, it might also be easy to miss the intensity beneath the regular-guy façade. Acquaintances talk about his wide range of interests, in particular his love of history and music. He has spent hours, for instance, listening to the soundtrack from Ken Burns's acclaimed documentary on the U.S. Civil War, says a friend. The Royal chairman has also devoted considerable energy to the Special Olympics. And he is the type of man who is determined to always be prepared. One of his favourite expressions seems to be "I like to try to anticipate the blowtorch rather than backing into it."

In the context of Cleghorn's whole career, his plunge into the shark pool of merger politics was not a surprise. In fact, it seems preordained. After graduating from McGill in 1962, the 220-pound, 6-foot-2 Cleghorn turned down a chance to play for the Toronto Argonauts and went to Clarkson Gordon to become a chartered accountant. But the lure of the wider world soon pulled him in other directions. "I never wanted to work for a bank, but I did want to work at something international," he once said. After working briefly as a futures trader for St. Lawrence Sugar, he went in 1965 to Mercantile Bank, which Citibank had recently bought from a company in the Netherlands. At Mercantile, which lacked the rigid hierarchies of Canada's big bureaucratic financial institutions, Cleghorn moved quickly upward. He drew assignments in places ranging from New York to Vancouver to Asia. At twenty-eight, he became Winnipeg branch manager, and was appointed western regional vice-president a few years later. In 1974, he returned to the Royal, taking a 10 percent pay cut to gain a spot in the project-financing department. Within twelve years, he was the bank's president, but the desire to play on the international stage never left him. As he moved up through the bank, he devoted a good deal of his energy to trying to search out U.S. merger partners. But such an acquisition never made sense financially. This was one of the big attractions to the Royal of a partnership with the Bank of Montreal, which already has a presence south of the border through Chicago-based Harris Bank. Cleghorn left no doubt that his aim was to turn the Royal into a North American player in the increasingly lucrative area of wealth management. "It goes back a long way," he said of his expansionary ideas during an interview in the clubby confines of the Royal's Toronto headquarters. More than ever, he said, he is convinced that international expansion is the key to a bank's strength.

Looking at the lives of Cleghorn and Barrett drives home the fact that while Canada's bankers still wear blue pinstripes, only individuals with strong, independent personalities are likely to emerge on top in a scramble for corporate ascendancy involving tens of thousands of other ambitious climbers. Anyone who still doubts that there is a lot more to the bank bosses than meets the eye should make the acquaintance of Charlie Baillie, the fifty-eight-year-old chairman of the Toronto Dominion Bank. While in the first months of 1998 Barrett and Cleghorn were grabbing national attention trumpeting their merger plans on the national stage, Baillie was quietly plotting what may have been the most Machiavellian move in the entire bank merger drama.

A white-haired, scholarly Harvard MBA who enjoys bird-watching and collects silver snuff-boxes, Baillie seems a far cry from the gung-ho, self-aggrandizing corporate merger artists driving the consolidation wave in international banking. In fact, when Cleghorn and Barrett had revealed their plans to join forces in January, Baillie drew attention across Canada by declaring there's no proof that bigger banks are better banks. In March, when Peter Gzowski wanted to stage a discussion of bank mergers for his CBC-TV program, it was Baillie who was invited to sit in as a foil for Cleghorn, the banker who was there to sell Gzowski on the merits of even bigger banks. But the program, which featured the three men relaxing around a coffee table in a cosy University of Toronto sitting room, took a curious turn. Right off the bat, Baillie told Gzowski, "I'm not saying we shouldn't allow mergers at this point in time."

No one in that room except Baillie knew that the TD chairman, despite his recently expressed scepticism about the need for bank mergers, was deeply engaged in behind-the-scenes merger talks of his own with Al Flood, the respected but somewhat dry chairman of CIBC. The two men, meeting regularly over an antique oak breakfast table in Flood's kitchen in suburban Toronto to avoid being seen by other bankers at Baillie's house in Rosedale, hammered out an agreement to merge their institutions. As it turned out, Baillie had announced the planned TD–CIBC merger long before the Gzowski program aired in May. Not only that, but Baillie, head of the country's fifth-largest bank, would under the terms of the merger agreement have wound up as the second most important bank chief in the country. "It's a huge coup for Baillie," one senior bank executive concluded when the deal was announced in April 1998.

The chairman's position in the would-be TD–CIBC combined bank was the reward Baillie was given for doing the deal. But the proposed merger was more than just a personal triumph for Baillie. It was widely seen as a political masterstroke that would have allowed TD and CIBC to regain the high ground in the battle for strategic advantage and market share in the fast-changing financial-services industry. There was also speculation – and this extended to the level of the federal Cabinet – that Baillie and his CIBC allies' intention was to scupper the Royal–BMO merger plan. That seems unlikely, but there is no doubt that the second merger greatly complicated the federal government's options. For his part, Baillie simply said the first planned merger changed the chess board and made it too risky for TD to go it alone.

Those who knew Baillie ought not have been surprised by his apparent about-face on the merger question. In fact, this was a vintage performance by Baillie, who is nothing if not unpredictable. Take holidays, for example. Rather than the average stint at the beach, Baillie and his wife, Marilyn – a niece of former governor-general Roland Michener and a successful author of children's books – prefer exotic travel. They have spent time in the wilds of Kenya, Botswana, and

Zimbabwe, a well as in the Andes and Papua New Guinea for bird-watching. And Baillie, an avid history buff who often surprises others with his impromptu remarks on Greek mythology or obscure events from Canada's past, doesn't just go out and buy some old magazines to amplify his interests. He recently purchased a copy of every issue ever printed of the British humour magazine *Punch.* He says this allows him to compare the contemporary treatment of an incident with descriptions in more recent histories.

In a world of exuberant, image-conscious corporate powerhouses, Charles Baillie – art lover, historian, theatre buff, country music fan, and soft-spoken thinker – seemed easily underestimated. "He was never a very flamboyant guy," recalled Catherine Swift, president of the Canadian Federation of Independent Business, who worked at TD some years ago. But Baillie is by most accounts one of the most astute executives ever to stroll down Bay Street. He first joined the bank in 1964, fresh from Harvard. It seemed a good fit. Baillie's grandfather had been an executive at the Dominion bank, which became part of TD in a 1955 merger. For fifteen years, Baillie had worked his way towards the top in an organization then dominated by chairman Dick Thomson, another Harvard MBA. In 1979, Baillie was appointed vice-president of the bank's U.S. division.

During the next few years, he pioneered TD's specialization in areas such as cable TV. These activities led to a ten-fold increase in the bank's American loans and made TD a recognized player in communications industries. In 1984, he was brought back to head office in Toronto to help build up the bank's increasingly important investment-banking group. Named president of TD in 1995, he added the title of chief executive officer in 1997 and took over as chairman in early 1998. "He had the support of the board and top management group here because he'd produced strong results in two major previous assignments," Thomson said. "The two major assignments, going back earlier in his career, were to start our U.S. corporate banking operations and . . . build our investment bank, and both of those were done brilliantly." Baillie seemed the perfect choice to lead TD, a company that could be described as "the thinking man's bank." A lean-and-mean operation, it stands alone among Canada's major banks in that it has survived not on corporate heft but on its shrewdness. In 1996, for instance, TD made more money than six of the largest ten banks in the world. And the bank's astute dive into discount brokerage – it now ranks as the biggest operator in Canada and one of the biggest in the world – paid dividends.

Although his pay packet ranges into the millions of dollars annually, Baillie eschews the trappings of showy wealth and corporate superstardom. Like Cleghorn, he sold his bank's jet, travels without an entourage, and is said by aides to seem a bit out of place in his tennis-court-sized sanctum in the TD tower in the heart of Toronto's financial district. And in what is perhaps even more strange for an individualist like Baillie, nothing in his office – not even the flower arrangements – can be altered. That was part of the contract agreed to when American architect Mies van der Rohe designed the eleventh-floor executive suite. For people used to the usual corporate go-getter, Baillie's thoughtful, unhurried, and straightforward demeanour can be unsettling. "With Charlie," said Christopher Newton, artistic director of the Shaw Festival in Niagara-on-the-Lake, Ontario, "you think that he's drifting, but he's not at all. He's taking in things in a slightly different way." The festival counts Baillie among its board of governors.

Ignoring the pressure from today's media for packagable sound bites and bland generalities, Baillie says what's on his mind. For instance, in February 1998, in a stunning departure from the usual politically correct pap, Baillie delivered an attempted wake-up call to Canadians about Quebec. Appearing at the Canadian Club in Montreal, he declared that his fellow countrymen were too worn out and afraid to challenge the separatist political line in the province. "I believe many of us have become hostage to a pervasive feeling that we must shy away from reality," he declared. "That calling it as we see it is impolite. That it is better, perhaps, simply to be quiet and go about our business. I apologize for being so blunt. But I am appalled by the self-censorship that has seeped into this debate. Too many, I believe, are willing to leave unchallenged the emotions and prejudices and fairy tales that are disguised as received truths [in Quebec]." Complacency or defeatism will never save Canada from being sundered by the separatists, he said. "I am a citizen of Canada, and if there is one thing that should pre-occupy a citizen, it is the future of his or her country. . . . The stark reality is clear. Canada did not exist at the beginning of the last century. There is no guarantee that we shall exist beyond the beginning of the next."

Baillie was no less blunt, or so it seemed, on the motivations behind TD's decision to seek a merger with CIBC. In a revelation that raised eyebrows throughout the financial community, Baillie said that consumers and business borrowers would be better off without bank mergers – but that change is making bank consolidations inevitable. "If we could go back to the way we were, then we don't need to consolidate," Baillie said in his laconic way as he and a number of journalists from the *Toronto Star* gathered for a chat in a boardroom looking out over the Toronto harbour. "We've got more consumer choice and corporate choice if we leave it the way it is, but I think it's too late for that."

Baillie, who visited the *Star* with CIBC chairman Al Flood, said the planned merger was set in motion by the Royal–BMO decision to go ahead with marriage plans before the landmark review of the financial-services industry was completed. "We wouldn't be here if the other announcement hadn't taken place," Baillie remarked in an allusion to the Royal–BMO deal. "They did the wrong thing, if it's the wrong thing, and they came in with their approach." That's what caused TD and CIBC to advance their plans to join forces, he explained. "We looked at it and said, 'Ideally, we could wait in the weeds and let them take the political heat and morale-management problems, and so on.' " But he said this would have complicated matters for the Ottawa officials who would have had to rule on the first announced merger without knowing another one was in the works.

The line that TD and CIBC had no option but to pursue a deal in the wake of the Royal–BMO agreement, was one Canadians would hear repeatedly as the merger debate deepened throughout 1998. This drove executives at the other pro-merger banks, who were trying to sell consolidations as a winning hand all around, to distraction. Said one executive about the actions of TD and CIBC, "I can't tell if they're getting married because they're in love or because their friends are getting married."

Baillie always got along well with Peter Godsoe, his rival at the Bank of Nova Scotia, but that friendship was certainly tested by Godsoe's all-out public campaign to sink the two proposed mergers.

No one was more a part of the establishment than Godsoe. He is the son of one of C. D. Howe's famous Second World War dollar-a-year men and can remember watching baseball with Lester Pearson in Ottawa in the 1940s. A graduate of the University of Toronto and Harvard's MBA program, he plays cards with the likes of Gerry Schwartz, the Liberal bagman and millionaire chairman of Onex Corp.; University of Toronto president Rob Prichard; and David MacNaughton, one of the country's best-connected lobbyists. His rise to the top at the Bank of Nova Scotia, where he started as a teller in Ottawa in 1966, was traditional but impressive, and until 1998 his pronouncements on the challenges facing Canada's banks echoed almost word for word those of his fellow bank bosses. Yet, in a move that kept Canada's financial community awash in speculation about his motives, Godsoe emerged as the pre-eminent foe of the merger strategies of his colleagues at Canada's other four biggest banks.

Godsoe at sixty is easy-going and open, with a self-deprecating wit. "I'm a failed mathematician and a failed accountant, but I became a banker," he once said. He reads voraciously – "mostly mysteries" – and is a seasoned world traveller who logged hundreds of days a year on the road when he helped run Scotiabank's international operations. His corporation's traditional business interest in the Caribbean has rubbed off on Godsoe and his family. "We go to Nassau at Christmas en famille," he disclosed. "We've been going there for years because of the bank. There's not much of the Caribbean we haven't seen." He also collects art, plays tennis, and enjoys cross-country skiing.

Strangely, despite his success in the corporate world, it is not always easy to figure out what Godsoe's talking about. His staccato delivery can be compared only with a comedian imitating George Bush: "One of the major problems of the mega-mergers is you're basically losing one-third of the banking system, the type of banking system we Canadians have had – and it was part of our country for close to one hundred years. We're destroying it overnight if we allow the mergers, and you say, 'What are the benefits?' Hard to find." Commenting on the implications of allowing mergers, he said, "It's not a small step forward, and you can wait and see proof. You've done it, boom, you've lost a third of your banking system, boom. ..."

To add to the confusion, Scotiabank has been, and continues to be, deeply interested in the merger game. "With or without mergers, we definitely want more organizational flexibility," Godsoe, in his gold-rimmed glasses and monogrammed blue shirt, said during an interview in a wood-panelled meeting room on the seventh floor of the bank's headquarters. "We have and we will [consider alliances with U.S. companies]," he added. "I think you're going to see more of that. You see it in the airline industry. Why is banking any different?" Godsoe also clearly thinks that the circumstances that determine a corporation's strategy can shift overnight. "The world is constantly moving," he said. "Anybody who says they can foresee what it's going to be five years out or ten years out – I don't know where they're from." In a reference to Microsoft's failure to see the full potential of the World Wide Web, he added, "We're in a world where Microsoft and Bill Gates missed the Internet four years ago."

Godsoe's critics can be forgiven for thinking that his opposition to mergers arises from the fact that Scotiabank was the only one of the five biggest banks not picked as a partner. This is borne out by any search of the records, which shows that not long ago the Scotiabank chairman was as vocal as any other banker about the business trends that were prompting talk of mergers. In 1996, at a time when the federal government had just denied banks the right to expand into auto leasing or to sell insurance through their branches, Godsoe gave an interview to the *Globe and Mail.* In it, using language that the pro-merger banks would adopt to justify their actions two years later, the Scotiabank chairman depicted a banking landscape so fiercely competitive that Canada's banks would survive only if they were allowed to throw off the chains of government regulation. "Is my competitor ten years from now Microsoft or Royal Bank?" he asked. "I can't honestly tell you. I can tell you that I don't discount Microsoft, and I sure as hell don't discount Fidelity." Fidelity Investments, one of the world's biggest mutual-fund companies, was moving into Canada in a major way at the time. "Fidelity is a giant, T. Rowe Price is a giant, and they are coming here. They just view it as California North, and they're going right after our savings."

Scotiabank's role in the acquisitions game was not just rhetorical. In 1994, it bought Montreal Trust. Then, in 1997, after three years of secret talks with former Ontario lieutenant-governor Hal Jackman, Godsoe added National Trust to Scotiabank's stable. In August 1997, when Ottawa approved the National Trust takeover, Godsoe told the *Toronto Star* that "he was glad to have it over with," and he observed that federal regulators had been relatively quick to approve the deal. Ironically, Godsoe cited his own bank's need to cut jobs at Montreal

Trust and National Trust to support his contention that the executives of the Royal, the Bank of Montreal, CIBC, and TD could not be believed when they said their mergers would not lead to mass lay-offs. Referring to Montreal Trust, which had three thousand employees when it was purchased by Scotiabank in 1994, Godsoe said, "Three years later, 25 percent of the jobs were permanently gone." He added, "I'm not saying that with pride. I'm just saying that's a fact." With National Trust, he said, Scotiabank was, by mid-1998, moving to eliminate two-thirds of the trust company's 175 branches. Without revealing the slightest hint that he understood the irony of what he was saying, Godsoe told the *Toronto Star*'s editorial board that Royal–BMO and TD–CIBC would find it "virtually impossible" to merge without cutting jobs, no matter what they promised.

Godsoe claimed he opposed the two mega-mergers on the grounds that they would be anti-competitive and bad for Canadians. But many believed that there was a lot more to it than that, and that it was, as they say, personal. In the wake of the Royal–BMO announcement in January 1998, Godsoe and Baillie entered into merger discussions but, according to senior bankers, were unable to agree on who would end up with the top job. That's interesting in light of the fact that Baillie did eventually land the promise of the top job at the proposed CIBC–TD bank, announced some weeks later. It is also fascinating, given how things played out, to pore over the 1996 *Globe and Mail* story in which Godsoe says that a decade ago, Cleghorn, Baillie, and he discussed how many Canadian banks would survive if the 10 percent rule blocking foreign takeovers was ever lifted by the government. The three men, Godsoe says, agreed that only two or three Canadian banks would be left standing. "I sort of had the idea they were telling me informally I was going to be working for them," Godsoe told the *Globe*.

Godsoe has expressed considerable anger and frustration at the verbal slights he has taken from the media and his colleagues as a result of his opposition to mega-deals (one columnist even labelled him "dead man walking"). "As it is, I'm going to get attacked personally," he said. "What am I, the odd man out? Canada's loneliest banker?" Despite criticism of his position from other banks, he persisted because "there's a lot of fear out there. Nobody else in big business will speak against this – they can't." When it comes to the pro-merger banks' argument that consolidations are needed so Canadian banks can compete domestically against increasing foreign competition, Godsoe seems to have changed his tune from the days when he raised the spectre of giant U.S. financial operations targeting Canada. Of Canadian banks, he now says, "It's hard to feel sorry for us in our country, with the amount of money we make." Already, he says, "Canadians think banks are too big, too concentrated, and [have] too much power in Toronto." And of Paul Martin's handling of the merger proposals, Godsoe asserted in mid-1998 that the finance minister "should have said no at the outset."

Of all the critics who accused the pro-merger banks of a blatant grab for more market power at the expense of average Canadians, Godsoe was seen almost universally as the most effective at rallying opposition. That makes it all the more curious to consider that as recently as early 1997, Godsoe was telling his shareholders that bank-bashing "is a blood-sport in this country," a practice so pronounced that it has undercut Canada's ability to establish an enlightened public policy towards its financial institutions.

That was a thought that would have been thoroughly endorsed by Al Flood, the CIBC chairman. Although a traditional banker with a subdued corporate demeanour, Flood was said to be a passionate Canadian nationalist. At the height of the merger debate, his frustration over the tendency of parliamentarians to take the side of Canadians working for American-owned companies at the expense of Canada's banks appeared to get the better of him. On a strictly commercial basis, it doesn't matter who owns the banks in this country, he told the Senate banking committee. But in an unusual public display of emotion, he added, "Personally, I'm still a Canadian." He said bank policy must treat the bank-ownership issue in a nationalistic way. "I think we have to be Canadians."

Then he told the senators that his bank's merger plan was intended to establish a strong, domestically owned bank capable of competing in the global market. "Let's look at Canada as a country and make it competitive, and the way we are going to make it competitive is [to] make it more productive," Flood went on. No other country, he said, is going to look after Canada's interests. Flood noted that foreign-owned insurance companies and American-owned car companies are opposed to the expansion of bank powers here. "I'm always amused when I hear that we're upsetting the foreign insurance companies or we're upsetting the foreign automobile companies on leasing powers. When I go to Washington or I go to London or I go to Tokyo or Frankfurt, nobody gives a damn about the Canadians, I can tell you that." He continued angrily, "They worry about the Germans, the Japanese, the Americans, the French, and they look after them. Why don't we look after Canadians?"

It was a rare outburst from Flood, a down-to-earth individual who normally eschews hyperbole and flowery language in his public utterances, and the emotional explosion left the senators a bit stunned. Sen. Colin Kenny, a Liberal, told Flood he should run for office. A keen student of public issues, Flood helped spark the national debate on government overspending with a 1995 speech in which he termed the federal deficit a "fiscal cancer." He also spoke out on youth unemployment.

Flood is from the old school. He began his career at sixteen, earning twenty-five dollars a week as a teller in the farm town of Monkton, Ontario, in a branch where they kept a gun under the counter. Computer banking was not on the agenda. "When I joined the bank, I was criticized for poor penmanship," Flood was quoted as saying in *Canadian Business* magazine. "Today, I don't think anybody would worry about that." From there, he worked his way to the top, one rung at a time, exactly the way successful Canadian bankers did for most of the last one hundred years. He is a dapper, meticulous man, so much so that he gets his hair cut by the same barber every three weeks like clockwork. When not working, he devotes himself to sports – he especially enjoys watching baseball and the National Football League – and community activities, especially charitable activities. Now sixty-three years old, he has planned for some time to retire in 1999.

Flood has only a grade ten education, though he did do a stint at Harvard's management-development program. But he is said to have an ability to digest statistics that leaves observers amazed. For a man who might seem a bit dry, he exhibits a fine, understated sense of humour. "One could argue that the branch of the future should have a full-service broker, should have an insurance agent or broker, should have a personal banker, should have a full-service banker," he told journalists during the height of the gruelling merger debate. "Isn't that the way you were going already with the ending of the four pillars?" Flood was asked provocatively. "Well, it's moving there," he replied. Then he added, "But there's been a little bit of blockage along the way. You know, there's been the odd obstacle thrown up in there."

Being cast in the mould of the traditional banker has not prevented Flood from recognizing and grasping the tremendous forces of change that have turned bankers into futurists. As far back as 1996, he was drawing the public's attention to the technological and competitive trends that a few years later sparked the global merger craze. "Economic forces have been unleashed that are unlike any we've seen before in human history," he told CIBC shareholders that year. "Their impact will likely be as profound as the impact of the Industrial Revolution. No individual, no business is immune."

And he has continued to draw links between what he sees as the need to adjust to change and Canada's ability to prosper in the Information Age. "Technology, knowledgeable people, and productivity are the key prerequisites for any successful economy in the twenty-first century," he said recently. "One major task ahead is to find a way to ensure that our financial-services industry can make the maximum contribution to enhancing these three prerequisites." Flood maintained, of course, that the best way to do this was to allow mergers that would give financial institutions the investment clout to keep Canadian banks competitive with increasingly bigger banks elsewhere. Canadians, Flood stated in a comment that remains germane even after Martin's decision to disallow bank mergers, must make some choices about their industrial policy and their future. "I don't think it would be either good public policy or good business to place all our faith for future growth in natural resources or manufacturing," he said. "Financial services is a logical choice" to maximize this country's capabilities in knowledge-based businesses, Flood added. "If Canada does not produce at least some first-tier players from this knowledge industry, then my question is, where will they come from?"

Apart from Godsoe, then, these were the empire builders who sought, through corporate consolidation, to enlarge their hold on their businesses and their market. Were their strategies appropriate for Canada? Did the privilege and arrogance sometimes exuded by these millionaire bosses make them the least likely salesmen for their dream? Or were they just too far ahead of the public's understanding of the economics of banking and the epochal shifts under way in business around the globe?

FIVE

REAL MEN MERGE AND BARBEQUE

On a rainy February day in 1998, Lance Haver, a forty-two-year-old American who grew up in the activist tradition of Ralph Nader, stood in the gleaming headquarters of CoreStates Financial Corp. in downtown Philadelphia. Haver, dressed in a black sweatshirt with the slogan "Consumer Power" printed on the chest, was surrounded by a small group of bank customers and local politicians. As he spoke on behalf of the protesters, Haver's voice echoed angrily through the mall-like bank office. "Don't put your money in a bank that hurts you. Don't support a business that will close down your neighborhood and refuse to invest in the very people who live in this city." His tone carried the anguish of many of his fellow citizens as they watched a banking tradition that began in Philadelphia in the era of Ben Franklin and Thomas Jefferson disappear in the merger craze that was sweeping through the financial-services industry.

CoreStates Financial, which called itself the oldest bank in the

U.S., had the unhappy distinction of being the last major bank with its headquarters in Philadelphia. Now it was about to be snatched up by Edward E. Crutchfield, the most aggressive acquisitor among the many buy-out artists rampaging across the United States like so many power-hungry Monopoly players. A no-nonsense businessman who looks very much at home sitting in a rocking chair on a porch in the North Carolina countryside, Crutchfield had earned the nickname Fast Eddie by leading Charlotte-based First Union Corp. on one of the most legendary corporate buying sprees of modern times.

After taking over in 1984 as chief executive officer of what was then the city of Charlotte's third-largest bank, Crutchfield forged more than eighty mergers and acquisitions in twelve years and turned First Union into the sixth-largest bank in the U.S., one with more than $200 billion in assets. Defying convention and caution (and pocketing $19 million U.S. in compensation in 1997 alone), he experimented with the latest in high-tech banking concepts and paid mind-bending prices to bag his quarries. In recalling his negotiations with the boss of one major East Coast U.S. financial institution, Crutchfield told *Business Week*: "I had a stack of billion-dollar bills and just laid them out for him one by one until he said yes."

The gung-ho takeover mood at First Union seemed pronounced by any standard. One Canadian banker remembers chatting with two senior First Union executives, one who pursued acquisition targets and another whose job was to handle the administration of the companies after their purchase. "I catch 'em," the first man said, and then, glancing at the second man, boomed, "and he skins 'em." By late 1997, Crutchfield had erected an empire of twenty-seven hundred bank branches stretching from New England to Florida. And he was about to complete the puzzle by buying the five hundred branches in Pennsylvania, New Jersey, and Delaware owned by Philadelphia-based CoreStates. The takeover – at $16 billion (U.S.), it was the most expensive in American banking up to that date –

would give First Union the biggest branch network in the eastern United States.

For many in Philadelphia, the fifth-largest U.S. city, the sale of CoreStates loomed as a tragic watershed. Not only did it mean the end of the city's role as a banking centre, with all the prestige and valuable head-office jobs that went with that, but it was also seen as another setback in Philadelphia's long fight to overcome the urban decay and decline in manufacturing industries that had sapped its vitality for many years. It was not just the anticipated loss of CoreStates bank branches and thousands of jobs – cost-saving measures that are accepted as all part of the acquisitions game in American financial circles – there was also the unhappy prospect of trying to convince a bank headquartered in faraway rural North Carolina to use its financial power and civic clout to help address Philadelphia's intractable urban social problems. "Consumers and low-income people get royally screwed by the First Union corporate culture," asserted Jonathan Stein, a lawyer with one of the community groups opposing the merger. "It's a bank that's out of a southern state, North Carolina, and it's going to be much less closely committed to needs here." A First Union spokesperson, Sandra Deem, denied this, saying the bank had a respectable record of community action.

Nonetheless, in the months after the bank buy-out was announced, activists in Philadelphia raised a storm of protest, enlisting the support of powerful congressional figures in a bid to block the deal. But as with other U.S. bank mergers, concerns about community well-being and job cuts seemed quickly forgotten in the heady, high-stakes merger mania that roared from Wall Street through North America's Main streets in 1997 and early 1998.

Almost with each passing week, the merger frenzy reached new heights on this continent and around the world. In the United States, where the wave of bank consolidations could be traced to the easing of barriers to interstate expansion in the 1980s, it was a stunning phenomenon. The dollar value of bank mergers and acquisitions in the U.S. shot up from $15 billion (U.S.) in 1994 to $95 billion (U.S.) in 1997. As for 1998, it had surpassed all previous annual records even before the stock-market slump slowed the pace of deal-making halfway through the year. Five giant financial-services merger proposals in the early months of 1998 doubled the value of all 1997 transactions. These were deals to join NationsBank and BankAmerica ($60 billion U.S.), Banc One and First Chicago ($30 billion U.S.), Norwest and Wells Fargo ($34 billion U.S.), Sun Trust Banks and Crestar ($10 billion U.S.), and Citicorp and Travelers Group ($70 billion U.S.).

This last agreement, which brought together one of the biggest U.S. banks with one of the country's largest insurance and brokerage companies, was breathtaking in size and scope. The most expensive pact of its kind ever, it created the first international supermarket for banking, insurance, and other financial products. Travelers-Citicorp, as defined at the time of the merger announcement, would have $698 billion in assets, 100 million customers in 100 countries, and nearly 162,000 employees. Word of the agreement to put all those assets under the famous Travelers logo, the red umbrella, rocked Wall Street and the world. "I have been doing this for twenty-five years, and this is the most dramatic transaction I have ever witnessed," gushed Thomas Hanley, a banking analyst at Warburg Dillon Read in New York, in an interview with Reuters news agency. The United States had seen nothing like it since the Great Depression, when American legislators, bitter over the collapse of the financial system, passed a law to keep banks, Wall Street, and insurance operations separate from each other. In fact, the Travelers-Citicorp deal wasn't even legal. But analysts guessed correctly when the transaction was unveiled in April 1998 that its momentum would add new urgency to efforts to sweep away the political log-jam that had kept the U.S. Congress from updating its banking legislation for twenty years.

The psychological impact on Canada's Bay Street was intense. Backers of the proposed Royal–Bank of Montreal consolidation took it as a sign that the merger wave was unstoppable anywhere on the globe. "The forces that are driving this trend towards mergers around the world are the same everywhere – technology, globalization, and demographics," Hugh Brown, a banking analyst at Nesbitt Burns brokerage in Toronto, told the *Financial Post.* "Canada obviously has got to recognize those forces. Are we going to look in the rear-view mirror or the windshield?" And the huge deal south of the border appeared to give comfort to Toronto Dominion Bank chairman Charles Baillie, who by then was only ten days away from announcing his own deal to join with CIBC. The gigantic, dazzling Travelers-Citicorp consolidation made it more difficult than ever to question the notion that big is better, Baillie told the *Post.* In a world of giant financial conglomerates, he said, "You might be able to make a great intellectual case that the little guy could compete, but . . . it might be [that] the big guy could make one mistake after another and still clobber you, or if he executed well it could be devastating for you." Baillie said the sense of inevitability injected into the merger craze by the mammoth transaction in New York would make it more difficult for the federal government in Ottawa to buck the trend. "The chances of approval of the BMO–Royal deal are probably higher than they were before the Travelers deal," he remarked.

Big as it was, however, the Citicorp-Travelers consolidation was only one act in a worldwide corporate shake-up unlike anything ever seen before. Through 1997 and early 1998, the trend towards massive global corporate consolidations defied all expectations and catapulted ahead with a fury that left investors, analysts, and average citizens in awe, and sometimes in fear. Driven primarily by the belief that bigger is better in the global marketplace, companies chalked up worldwide mergers and acquisitions totalling $1.6 trillion (U.S.) in 1997. But that was soon left in the dust by the activity in the first half of 1998. By June of that year, according to Securities Data Corporation, merger values around the globe had reached $1.3 trillion (U.S.), double the total for the same period of 1997 and almost equal to the value of all deals recorded in 1997. How heated was the action? In the United States, on a single day – May 18 – eleven mergers worth about $17 billion (U.S.) were tallied.

In the frenzy of buy-outs, there were more expensive deals than German automaker Daimler-Benz's merger with the venerable Chrysler Corp. or the purchase by Germany's Bertelsmann of New York–based Random House publishers, but these two agreements seemed more than any others to awaken the public to the phenomenon of huge cross-border corporate marriages. And there was little doubt that these deals were one more stunning reminder of the triumph of global capitalism as championed by the U.S. corporate colossus. It all seemed to go hand in hand with McDonald's blitzkrieg through Europe, the struggle for market expansion around the world between Coca-Cola and Pepsi, and the stunningly successful inroads of America's Hollywood-style commercial culture everywhere from France to Brazil to India.

Indeed, with communism vanquished, the old saw about making the world safe for capitalism was in fact being realized, and corporations everywhere were jumping on the merger bandwagon with the same macho corporate abandon as their American role-models. Bank of Nova Scotia chairman Peter Godsoe, the lone anti-merger hold-out among major bank chairmen in Canada, caught the tone of it all in September 1998, when he quipped: "Real men merge and barbeque."

The bank mergers of the 1990s bore characteristics that were markedly different from those of earlier buy-out sprees. In the 1960s, the corporate world witnessed a wave of outrageously greedy takeovers that mixed and matched all kinds of companies indiscriminately. This was followed two decades later by the era of the leveraged buy-out, when acquisitors used junk bonds and other questionable financial tools to effect what were often hostile takeover bids for companies that, once purchased, were carved up and sold off to the highest bidder. But the latest round embodied a much more positive-sounding trend. It was, more than anything else, a quest to establish conglomerates with the size and scope to sustain world-class marketing savvy, technology, and productivity. In the financial-services industry, this meant achieving adequate corporate size to cost-effectively develop and install the new technologies needed to stay competitive in fast-developing business areas such as credit-card distribution, wealth management, and electronic commerce. As corporations expanded, their size would allow them to lower their costs and thereby raise their profits – or so the theory went. Mergers were also about finding ways to stay big enough to ensure the market capitalization needed to guard against being taken over by even larger conglomerates in the next round of consolidation. In 1998, there was no end in sight to this trend.

Harold MacKay, who headed the government-commissioned task force on the future of the financial-services industry, put it this way: "Driven by technology and globalization, change is having a profound effect on the world and all of its citizens." Addressing a group of reporters assembled in the national media theatre across the street from Parliament, MacKay said, "Jets and fibre optics and satellites have made the world a smaller place. And as the world is shrinking, it's also changing. Change is forcing countries to reinvent themselves. Not that long ago there were two Germanys and Russia was a formidable player. A dozen years ago, only one country in four had a democratic government. Today, two-thirds of the countries in the world are democracies. Ten years ago, one billion people lived in a market economy; today five billion do.

"The same forces of change," MacKay continued, "are clearly

affecting the financial-services sector. Capital markets have become global . . . new competitors with advanced technology are threatening existing players . . . consumers have new means to access financial services . . . and a whole new range of consumer needs and issues are looming."

MacKay's report on the financial-services industry picked up this theme: "Many observers are predicting that, within a decade, a small number (perhaps ten to fifteen) of significant, global financial institutions will emerge. Very large regional (North American, European, or Asian) players will complement these institutions, as will a large number of local players and many niche players, some of them operating globally. All institutions, facing this paradigm, are trying to determine their own strategy, as a matter of survival and value-enhancement."

For financial companies, numerous factors were behind the consolidation craze. While almost half a decade of impressive profit totals in the mid-1990s obscured this development, banking had become a mature industry. It faced the prospect of slower revenue growth in its traditional business activities while at the same time confronting skyrocketing costs for new technology. "The old physical model of banking – with branches, proprietary products, and back rooms – is continuously being reshaped by technology developments and changing customer preferences," wrote Ernst & Young consultants in a study on technology in banking. In Canada, according to the MacKay report, financial institutions have in recent years been generating only average profits when stacked up against efficient North American and European competitors. The MacKay report calculated that the five largest Canadian banks' overall profitability (measured as net income divided by total revenue) rose from 9.7 percent in 1992 to 19.5 percent in 1996. However, this compares with profitability ratios of 22.2 percent in Britain and 20.2 percent in the United States.

Just as important to the strategists eyeing the $1.4 trillion in

Canadian household financial assets, the last decade has witnessed a profound upheaval in the habits of investors. Low returns on interest-sensitive investments and an ageing population's concern about retirement combined to steer Canadians increasingly away from bank deposits to more risky investments in the stock market. While the chartered banks' share of all financial assets declined, the eighty-five mutual-fund companies operating in Canada enjoyed a stunning upsurge in sales. By 1998, slightly more than one-third of all Canadian households owned a part of the country's $300 billion worth of mutual funds. The fund companies' share of total financial assets in Canada shot up to 11.5 percent in 1997 from just 2.9 percent a decade earlier. In addition, large corporations were turning to the capital markets to borrow funds, and many small- and medium-sized businesses looked increasingly to credit unions and asset-based financing companies instead of banks for credit financing.

These historic changes were being felt not only at the banks. For many of the same reasons, the life-insurance industry was in the throes of a period of intense consolidation. The Canada Life Assurance Co., for example, acquired seven companies in the 1990s, but by late 1997 had nonetheless gone from being the fourth-largest insurer in Canada to being the sixth-largest. At Manulife Financial, chief executive officer Dominic D'Allesandro cemented his company's stature as one of the giants with a 1996 merger with North American Life Assurance Co. And Winnipeg-based Great-West Life Assurance, the largest player in the accident- and sickness-insurance sectors, outbid the Royal Bank for the London Insurance Group to shore up its position in the life-insurance market. How cut-throat could the game be? Some believed that Power Financial Corp., the Montreal holding company controlled by the well-connected Desmarais family, had Power-owned Great-West Life buy London Insurance expressly to keep the banks from expanding into insurance. Power Corp. officials denied this.

By the late 1990s, the insurance shake-up took on an even more dramatic tone with the announcement that some of the major life insurers planned to do away with their long-time structure as mutual companies owned by their policyholders. Instead, they intended to become publicly held stock companies, a process that would pump an unprecedented $10 billion dollars into the hands of two million lucky Canadian policyholders. But going public would be a lengthy, complex process, one that Sun Life chairman John McNeil likened to "planning the invasion of Normandy." This restructuring was designed to enable the companies to become more disciplined and raise capital more readily, but it also heaped new uncertainty on the insurance industry's future. "This is a pivotal time in the history of this industry," Robert Astley, the lean, athletic-looking president of Mutual Life Assurance Co. of Canada, told a business audience in the spring of 1998. "What will happen in the next couple of years will have a marked impact on the shape and texture of all financial services. As we enter this new phase, uncertainty is at an all-time high. We need to be clear on the principles we use as a compass to guide us through the fog."

Six

BATTLEGROUND

One of the many unknowns in the future of financial services is the potential impact of the new specialty competitors – the so-called monolines – that are challenging traditional banking and insurance roles in Canada and the United States. As they mass-market such products as mortgages or credit cards, these companies use their huge scale to bring prices down to extremely competitive levels. By 1998, this trend had reached the stage where only those banks big enough to keep their own costs and prices very low through economies of scale had a chance against the monolines. In Canada, these challenges were heightened, bankers said, by the need to continue to operate traditional bank branches. "Competitive pressures and the demands of different groups of customers present us with stark choices: invest in new technology or drop out of the competitive race; maintain traditional banking branches or lose a significant portion of our customer base," Matthew Barrett explained. Indeed, the MacKay task force concluded: "Taken as a whole, it is clear to us that Canada's financial institutions will have to work hard to become more efficient in the future. If they do not become more productive, their competitive position is likely to erode."

The competitive demands of the industry, it seemed, would only intensify as executives searched for better ways to appeal to fickle customers in an era when everything in retailing was up for grabs. No one articulates this trend better than Richard Kovacevich, the no-nonsense former Citicorp executive who makes his Norwest Corp. bank employees refer to their outlets as "stores" – not "branches." Kovacevich, who made his name as an aggressive marketing man, came out on top in one of the most notable mergers of 1998, the $34-billion (U.S.) plan to join Minneapolis-based Norwest Corp. with San Francisco–based Wells Fargo. Kovacevich believes that financial services are simply commodity products, and that the key to healthy growth in banking is competition unhindered by overzealous government regulators. His watchword is "Let the banks fight it out. The only winner will be the consumer."

In assessing the current state of banking, he starts from the position that changing customer preferences, tough new entrants in the market, and technological advances are redefining the sector. "A bank certificate of deposit, an insurance annuity, and a mutual fund are all basically satisfying a similar need – some sort of savings for the long term," the tall, energetic banker explained. "The consumer in the U.S. paid three different distribution systems to come to the door to explain these three products, yet they had to figure out which of the three products made the most sense for them, because each has different risks and rewards. If you could offer all three products at, let's say, one-third the cost and help the consumer decide which of those is best, you're giving better service at lower cost, and that's what it's all about."

Kovacevich grows testy discussing how government regulators in the United States and Canada have traditionally sought to separate such financial services as deposit-taking, insurance sales, and stock brokerages. "No one," Kovacevich growled, "would have designed these distribution systems separately other than government regulators. Fifty years ago, there may have been good reasons to keep all these things separate. But the customer and technology are driving you not to do this any more. They want you to give them better service at lower costs, just like the Home Depots, the Wal-Marts, and others do." He said it is ridiculous to worry about whether a few large companies can completely dominate a competitive market. As an example, he cites the retail market in the United States, with its thousands of different stores of every size and variety. No matter how large a company may be, he argues, "If you don't continue to serve customers and do it well, you're going to lose market share. There's too many nimble players out there who are going to find a way to get you. It's the little companies who keep picking off the big companies because they become so bureaucratic, so big, and so unresponsive. Did Sears have a competitive advantage over the Gap?"

As they tried to stir up support for mega-mergers in Canada, bankers never missed a chance to point to the dramatic changes in the United States as proof that a failure to update financial-services regulations could have enormous consequences. On the one hand, there was Charlotte, North Carolina, where the spinning construction cranes on the new skyscrapers symbolized the meteoric rise of the once minor regional transportation hub that had, in only a few years, emerged as the second most powerful financial capital in the U.S. This was the handiwork of Edward Crutchfield, First Union Corp.'s empire-building chairman, and Hugh McColl, a similarly aggressive executive at the other major banking power in Charlotte, NationsBank. (In April 1998, McColl stunned American financial circles when he unveiled a $60-billion (U.S.) deal with San Francisco–based BankAmerica Corp. to establish the first coast-to-coast banking colossus in the United States, with $570 billion (U.S.) in assets.) The city of Charlotte's speedy rise to the top of American banking could be traced to a legal framework established there in the nineteenth century. In contrast to many other states, where banks were limited to a single region or even to having only one branch, North Carolina permitted branches across the state. This allowed the creation of relatively big banks in Charlotte, giving Crutchfield and McColl an advantage when, in the 1980s, Congress cleared the way for interstate banking – and aggressive expansion – in the U.S.

While Charlotte boomed, other cities watched as their homegrown banking industry was swamped by bigger competitors from other jurisdictions. Look at what happened in Chicago, said Al McNally, the Canadian-born chairman of Harris Bank, an Illinois-based financial institution owned by the Bank of Montreal. As one of the last states to begin liberalizing its laws, Illinois still had so-called unit-banking statutes in force into the 1980s, McNally explained. These rules decreed that a bank could have only one branch, and that no bank could exist within two miles of another.

"Illinois banks were not allowed to grow, expand, and develop distribution networks and all the kinds of things that were required to play an increasing regional role, and then to be part of the nationwide consolidation now taking place in the U.S.," said McNally, who can look out his office window at the towers of one bank chain owned by a Dutch conglomerate and another belonging to Ohio-based merger giant Banc One Corp. Chicago, as a central U.S. transportation and service hub and with its tradition of financial and commodities exchanges, should "have given New York a heck of a run in the development of itself as the money centre of the United States," McNally said. But this hasn't happened. Chicago banks "weren't able to develop with the New York money-center banks and the banks that are headquartered in Charlotte that are driving the nationwide consolidation now under way in the United States."

Instead, "there is a not a single major, local Chicago bank left" serving the average bank customer. The full-service banks in Chicago are owned by "the Dutch, the Canadians, folks from Ohio and California."

What does that mean for Canada? McNally asserted that Canada could find its bank head offices disappearing as well if the government fails to update its laws to allow banks to become big enough via mergers to compete with other conglomerates. However, many opponents of bank mergers say governments in Canada have already permitted Canada's major banks to achieve more than enough size and concentrated market power to survive and prosper.

For all the Economics 101 rationales for mergers, there is a nagging undercurrent of cynicism that attributes much of the craze to the ego-driven excesses of the top financial-services executives. Some analysts say that the ever bigger and more outrageous merger plans, far from being a competition issue, should be picked apart as an example of questionable corporate governance. What's more, there is no proof that mergers are likely to produce more efficient corporations or greatly enhance long-term shareholder value. "Now, I do not quarrel with the proposition that the movement toward consolidation of already large financial institutions is firmly entrenched and will probably continue," said Henry Kaufman, the president of Henry Kaufman & Co. of New York. "However, it is worth bearing in mind that it is hardly a foregone conclusion that every one of the large mergers that have been done or will be done can be carried off successfully. Many potential pitfalls can intrude."

Of nineteen bank mergers made between 1990 and 1993 and studied by the U.S. Federal Reserve Board, only six resulted in improved profitability. In another often-cited research project, Michael Porter of the Harvard Business School looked at acquisitions by thirty-three large, successful companies from 1950 to 1986. Within a decade of the acquisitions, he found, more than half of the acquired companies had been put on the auction block or were liquidated.

The problems created by mergers are legion, experts say. They can come in the form of power clashes among the most senior managers in the merged entity or in disputes over staffing. The latter problem was so pronounced in the case of the Swiss Bank Corporation/ Union Bank of Switzerland merger that employees of UBS accused their new-found partners of nothing less than "ethnic cleansing." Problems may also take the form of customer loss, internal operating frictions, or trouble reaching efficiency goals. Stockholders in the companies being acquired tend to do well as a result of acquisitions, while owners of shares in the company doing the buying often do not.

In financial services, the best-known example of a merger gone awry is San Francisco–based Wells Fargo & Co.'s $11.3-billion (U.S.) takeover of its California rival, First Interstate Bancorp. In the aftermath of the deal, records disappeared when the two banks' combined computer systems froze. Deposits failed to show up in the banks' records, customers were forced to wait in interminable lines, and tens of thousands of disgruntled consumers bolted to other institutions. With the corporate marriage in trouble, Wells Fargo signed on with powerful Norwest Corp. in mid-1998.

In Canada, the most important study so far on mergers, the MacKay task force, reached a somewhat ambiguous conclusion. After an extensive look at the existing research on the issue, it concluded: "The evidence we have reviewed does not sustain a case that, for most purposes, size is a strategically important variable or that all, or even most, mergers tend to bring about gains in efficiency." However, the task force did conclude that larger institutions have more opportunities for improved performance, and that an increased capital base can provide financial-services companies with the chance to reduce operating costs and, in some cases, increase their profitability.

Looking back over the 1990s, it is clear that another major driving force in the merger phenomenon was the booming value of financial-services stock in the decade's long bull market. Rising bank share values made stock-for-stock deals the preferred way of paying for mergers. This contrasts sharply with the 1980s, when most mergers or acquisitions were completed with straight cash. With equities markets in such a bubbly mood for much of the 1990s, corporate bosses could drive up the value of their companies' stocks simply by announcing a consolidation. Shareholders, of course, loved riding this bandwagon ever higher, and the upsurge in stock price had the added benefit for top executives of boosting the value of their stock options, often by many millions of dollars. Not least among the beneficiaries were the investment bankers who helped put the deals together. On May 11, 1998, for instance, the bankers at the Salomon Smith Barney division within Travelers Group were said to have been involved in a record $90 billion worth of mergers and acquisitions. With fees usually calculated at one percent of the value of a transaction, it was estimated that Salomon Smith Barney earned some $900 million in a single day.

Merger fever stoked the fires of appreciation on the Toronto Stock Exchange all through early 1998. Bank stocks soared in anticipation of consolidations and because of what looked in the first few months of 1998 to be another year of sharply higher record profits at the major banks. However, the outlook lost much of its lustre as the year unfolded. The worldwide economic malaise arising from the financial crisis in Asia unsettled capital markets in North America, prompting a summer of slaughter on both the Toronto Stock Exchange and Wall Street. As far as the Big Six Canadian banks were concerned, analysts correctly downgraded their expectations. The combined 1998 profits of these six major banks totalled $7.03 billion, marking the first time in years that their collective profit had not set a new record high. This contrasted sharply with the increase in total profits in

1997, when the $7.5 billion in net earnings represented an 18 percent jump over the previous year. In this atmosphere, bank shares were hardly immune to the plunge in shareholder confidence. CIBC, which had closed at $55 a share on the day its merger with TD Bank was announced in April, hovered at $32.40 on the Toronto Stock Exchange on November 20. On that same day, TD shares, at $69 when the merger was revealed, had slid to $46.40.

Nonetheless, as the banks began one by one in late November to release their 1998 fiscal results, investors saw that bank profits, while not spectacular, had in general weathered the storm on the markets better than many had expected. Bank stocks bounced back as part of a wider resurgence of prices on North American stock markets in late November.

A similar phenomenon was experienced with the merger trend. In mid-1998, the unexpectedly persistent turmoil on world capital markets had punctured the very merger balloon that appeared, only a few months earlier, to be soaring towards record heights around the globe. The frenzy of the previous few years suddenly screeched to a near halt. Mergers and acquisitions dwindled in number, initial public offerings of shares slowed drastically, and North America's investment bankers suddenly found themselves contemplating whether they would have jobs by year-end, rather than how fat their bonus would be come Christmas. The aura of doom and gloom was not aided by the announcement of thousands of lay-offs by the new Travelers-Citicorp conglomerate, or by the resignation of David Coulter, president of BankAmerica, the product of one of the most prominent 1998 bank mergers (the amalgamation of BankAmerica and NationsBank). Coulter quit after the new combined institution announced an unexpectedly steep 78 percent drop in earnings in the third quarter of 1998, owing to a mammoth loss on a loan to a risky securities-trading operation called a hedge fund. But his departure was also said to be the result of bitter post-merger internal problems.

In Canada, meanwhile, the alarming slide in the value of shares on the TSE in mid-1998 did little to help the four Canadian banks seeking mergers. The optimism that had drawn so many investors into the euphoria over the market in general, and over merger-prone banks in particular, seemed to be evaporating. Coupled with this was an increasing distrust on the part of Canadians – who had seen their dollar crash to almost unheard-of levels against the U.S. currency early in 1998 – of global market forces. Popular support for mergers was obviously derived in part from the belief that globalization and free trade were creating ever-larger markets with the potential for ever-greater prosperity in those nations prepared to take advantage of this new economy. Thus the disturbing, seemingly unstoppable spread of recessionary conditions from Asia during 1997–98 shook public confidence in world markets and giant financial organizations.

Despite these difficulties, however, the pendulum of events behind the merger phenomenon began to sweep back as the year wore on. North American stock markets survived the international economic storm. Citigroup was working hard to overcome the leadership turmoil spawned by the Citicorp-Travelers amalgamation and integrate the two giant companies. In early November, the Daimler-Benz/Chrysler pact was finalized. Then, on November 23, the day some observers called Merger Monday, ten transactions – each valued at more than $1 billion (U.S.) – were announced by American companies. The deals prompted talk that the hiatus in mergers might be coming to an end. "The engines seem to be firing up again," Herald Ritch, co-head of mergers at Donaldson, Lufkin & Jenrette Securities Corp., told the *Wall Street Journal.* Indeed, a few weeks later came news of the monster of all mergers. Exxon, the largest American oil company, moved to buy the second-largest, Mobil, in a deal worth $80 billion (U.S.) that would create the world's biggest conglomerate.

As encouraging as these developments may have been for

financiers, they were unlikely in the short run to erase the gloomy memories Canadian investors retained from the panicky days of steep losses earlier in the year. And these memories would do little to improve Canadians' attitudes towards bankers who said they had to merge with their competitors to be big enough to play on the global stage.

SEVEN

FOREIGNERS AT THE GATES

One by one, they come into the bright, sunny room on the first floor of the modern office tower in the sprawling suburbs north of Toronto. There are the business people, the retirees, the elderly couples, and the single women. Curious but wary, they peer at the orange Harley-Davidson motorcycle, the free computer terminals, the bustling coffee bar, and the signs on the walls urging people to be their own bankers. Before long, they're sipping lattes and listening carefully as the woman behind the counter tries to explain the concept of a bank with no tellers, no cash drawers, no branches, and no service fees.

This was the scene every day at the Toronto-area café that was the only public presence in Canada of ING Direct, the branchless nationwide bank that opened for business in April 1997. Arkadi Kuhlmann, the hip fifty-one-year-old banking maverick who heads ING, had set up the coffee bar for customers – not for their convenience, but because there were so many of them who just had to see something at the end of the telephone line. "The biggest problem is that people wonder if it's too good to be true," said Kuhlmann in a reference to the bank's products, such as its no-fee daily-interest savings account. In 1999 this account was paying 4.2 percent annual interest – a rate that, as ING loved to point out, was up to six times higher than rates available at other Canadian banks.

Kuhlmann, known for his poetry-writing, his self-painted canvases, and his silver Porsche, takes delight in demonstrating how his company has thrown off the traditionally dour, repressive strictures of consumer banking. For example, there were the unsecured loans of up to fifty thousand dollars that ING was offering on the basis of a ten-minute approval over the phone. "There are no fees, no service charges – just call straight up, use the money for whatever you want," Kuhlmann enthused. "You can go and buy your car, buy your piece of furniture, whatever." ING's strategy, as explained in TV advertising spots that featured the notably grainy visage of a popular star of Dutch cop dramas, was straightforward: save your money. "I'm running the first discount bank in Canada," Kuhlmann said. "I'm opening up a brand-new category. We've seen it in brokerages, but we haven't seen it in banking."

An early proponent of electronic banking, Kuhlmann is said to have installed one of the first-ever multi-cash machines at John F. Kennedy Airport while working for New York–based currency trader Deak International in the early 1980s. With his no-frills electronic bank in Canada, he delights in playing the role of the little people's banker. Of the customers who come to the coffee shop seeking reassurance about ING, Kuhlmann said, "It's Martha and Billy and everybody else, and they want to make sure, 'cause Charlie told them, 'Like, leave this money in term deposits, don't invest it.' So now, of course, Martha's term deposits all matured, right? She's deciding what to do. And she's asking, 'Are we CDIC insured?' Yes, we are. 'Are we federally regulated?' Yes, we are. We're not sort of a mutual fund, or an investment planner, or anything like that. We're a bank, okay?"

But for all the folksy treatment, ING's venture into the Canadian market is not that of a struggling upstart. The new telephone-banking operation is located in Canada because the country was chosen as a test market by one of the world's biggest financial institutions, Amsterdam-based ING Groep NV. In its first year in Canada, ING spent $50 million on promotion, including print and TV ads and the dispatching of eight kids (four in Toronto and four in Vancouver) to ride around on bicycles handing out ING leaflets and orange Tic Tacs (orange is the company's, and the Netherlands', colour). All this hasn't made Kuhlmann too popular among his colleagues in the traditional financial services. Other bankers, he joked, "generally leave restaurants when I walk in."

As intriguing as ING's operations were, the Dutch-mandated experiment in branchless banking was only one sign of the growing interest in Canada being shown by some foreign financial institutions. Facing stiff competition at home, these corporations from the U.S. and, to a lesser extent, Europe were by the late 1990s eagerly eyeing the Canadian market as a potential expansion target. Their appetites were whetted all the more by the federal government's effort to gradually rewrite the rules that have protected Canada's big banks for decades from some forms of competition from abroad. By 1998, it was clear that, at least in a number of vital business lines, the challenge from abroad would continue to grow. The foreigners, in fact, were already here in certain areas of banking, as anyone who bothers to examine the credit-card mailings that land on his or her doorstep every month has surely noticed.

In addition to ING, one of the more formidable entrants was MBNA, the giant Delaware-based credit-card provider that was sending out thirty million card solicitations a month. After only sixteen years in existence, it was by 1998 the second-largest credit-card lender in the world after Citibank. MBNA specializes in affinity credit cards. This type of plastic, as opposed to a points-reward card, bears the issuing bank's name along with the name of another organization that the cardholder wants to support. In exchange for the consumer's use of a particular credit card, the card issuer agrees to pay a small percentage of every dollar spent on the card to an organization endorsed by the consumer. Said to have originated twenty years ago with the Sierra Club conservation group in the United States, the often colourfully designed cards have become a powerful and increasingly common marketing tool. They are endorsed by groups of all kinds, from universities to sports organizations to auto clubs, and MBNA has experienced a dizzying rise in business. By 1998, the company had amassed endorsement deals with 4,500 groups in the United States, Canada, Britain, and Ireland, with total membership exceeding 150 million. In the U.S., 54 percent of doctors, 60 percent of dentists, and 36 percent of lawyers were said to carry an MBNA card.

MBNA Canada Bank got rolling in the Canadian market in late 1997, operating out of its new office in Gloucester, near Ottawa. "MBNA's expansion into Canada is a natural extension of our business of marketing to people with a strong common interest," declared Patrick O'Dwyer, president and chief executive officer of the Canadian subsidiary. "The time is right to enter the credit-card business in Canada. The Canadian credit-card market provides an attractive opportunity to offer a highly competitive product backed by superior customer service."

The company signalled its arrival north of the border by wresting the endorsement of the 150,000-member Ducks Unlimited Canada away from the Bank of Montreal, which had provided the well-known conservationist group with an affinity-card program of its own for eight years. It was well understood that Ducks Unlimited Canada might switch to MBNA on the basis of the long relationship between the U.S. wing of the conservationist organization and the Delaware company. But the Bank of Montreal was still demoralized to lose what had been its first, and its most prestigious, affinity-card endorsement, executives there said.

Because of its size, MBNA is able to offer very competitive contracts to prospective affinity groups. These include a higher percentage rebate on every purchase than is usually offered by other card issuers. "It was a much better deal for the ducks," explained Wayne Doherty, manager of licensing programs for Ducks Unlimited Canada. "They've brought competition into the marketplace," he said of MBNA. In addition to higher rebates, MBNA also offered the consumer a low introductory interest rate on overdue card balances. Within five months of opening shop in the Ottawa suburbs, MBNA landed endorsements with forty organizations, according to company spokesman Peter Frank. Among these were the National Hockey League, MADD (Mothers Against Drunk Driving), the Canadian Nurses Association, and the Air Force Association of Canada.

MBNA was a prime example of the kind of high-powered, supercompetitive one-product specialist that bankers had in mind when they referred to "monolines" or "category-killers." But MBNA was not by any means the only impressive business giant on the list of foreign competitors operating in Canada by the late 1990s. On the credit-card front, another formidable U.S. firm was vying for part of Canada's $20-billion card market. Virginia-based Capital One Financial Corp., which has more than $23 billion in assets and 14 million customers in the U.S., Canada, and Britain, made its mark with low-rate cards. It started distributing card solicitations in Canada in 1996, and a year or so later initiated an instalment-loan business. There was also Banc One Corp., an Ohio-based financial player with fifteen hundred banking outlets in twelve U.S. states. Banc One began marketing credit cards in Canada in September 1998. "Over the long term, international markets present significant growth opportunities for credit-card lending," said chairman John McCoy. "It is very natural for our international efforts to begin in Canada, which has many similarities to U.S. consumer markets. We are enthusiastic about the opportunity to serve consumers in Canada," he continued. "Our efforts will reflect the uniqueness of the Canadian people, and at the same time will be an extension of [Banc One's] successful strategy of providing products with superior pricing as well as excellent features and customer service, all of which are enabled by our emphasis on technology."

As John Cleghorn and Matthew Barrett travelled the country trying to drum up support for their merger, they never stopped trying to drive home the point that the size of their foreign competitors alone meant tremendous competitive advantages, allowing the companies from abroad to create low cost structures that permitted very aggressive pricing strategies. Whether the two bankers were talking to newspaper editors or members of Parliament, nothing seemed to shock as much as the revelation that the Canadian government had itself opted for foreign-owned providers on some of Ottawa's own multi-million-dollar credit-card contracts. In late 1997, the Canadian subsidiary of U.S.-based Citibank, which has issued more than fifty million credit cards worldwide (almost twice the number of all Canadian card issuers), won a much-sought-after card contract for a portion of the federal government's purchase-and-supply business. And American Express was re-awarded the government's expense-card business. In the process, the U.S.-owned conglomerates beat out a number of Canadian banks. Speaking to members of the House of Commons finance committee about this, Barrett said, "Am I criticizing the government? No, I'm not. They got a better deal. But I'll give you an inside story. I ordered our people to bid break-even because I wanted the prestige of having the government's business." And at break-even, Barrett said, the Bank of Montreal still couldn't compete.

In addition to the credit-card giants, there were other well-established foreign entrants in the Canadian market. Fidelity Investments, the world's largest mutual-fund company, held a substantial chunk of the burgeoning Canadian market for that product. Franklin Templeton Group was also a major mutual-fund company in Canada, with more assets under management by 1998 than the Bank of Nova Scotia and the Bank of Montreal combined. In the lending business, Canada's banks were up against the likes of GE Capital Corp. It's a subsidiary of Connecticut-based General Electric, which vies with Microsoft for the title of most profitable U.S. corporation.

In June 1998, New York–based Merrill Lynch, the world's largest brokerage firm, returned to the Canadian retail brokerage business by acquiring Midland Walwyn Inc. in a stock offer valued at $1.26 billion. Eight years earlier, Merrill Lynch had sold its Canadian retail investment operations to CIBC Wood Gundy. The unusual reactions prompted by Merrill's much-publicized decision to purchase Midland illustrated the strange state of Canada's financial-services industry by 1998. Despite the fact that the last independent brokerage in Canada was joining forces with American interests, many otherwise nationalistic Canadians applauded the move. They did so on the grounds that it would preserve Midland from the clutches of Canada's big banks, which had taken over every other major Canadian investment house since being allowed into that business in 1992. Executives of those Canadian banks with merger plans grumbled fiercely when Merrill's takeover was completed, with official government approval, in only a few months while the federal government's decision-making process on the proposed combinations of Canadian-owned banks dragged on and on. For its part, Merrill Lynch made no bones about its intention to take advantage of an increasingly open Canadian business environment. "The nature of Canadian markets will change significantly over the next few years, with continuing deregulation, industry consolidation, and strong growth in demand for personal financial services," Merrill Lynch president Herbert Allison said. "With this acquisition, we will be ideally positioned to help clients in Canada and worldwide take advantage of the many new opportunities in the Canadian market, while achieving strong returns for shareholders."

Other U.S. players loomed as challengers to Canada's financial institutions. There was Wells Fargo & Co., the storied San Francisco bank that got its start running stagecoaches in the Wild West in 1852. Through telemarketing, Wells Fargo had become the largest lender to small business in the U.S. It featured unsecured loans based on a half-page application, no meetings with credit officers, and no restrictions on the use of funds. Leap-frogging the border into Canada via mail and phone, Wells Fargo lent $50 million to Canadian firms in one year, with most of the loans for less than $75,000 apiece. And another potential competitor of formidable size waited in the wings: California-based Countrywide Credit, which services $200 billion plus in mortgages – more than the total held by all Canadian banks. Countrywide had expressed an interest in the Canadian market, but as of late 1998 had not followed up with concrete plans. The threat is still raised, however, as justification for Canadian banks' need to grow bigger. Of Countrywide, the Bank of Montreal's Barrett says, "Think about the economies of scale a company like that can achieve, and the range of mortgage products and services it can offer."

Yet another company that is often mentioned is Norwest Financial Inc. One of the biggest and most aggressive U.S. bank holding companies, it is poised to expand north of the border. Through its ownership of Trans Canada Credit Corporation, Norwest has 143 consumer-finance stores in Canada. It is also affiliated with T. Eaton Co.'s credit operations for its 1.2 million customer accounts. As well, U.S.-based Associates First Capital Corp. has been on a shopping spree that has made it the largest non-bank consumer lender in Canada. And commercial lenders have also been looking to expand northward. Finova Group Inc., a highly regarded commercial-finance and leasing company based in Phoenix, set up shop in Toronto in mid-1998. Heller Financial Inc. of Chicago, another formidable competitor in commercial lending, with subsidiaries in nineteen countries, was also preparing to move into Canada.

There was no arguing with the fact that foreign banks were expanding their operations in Canada and would likely continue to do so. Rodgin Cohen, a merger expert who has been involved in some of the biggest deals in the United States, explained: "As consolidation continues here and ultimately nears completion, there will be more pressure from the United States to the north." It would be the rare U.S. bank "that wouldn't find Canada an appealing place to do business," observed Cohen, a diminutive lawyer whose office at Sullivan & Cromwell in New York's financial district provides a spectacular view out over the East River. "If they are comfortable at all with expanding to another country, Canada would clearly be the one that you would be most comfortable with – there's the common border, the common language (outside Quebec), and so forth."

The pro-merger Canadian banks themselves played up the threat from abroad with a fervour that sometimes bordered on hysteria. "This is a time of momentous change in financial services," intoned CIBC chairman Al Flood. "Our industry is going through massive structural adjustments that amount to a virtual revolution in the way we do business." He went on: "Powerful new competitors are entering our markets. Many are financial-service giants whose size and resources dwarf those of Canadian banks. They are the products of a huge wave of global consolidation that's occurring in my industry. We can hold our own today against any of the new players operating in Canada. But these competitors are growing rapidly . . . and they are growing stronger." The Royal's Cleghorn, who illustrates his speeches with a video on foreign competition accompanied by music fit to dramatize an invasion from Mars, summed up his bank's urgency in much blunter terms. "You don't wait until you're dying to pick your cemetery plot," he told the *Toronto Star.*

And the would-be merger partners got some support from an unlikely corner. Ed Clark, who as president of the holding company of Canada Trust was a direct competitor of Canada's banks, said, "We recognize the forces of consolidation which are sweeping all industries. We believe some further consolidation is inevitable in Canada and is in the public interest in order to ensure strong Canadian-based institutions."

Bank analyst Hugh Brown, of the Bank of Montreal–owned brokerage Nesbitt Burns, could hardly be expected to oppose mergers. But as a respected analyst, his words are worth considering. "By denying Canadian banks the ability to evolve with the massive changes occurring in the banking world, including mergers," he said, "we effectively are helping the competitors of Canadian banks, many of which are foreign-owned (i.e., MBNA, Fidelity, GE Capital, Wells Fargo, ING, etc.)." Foreign competition was also an important topic in the MacKay task force report to the federal government. The study detailed some of the challenges from abroad facing Canada's financial institutions and concluded: "What we can say with certainty is that it will be an increasingly difficult challenge to succeed in the world we are quickly moving into. It will not be easy for Canadian institutions to adapt."

While no one could dispute the fact that foreign institutions were making inroads in Canada, there was fierce disagreement about the size of the threat they posed and the implications for policy-makers. Many observers, both within and outside of the industry, just did not believe that Canada's major banks, with their extensive retail networks, healthy profits, and dominant market position, were in any real danger from non-Canadian financial players. For instance, ING had indeed been a success in Canada, signing up more than one hundred thousand clients in its first two years of operation. But Kuhlmann nonetheless scoffed when the bankers planning mergers raised ING's name to justify their proposed consolidations. "There isn't a speech that gets done in the industry that doesn't trot out our name as, you know, the reason Canadian bankers are going to be doomed," he said. "What's the Royal Bank got? Like, eight million customers. I mean, we've got a few tens of thousands. I think it's just way out of proportion. We're not going to take over the marketplace." (Royal Bank actually has ten million customers.)

Many analysts agreed. Commenting on the big banks' characterization of Wells Fargo's efforts to develop business in Canada as a threat, Ottawa economist Mike McCracken said, "This is like a gnat crawling up an elephant's leg with rape in mind."

Indeed, the recent history of foreign banks in Canada does not convey the image of a group of voracious attackers. After being prohibited from entering the country at all for thirteen years, foreign banks were allowed, as of 1980, to do corporate and, contrary to popular belief, retail banking in Canada. The only stipulation was that they could not operate through branches of their parent company, but instead had to set up subsidiaries in Canada, with a separate allocation of capital. Foreign entrants reached a peak of fifty-nine in 1987, but after that a number of factors combined to reduce Canada's attractiveness. These included the early 1990s recession, the debacle in real estate, and the disadvantageous rule forcing them to operate through subsidiaries, not branches. Non-Canadian banks gradually exited the country. Their number had fallen to forty-four by early 1998. At that time, foreign banks in Canada accounted for about 10 percent of total assets in the banking sector, 7.3 percent of business credit, and only 2.8 percent of credit to small- and medium-sized businesses, according to the MacKay task force. Commercial lending to large corporations doing business in the major cities has been the primary focus of the foreigners who stuck it out. Of these, only one institution – Hongkong Bank of Canada – has tried to compete with Canada's major banks in the retail, or consumer, banking sector, a sector that has traditionally required an extensive network of branches, which are very costly to build and operate. "Generally, the Canadian marketplace is considered to be extremely competitive," remarked Kevin Choquette, a bank analyst at Scotia Capital Markets. "The margins in Canada are a lot lower than in a lot of other countries. So I think foreign financial-service companies looking at Canada would only be doing so on a business-by-business basis – that is, credit cards, or perhaps mortgages in the future, or mutual funds and those types of select businesses. In terms of setting up shop in the same context as the large Canadian banks, I would think it would be unlikely."

Finance Minister Paul Martin agreed, and all but dismissed the idea that foreign banks would come into Canada to offer consumers, especially those outside the big cities, new banking options to offset the possible loss of competition as a result of the proposed Royal–BMO and TD–CIBC mergers. "No country in the world has had foreign banks come in and open up extensive branching networks outside the major metropolitan centres," he said in an interview with the *Globe and Mail*.

Most industry observers concluded that the only way a new foreign financial institution would engage in large-scale consumer banking in Canada would be if it was allowed to take over an existing Canadian bank. And that would mean revising the existing rule preventing bank takeovers by foreign interests. This is the famous 10 percent rule, put in place in the mid-1960s by Liberal finance minister Walter Gordon. Introduced after Mercantile Bank was bought by

Citibank of New York, it was meant to keep Chase Manhattan Bank of New York from buying Toronto Dominion. It decreed that no single shareholder could own more than 10 percent of the shares of a major bank's stock. The measure effectively eliminated the possibility of a foreign acquisition of a Canadian bank. Despite the MacKay task force's general preference for a more open, less regulated financial system, the influential study group recommended only that the government modify this rule – not do away with it. As the Liberals well knew, the 10 percent measure was a sacred cow to Canadian nationalists. A hint of the reaction Ottawa could expect if it changed this rule was contained in the September 1998 report by a task force on bank mergers headed by British Columbia small business minister Ian Waddell. Commenting on the possibility of a foreign acquisition of a major Canadian bank, the task force concluded: "Such a takeover would not increase competition or reduce concentration [in the banking industry], but it would raise broader concerns about the acceptable level of foreign ownership in the Canadian banking sector and the continuing viability of national regulation of the Canadian financial system."

TD's Baillie and the other senior bankers in favour of mergers were pragmatic about the 10 percent rule, saying they welcomed a wide-open playing field in Canada. Cynics would say this was an easy position to adopt, since the bankers must have known the Liberals were reluctant to scrap the protectionist ban. But by 1998, the men who ran Canada's big banks had little option but to oppose the 10 percent stipulation. This was because Canadian bankers were in the midst of their own aggressive invasion of the lucrative U.S. market, where there were no legal bars to foreign ownership. In 1984, the Bank of Montreal established a beachhead south of the border with its acquisition of Harris Bank, a Chicago-based company operating throughout the Midwest and Florida. In a major foray into

Wall Street, the CIBC bought Oppenheimer & Co. of New York in mid-1997 for $525 million (U.S.).

Looking ahead, the U.S. market loomed large in the planning of both sets of would-be merger partners. The Royal and the Bank of Montreal hoped to become a continental force in wealth management, personal banking, and commercial banking for small- and medium-sized businesses. More U.S. acquisitions or mergers south of the border were definitely part of the plan. It was this notion that led to Barrett's unfortunate claim, in a meeting with the *Globe and Mail* editorial board a few days after the merger announcement, that a merged Royal–BMO intended to "kick ass" in the U.S. As for CIBC and TD, they hoped to expand their North American activities in the retail brokerage business through TD's discount network, one of the biggest in the U.S., and in investment banking through Oppenheimer.

Whatever an individual bank's strategy, there was no doubt that change was the order of the day. But beyond that, there was little agreement in 1998 on how far Ottawa should go in opening up the Canadian financial-services market, or on what kind of role foreigners should, or would, play in advancing competition north of the border. The idea that the pro-merger banks tried above all to drive home was that, from a competitive point of view, it did not matter if Chase Manhattan or Citicorp or others had little interest in opening nationwide, full-service consumer banking in Canada. What worried Flood, Baillie, Cleghorn, Barrett, and others was the ability of the large, fiercely competitive foreign players to skim off the cream of Canadian financial services by concentrating on profitable niche businesses while ignoring the less economical parts of banking. As CIBC's Flood put it in a speech, "Bit-by-bit they chip away at our core business lines . . . until eventually we'll become marginal players in our home market. It happened to Eaton's. For decades, Eaton's was Canada's premier department-store chain. Last year, it was on the verge of bankruptcy due to intense pressure from new competitors like the Gap, Future Shop, and the 'big box' discounters. We don't want this to happen to us."

Canadians, however, seeing the dominant position, competitive strength, and profitability of Canada's massive banks, would clearly need some convincing before they accepted the validity of this threat.

EIGHT

EL DORADO NORTH

Wearing a wool toque and gloves to ward off the December wind, Matthew Behrens stood on a corner at the heart of Toronto's financial district hoisting a hand-lettered placard with an imitation balance sheet. On one side, in large blue letters, were the words "1997 Bank Profits = $7.1 Billion." On the other side of the imitation ledger was written: "Cost of Ending Child Poverty in Canada = $7.1 Billion." Behrens, a young man who belonged to a local social-action group, was demonstrating with a handful of others on the day in late 1997 when the last of the Big Six banks reported their annual profits. That year, the total came in at $7.5 billion, surpassing all previous records by a wide margin. "There's one and a half million kids living in poverty," Behrens explained. "If there's that much profit around, why don't we take care of the problem of child poverty?" His was a lonely voice in the booming centre of a financial industry that was busy celebrating one of its best years ever, a year of skyrocketing stock markets that spurred unheard-of net earnings – and unheard-of salaries – in brokerages and banks across Canada.

But Behrens and his small band of colleagues were not the only ones making their voices heard as Canadians confronted the geyser of profits cascading down around the men and women at the top of the financial-services industry. "The banks' profits look outrageous," exclaimed Peter Bleyer, executive director of the Council of Canadians. "They are making profits beyond the needs that any bank CEO or shareholder should have." And they're doing it at a time when poverty is on the increase and governments are cutting social programs, he said. On that same day in late 1997, in Toronto, Vancouver, and Winnipeg, the council held small demonstrations against the banks' huge take.

Those concerned about the money machine that funnels wealth upward in the banking industry have had much to protest in recent years. Ever since 1993, when these corporations were first forced to publicly report the compensation given their top executives, Canadians have watched in awe as the salaries and bonuses of senior bankers climbed to stratospheric levels. With stock markets in turmoil for much of 1998, the preceding year may have been the high point in this sweepstakes of wretched excess. The 1997 figures, in fact, defy the average person's credulity.

At the top of the pack in 1997 was Tony Fell, head of the Royal Bank's investment arm, who pulled in a bonus of $6 million. In addition to his bonus, Fell, chairman of RBC Dominion Securities, received a salary of $302,000. As with many in the brokerage industry, his earnings were tied directly to the results at RBC Dominion in a year of roaring stock-market returns. In fact, Fell's earnings easily eclipsed the compensation package of his boss at the Royal Bank, chairman John Cleghorn, who took home $3.2 million that year. Among bankers who had to report their earnings publicly, Fell was rivalled only by John Hunkin, the smooth, affable president of CIBC World Markets, who was paid a $4-million bonus plus $299,000 in salary. Hunkin was also given almost $6 million in CIBC shares, but they were to be issued over the following three years.

While the investment dealers stole the show, the bank presidents did not do badly by any measure. Cleghorn's $3.2 million put him in the middle of the pack among the bosses of Canada's biggest financial institutions. At the pinnacle was Matthew Barrett, who was awarded a $4.2-million pay packet. And that was not all the flamboyant executive had in the way of financial support. At the time the annual compensation numbers were made public early in 1998, Barrett was sitting on $25.3 million in stock-options gains that could be cashed in at some future time. In that department, the Royal's Cleghorn was also looking good, with $16.1 million in stock-options gains that could be exercised at some future date. As for the other top bankers, Bank of Nova Scotia chairman Peter Godsoe's compensation package for 1997 was $3.4 million, and Toronto Dominion boss Charlie Baillie got $2.7 million. (It is worth noting, too, that Baillie's former boss, forty-one-year TD veteran Dick Thomson, who stepped down as chairman in early 1998, had no less than $40.3 million in unexercised stock-option gains at the end of 1997.) Canadian Imperial Bank of Commerce chairman Al Flood pocketed $3.2 million in 1997. In 1998 Flood's compensation fell sharply, however, after he refused to accept an $800,000 bonus for which he was eligible. CIBC had a rough year in 1998, with net earnings dropping 32 percent, but Flood still took home a base salary of $1.01 million. CIBC's Hunkin also went without a bonus for 1998.

As stunning as these numbers were, they were only the tip of the iceberg in the decade of widespread largesse in financial services. Experts estimated that across the country in 1997, for example, the "million-dollar club" included roughly four hundred brokers, bankers, number crunchers, and power brokers. One of the few bankers who said anything about this for the record was Hunkin, who, in the heat of a discussion about the outrageous size of these salaries, told reporters that at CIBC, "We have many people who are paid in the millions of dollars, and quite a number who are paid more than our chairman is paid." He was referring to Flood's 1997 $3.2-million compensation package.

At investment dealers across the country, the big pay packets were part of a gung-ho, hard-driving culture that handsomely rewarded the people who brought in the profits in the good years. "It's very transactionally driven. It's very much 'What have you done for me today?' " explained Rick Moore, managing partner at Russell Reynolds Associates, an executive search firm. "Some firms are very much 'Eat what you kill' – it's what you've done and only what you've done," he said, meaning that compensation is based on individual sales. Other companies work on a group system, with bonuses determined by how well a sales group or division performed over the year. While such schemes are common in the investment industry, Canada's major financial institutions are relying more and more on incentive pay programs to build employee commitment and satisfaction across their various divisions.

Morale could hardly have been higher in the upper reaches of banking and in all the businesses that depend on bankers and brokers in 1997 and early 1998. What might be called the Porsche-o-meter – a reliable measure of how freely the money is flowing in the brokerage houses – was right at the top of the dial that fall. "They had a good year and bonuses are big, big, big this year," enthused Günther Müller, who sells Porsches at a dealership in Toronto. "You always get them when it's stock-market bonus time," he said of the investment dealers. "Of course, it's the Porsches they're interested in." By that time in 1997, Müller's dealership had just about run out of the German sports cars. If you wanted a new Porsche 911, valued at $100,000, you would have to wait until well into the next year. It was an even longer wait for the new Porsche Boxster, the two-seater model with a $65,000 price tag. Dealers of Mercedes, Jaguars, and other status vehicles were also selling cars months in advance. And it was not just the car dealers who were making a killing. Real-estate brokers, expensive restaurants, and top-end tailors all shared in the wealth as the investment bankers enjoyed the fruits of one of the longest bull markets in history. "The salaries that are being paid are unbelievable," Stephen Jarislowsky, a well-known Montreal brokerage boss, told the *Financial Post.* By mid-1998, the market had peaked and then plummeted as the Asian financial flu spread. But even though the investment community was starting to talk about lay-offs and belt-tightening, the money was still gushing out of the stock market, at least according to car dealers, restaurant workers, and others.

Despite the huge bank profits and the lopsided executive salaries, there were not very many Canadians out on the streets protesting as Matthew Behrens had done the day CIBC announced its record $1.6 billion in net earnings. But that isn't to say that a great many Canadians were not quietly appalled by the million-dollar pay-outs in an industry where a teller's salary averages about $21,000 a year. And the banks were starting to hear more and more about this from disgruntled shareholders. At CIBC's annual meeting in a posh Toronto hotel in early 1998, senior executives were berated for their "obscene" and "outrageous" salaries during a fractious gathering that was indicative of the new, restive mood among shareholders.

The catalyst for much of this grumbling was Yves Michaud, a Parti Québécois founder and relentless critic of bank profits and practices. Self-possessed and imperturbable, the mustachioed separatist dominated the question-and-answer sessions of the annual meetings like a star lawyer defending a client in a dramatic case. His interjections were flamboyant, lengthy, and provocative. Largely because of his presence, the 1998 CIBC annual meeting dragged on for four hours.

But as Michaud has proven repeatedly, he is not to be trifled with. His self-described quest for shareholder democracy took on new force after a precedent-setting decision by a Quebec court in 1996 forced financial institutions to allow shareholders to vote on proposals put forward from outside the ranks of a bank's management. Michaud has taken full advantage of this ruling, demanding votes at the major banks' annual meetings on various propositions, including one that would place a cap on the salaries of top executives. Another of his proposed reforms would allow shareholders to vote for members of the board directly, as opposed to the traditional practice of voting for or against a slate of directors chosen by management.

While none of his proposals passed in shareholder voting in 1998, support for Michaud's goals appears to be growing. In particular, many shareholders seem angered by the size of the compensation packages going to senior executives. At CIBC's 1998 meeting, Sandra De Zen, a thirty-three-year-old shareholder and mother of three, stood to comment on the package granted the CIBC's Hunkin, which included the $4-million bonus. "This is ridiculous," she declared. "You can't possibly spend $4 million in one year." She also told CIBC's Flood that the bank needed more women and young people on its thirty-two-member board of directors. "We are the future, not you," De Zen blurted. In a surprise appearance as a proxy shareholder, New Democratic Party leader Alexa McDonough was applauded by CIBC shareholders when she labelled the huge salaries paid to executives "a display of unspeakable arrogance and insensitivity."

Talking with reporters after the meeting, Flood and Hunkin acknowledged the shareholders' impatience. "There is a high degree of sensitivity about these issues, no question about that," Flood said. But Hunkin was unfazed when asked how it felt to be told his salary and bonus were obscene. "The emotionalism around it is not surprising," he said. Of his $10-million total compensation package, he said, "It is a big number," agreeing that "there is a very substantial disparity" in incomes in Canada. However, Hunkin was not giving any ground. "If what we're trying to accomplish is some kind of social goal in terms of disparity of income, that's one thing. But what we are trying to do is build a great organization," he argued. He said substantial salaries are needed if the bank is going to hang on to its best employees.

Of course, CIBC was not the only bank to hear from shareholders on these issues. At the Bank of Nova Scotia's annual meeting a few days later, one questioner noted that chairman Peter Godsoe had been awarded a 20 percent increase in compensation over the previous year. Some of the listeners clapped when the man said, "It would seem to me you would want to give a 20 percent bonus to all your employees." Godsoe responded that it was the bank's directors who made these decisions. At the Royal Bank's annual meeting, New Democrat MP Patrick Martin showed up to criticize the banks wearing a lapel button that read, "Monster Banks, No Thanx." At that meeting, Michaud nearly pulled off a major coup. Some 49 percent of shareholders supported his proposal to allow open voting for members of the bank's board of directors. Michaud, who had referred to the existing practice of voting for management-picked slates as a "Fidel Castro–like system," declared the result a great victory for all shareholders in Canada. "It opens the next millennium with a new era with better participation and shareholder democracy – not only in the banks but in all corporations," he told reporters. As exaggerated as that claim may have been, John Cleghorn responded to the close vote with a promise to look into changing the traditional means of choosing his bank's directors.

Under pressure from activists, the political Left, and much of the media to justify their mammoth profits, the big banks fought back with a barrage of statistics and explanations. They said their profit numbers reflected the size of banks that held deposits in the $700-billion range and assets in the $900-billion range. With numbers that large, net income figures are also likely to be huge, the banks said. They liked to point to a Statistics Canada survey of the financial performance of large companies. The study, released in October 1997, said that independent investment dealers (i.e., those not owned by the banks) were the most profitable businesses in Canada, with a 26.5 percent return on capital employed. Next in line were marine operators and salvage companies, with an 18 percent return on capital, and in third place were fertilizer and explosives manufacturers, with a 17.3 percent return. The chartered banks stood thirteenth, with a return on capital of 12.9 percent. The investment dealers owned by the banks were very high on the list, however. They ranked fourth, with a 15.7 percent return on capital.

While figures like these might have swayed some bank critics, billion-dollar profits were still a sore point with many Canadians. And they were one of the factors contributing to the widespread public unease over the idea of bank mergers. In fact, as they contemplated their flawed image with Canadians, the leaders of the major banks may have wondered if they were not in many ways victims of their own success. For decades, the big chartered banks had been the beneficiaries of government regulatory change so often that the few times they had been thwarted – such as with the 1996 decision by the federal government to keep the banks out of auto leasing and insurance sales through their branches – stood out as landmarks in the evolution of financial services in this country.

Banking in Canada, which for historical purposes could be said to have officially begun with the creation of the Bank of Montreal in 1817, developed for more than a century through periods of instability, skulduggery, failures, mergers, expansion, and hard times. Its characteristics – a national banking system that meant branches of Canada-wide institutions on every corner and dominance by an oligopoly of corporate behemoths – are well known. This structure essentially took shape during a long stretch of bank collapses and intense merger activity that started in the later years of the nineteenth century and continued through to the Great Depression. "The big merger move took place between 1890 and 1920," observed David Bond, a University of British Columbia professor and consultant to the Hongkong Bank of Canada. "In 1890, there were forty-eight banks; by 1920 the banking industry as a whole had quintupled in size, but the number of banks had gone down to nineteen."

While there were many reasons for this, Bond said in an interview, the main cause was the inability of smaller banks to chart a future course. "Basically, many of the smaller regional banks – the Bank of New Brunswick, the Eastern Townships Bank, the Bank of Ottawa, the Metropolitan Bank, the Sovereign Bank, the Crown and Northern Crown banks, and a lot of the little bitty eastern banks – just saw that, one, they didn't have a planned succession, so they didn't see who could take over, or they simply lacked the capital and the vision to make the major move into significant branching in the expanding West." As the country evolved from an agricultural to an industrial nation, the smaller banks also found it hard to meet the credit needs of increasingly large industrial clients, Bond added. "So the smaller banks had limited prospects in the future, and the bigger banks could offer the shareholders a premium and offer several of the directors a position on the big bank board. The combination of those things – essentially, economies of scale – led to the demise of many of the regional banks."

If the structure that the banks eventually assumed became familiar to everyone, so, too, did the attributes that coloured Canadians' perceptions of these financial operations. Out of decades of resentment of tight loan policies, Depression-era foreclosures, holier-than-thou conservatism, and bankers' privileged wealth came the modern public view of banks as uncompetitive, immensely powerful, unyielding, and filthy rich pillars of the country's corporate and political establishment. Some of this was no doubt exaggerated, and it certainly ignored the better features of this country's banking system, such as its reliability and its national pricing and cheque-cashing structures. "One of the great strengths of Canada was a very stable banking system," commented historian Douglas Owram, a vice-president of the University of Alberta. "No banks failed in the Depression, unlike the States, where they had lots of banks fail." In contrast to the situation in Canada, where banks could open an unlimited number of branches across the country, U.S. bankers faced stiff limitations on branching, a restriction that made American banks more vulnerable to regional or local economic swings. But in Canada "we have also had lots of complaints about the lack of responsiveness [by banks] because of the lack of competition, especially in the Depression," Owram said. While the ability of Canada's banks to shift capital around the country gave them an important role in the development of the West, that did little to improve the esteem with which banks were held on the Prairies and beyond. "True westerners don't trust banks, any banks, ever," wrote Ted Byfield, founder of the *Western Report*, in the *Financial Post.* "If the Big Four announce mergers, westerners suspect a plot. If they'd announced plans to split into 40 little banks, westerners would have suspected a plot."

In addition to the advantages of a national banking system, life for Canada's bankers was also made easier by the fact that they were not subject to anti-combines rules, which meant that until recently there was no price competition, only competition between banks on services. "Remember, until 1980, if I were the Commerce and I wanted to raid one of your accounts and you were the Bank of Montreal and I went and called on your customer, I could be censured by the bankers' association," UBC's Bond said. "And if I went to rob somebody – in other words, hire one of your smart whiz-bangs – I also could be censured. I mean, there was an agreement that you just didn't do that. It was enforced because the banks controlled the [nationwide financial] clearing system."

But if Canada's approach to banking promoted stability, the lack of competition among the gradually shrinking ranks of financial institutions also fostered major mistakes, Bond pointed out. "The lack of price competition was a convenient little oligopolistic behavioural pattern, and I don't think they should have done that." As well, there were bankers who showed "immense arrogance towards their customers," he said. "And they were also excessively small-c conservative, which I suppose is the nature of bankers." But one of the major failings of the system is that Canada has not developed the capacity for providing sufficient risk capital for business, Bond remarked.

Whatever its pluses and minuses, the banking landscape in Canada has changed immensely in the last half-century. Looking back over that time, Canadians could be forgiven for thinking the banks had greedily gobbled up most of the financial-services industry and were intent on swallowing what was left as quickly as possible. These were the same banks whose former bosses, lulled by their own success and innate conservatism, had by the 1950s found themselves increasingly surrounded by more innovative competitors among the trust, finance, and mortgage companies. At that time, the financial-services industry was still strictly divided under the "four pillars" concept, but this segregation was starting to erode.

Allowed into mortgage lending on National Housing Act–insured loans on new housing in 1954, the banks began what would be a gradual but relentless forty-year drive to expand their operations, services, and customer base. Successive federal governments chipped away at the four pillars through a series of Bank Act revisions. One of the most significant came in 1967. For the first time, the banks were allowed to make conventional mortgage loans and the 6 percent interest-rate ceiling was lifted – both were changes that benefited the banks at the expense of finance companies, trusts, and insurance firms. Another set of revisions was passed in 1987. As part of a general liberalization that gave insurance and trust companies the freedom to expand their operations and holdings, the banks were allowed that year to buy securities dealers. And a further dismantling of the four pillars came in 1992, when the banks were given the right to set up insurance subsidiaries. However, the federal government would not budge on its refusal to allow the banks to engage in car leasing or sell insurance through their branches. Even so, the legislative changes made between 1987 and 1992 unleashed a furious round of expansion by the big banks. Within a few years of being allowed into the securities business, the banks had, in a series of billion-dollar deals, grabbed up all but one large independent brokerage house. And by the late 1990s, only one large trust company, Canada Trust, was left standing on its own on the financial-services battleground.

While the banks' presence in such areas as personal finance and mortgages benefited consumers by driving down prices, it was a record of aggressive expansion that did little to relieve the anxiety of the banks' competitors, not least those in the insurance business. Commenting on the recommendations put forward by the MacKay task force to further open up the competitive landscape, Guarantee Co. of North America president Jules Quenneville told members of Parliament that MacKay's reforms were really a disguised attempt to bring forward "protectionist policies which will further concentrate financial power in the hands of the banking industry." He said the banks' inability to compete had nothing to do with Canada's limited market. Rather, Quenneville remarked, "As in most oligopolies, the banking industry has not distinguished itself as innovative or responsive to consumer needs."

With their acquisitions of the brokerage houses in particular, the banks realized a tremendous financial advantage as they gradually moved away from their standard role as deposit-takers into the wealth-management business. As the bull market roared ahead in the 1990s, the banks raked in revenues from investors who were increasingly shifting to equities at the expense of traditional savings vehicles. How much of a boost did this give to the banks' bottom line? The $7.5 billion in profits reported by the Big Six banks in 1997, to take just one example, marked an increase of fully 43 percent over what they had earned only two years earlier.

While the pro-merger banks talked about their struggle to stay competitive, it was obvious that these financial institutions were in a very strong position. By 1997, eight banks – the Royal, CIBC, the Bank of Montreal, Scotiabank, Toronto Dominion, the National Bank, the Canadian Western Bank, and Laurentian – controlled 86 percent of the $776 billion in total domestic bank-sector assets, according to the MacKay report. Forty-six smaller, largely foreign-owned institutions held the remaining domestic bank assets. And between them, these fifty-four banks controlled 46 percent of all assets in the financial-services industry. According to the Canadian Bankers Association, the banks generated 55 percent of their revenues from net interest income. Another 44 percent came from revenue from services to clients through investment subsidiaries, currency transactions, and other activities. Then there were the service charges so hated by consumers and small business people. The CBA said 4 percent of bank revenue came from those charges. That didn't sound like much until people realized it was 4 percent of annual revenues totalling a whopping $83 billion – or $3.3 billion a year. That alone was enough to convince some Canadians that their bankers had long been too rich, too powerful, and too greedy for their own, and the country's, good.

NINE

GIVING CREDIT WHERE IT'S DUE

Many a newspaper reader in British Columbia can identify Markus Stoiber, the handsome, imperious bank chief executive who can be seen in advertisements peering out the window of his skyscraper office or hefting his tennis racket as he heads out for a quick game. "Thanks to my bank, all my retirement dreams came true," Stoiber says in one ad. Then there's another spot that features a gallery of photos of Stoiber, his chef, his gardener, his pilot, his food taster, his son, his masseuse, his personal trainer, his interior decorator, his equestrian coach, his first wife, his butler, his present wife, his dog, and his future wife. Above these snapshots is the headline "Bigger Bank Profits. They're Good for All of Us."

The ads are realistic. The only difference is that Stoiber and his company, Humungous Bank, are fictional. Both are the creatures of a Vancouver ad agency, which created the series of satirical print, radio, and outdoor promotions for Richmond Savings, a British

Columbia credit union. "We Built This Bank One Service Charge at a Time" was the headline on another newspaper ad for Humungous Bank, whose motto is Your Money Is Our Money. Underneath the ad, in small print, is the message: "If you think the big banks are getting bigger at your expense, it's time you talked to Richmond Savings. We believe in rewarding our customers with fewer charges. Not to mention service that's second to none. After all, that's how we built our business. We're not a bank. We're better."

This ad campaign for a company that doesn't exist caught on beyond all expectations, says Brent Cuthbertson, Richmond Savings' director of marketing. Humungous Bank has spawned an Internet following, given rise to a sharp increase in Richmond Savings' membership, earned awards, and added a new phrase to the B.C. lexicon. In 1997, for instance, the Vancouver Province published an editorial cartoon featuring B.C.'s New Democrat premier Glen Clark over the words "Humungous Government. Your Money Is Our Money."

The spoof ad campaign was dreamed up in the early 1990s by Palmer Jarvis Communications and Richmond Savings, now Canada's third-largest credit union. As it grew in popularity, the concept evolved. A few years ago the fictional Stoiber set up a Web site (www.humungousbank.com) at his imaginary Caribbean villa. On this site, visitors could sample the thoughts of Stoiber, such as: "If everyone saved a penny today and doubled it every day after that, by the end of thirty days I'd get a vacation in the Bahamas." Browsers also could approach an on-line Humungous Bank teller's booth, only to be met by a Closed sign. Or they could apply and be turned down for a loan. Also on offer were mutual funds like the Canadian Inequity Fund, which buys such investments as Humungous Vital Organ Sales and Humungous Repossession. In a recent phase of the campaign, Humungous Bank itself appeared to be running ads to fight back by attacking Richmond Savings. One of these was a written promotion for Richmond Savings, with the wording mostly blacked out by a huge imitation Warning stamp. In smaller print were the words "This subversive propaganda is dangerous. It is designed to lure you away from Humungous Bank . . ." A real Humungous Bank would have reason to worry. During the first five years the ads were in production, the number of people doing business with Richmond Savings ballooned 55 percent, to eighty thousand, and assets were up 125 percent, to $2.7 billion, the company said.

So how much did this bother the mainline banks? Enough that senior bankers trekked west in 1995 to try to persuade Richmond Savings to drop the campaign. The executives representing the big banks argued that the Humungous Bank ads were unfair and too harsh. Margaret Eckenfelder, regional director in Vancouver of the Canadian Bankers Association, complained that Richmond Savings was taking advantage of the "negative perception" Canadians have of their banks. And that was not the end of the tensions between the B.C. credit union and the big banks. When Richmond Savings tried to obtain trademark protection for its slogan (We're Not a Bank. We're Better), the banks challenged the application before federal trademark authorities. When asked why, Eckenfelder explained that Richmond Savings' tag line was "deceptively misdescriptive."

Humungous Bank tapped the deep vein of distrust and resentment Canadians have when it comes to their biggest financial institutions. This anti-bank feeling goes a long way towards explaining the popularity of credit unions. Owned by their members and dedicated to pumping their profits back into the communities they serve, these co-operatives became, in the years after the Second World War, an increasingly important alternative to mainline banks across the country. In Western Canada, particularly in B.C. and Saskatchewan, they are still a powerful force today.

In Quebec, le Mouvement des Caisses Desjardins, the equivalent of the credit unions, is both emblematic of and instrumental to

French-Canadian nationalism. From its meagre beginnings at the turn of the century, the movement, which was created by Alphonse Desjardins, has grown into a massive financial conglomerate with affiliates in Ontario, Manitoba, and New Brunswick. This unique, provincially chartered organization controls assets of $75 billion and includes 1,400 credit unions with 5.4 million members. With 42,000 people on the payroll, the Caisse is the largest private employer in Quebec. Its existence in and importance to Quebec's financial-services sector made the entire question of bank mergers less explosive in the province. "It's not an issue in Quebec," Finance Minister Paul Martin said in the summer of 1998.

Elsewhere, the planned mega-bank consolidations had the makings of a watershed for the credit union movement. When the Royal–Bank of Montreal and Toronto Dominion–CIBC merger proposals were announced, it wasn't long before credit union leaders turned their thoughts to the inroads they could make with the many Canadians who were alienated and alarmed by the prospect of even bigger banks. Perhaps spurred by the success of the Humungous Bank campaign, credit unions cast about for innovative ways to make their point. In downtown Regina, the Credit Union Central of Saskatchewan rented billboards saying, "Send Your Bank a Message: 1-888-i-switch!!!" Metro Credit Union in Toronto put out brochures that proclaimed, "Banks? No Thanks. (There's a Better Alternative.)" The Hepcoe Credit Union, Ontario's third largest, launched an ad campaign around the southern part of the province using such tag lines as "Imagine Finding a Banker Who Understands Your Small Business. Stop Laughing. We're Serious." And Ontario's Brockville Community Credit Union developed an ad it ran on the radio that went as follows:

(Phone rings.)

"Welcome to your new bank. Now that we've taken over your old bank, we've installed an easy-to-use, bank-by-phone system. Listen closely to the following options. To find out how many convenient services we've taken away, press 1. To find out about the all-new service charges and bank fees you have to pay, press 2. For information on exciting new ways of billing you for your service charges, press 3. To learn about the penalties for not paying those service charges, press 4. To contact an employee who will treat you like a number instead of an individual, press 5 and hold for at least eight minutes, at which time you will be disconnected."

(Beep. Music under announcer.)

"Isn't it time you said, 'No thanks' to banks? Hang up and call the Brockville Community Credit Union."

Such ads sought to exploit a bank-merger backlash that had the potential to provide credit unions with a significant boost in membership, and anecdotal evidence suggested in early 1998 that disillusioned bank customers were indeed responding. "The mergers have made everyone, all consumers, more aware of their banking choices and the alternatives that are out there," explained George Scott, director of market development at Credit Union Central of Ontario. This customer windfall was eyed hungrily. For although one in three adult Canadians already belonged to the century-old credit union movement, some of its leaders were convinced that more consumers, particularly in Ontario, would join if they only knew about the fast-evolving alternative to banks. "There's a real lack of awareness," said Howard Bogach, chief executive officer of the forty-thousand-member Metro Credit Union in Toronto. "People ask me things like: 'Do you have to belong to a union to join?' " But convincing people to sign on can be difficult, he added. "Unfortunately, the term 'credit union' is two words, 'credit' and 'union,' both of which individually can have negative connotations."

Also, organizations like Scott's were up against well-known and long-standing consumer inertia when it comes to banks. Scott said opinion polling has shown that 60 percent of customers never switch their financial institutions. And many credit unions lack the size and capital to stick with the growing businesses they help nurture. The Canadian Federation of Independent Business, in a statement to the federal Liberal party caucus task force on financial-services reform, said, "It is true that some credit unions offer good service, particularly in Quebec and Western Canada." But, the CFIB continued, credit unions "have very little national market presence or power, have underdeveloped commercial lending expertise and are not as well-equipped to grow with companies as they expand and specialize."

For these reasons, the country's credit unions remain small players in the Canadian financial-services sector, at least outside of British Columbia and Quebec. In addition to Quebec's caisses populaire, there are 870 Canadian credit unions, with 4.5 million members. Their combined assets of $49 billion are dwarfed by those of a single large bank, the CIBC, which boasts more than $280 billion in assets. Apart from their lack of profile among Canadians, credit unions are hampered by provincial regulations that differ from one jurisdiction to the next, lack of financial wherewithal, high operating costs, and a fractious membership built around local communities and their interests. They also complain that their best ideas – such as daily interest savings accounts, open mortgages, and mutual funds that choose only ethical companies – are simply grabbed up by the banks, who market the innovative products across their own huge national networks. In short, credit unions in most areas of the country have to work hard to lure customers away from the big financial institutions.

"Right now, you'd be kidding yourself if you said credit unions are stiff competition to banks," said Harri Jansson, president and chief executive officer of Richmond Savings and a former Bank of Montreal executive. "In my eighteen years at the Bank of Montreal, I never looked sideways at a credit union. They weren't on the radar screen." And ironically, there was another dynamic at work: Like the very banks whose size tended to smother their business aspirations, the credit unions were, by the late 1990s, confronting the need to adjust to technological change and increasing competition from new and more aggressive entrants in the financial-services market.

"In Richmond, we have four other credit unions, and every single bank is in here, plus Citibank has a retail operation here," Jansson said during an interview in the credit union's modest headquarters outside Vancouver. He told of playing golf with a banker who was surprised when he heard that Richmond Savings could have trouble surviving on its own in today's world. Jansson recalled explaining to his golf partner that the problem was that credit unions are expensive. He explained, "It costs us about eighty-two cents to make a dollar. It costs the Canadian banks on average fifty-seven cents to fifty-nine cents to make a dollar. [If] they combine [through mergers] and reduce the expenses, the overhead, they'll get that down to world class, which is around fifty cents. So, let's say that three years from now we wake up and we've got two or three banks in Canada and their costs of making a dollar is fifty; ours isn't going to be any lower and may be higher because costs keep going up. So, you could go down the road and say, 'Well, we're fine,' but our [profit] margins are shrinking, our competition is ourselves, . . . which is stupid, and . . . we've got the banks driving the costs down. It doesn't make any sense. First of all, in my mind, we have to stop competing against ourselves. We have to find a way to work together to compete against the banks."

In the wake of the announcements of merger plans by Royal–BMO and TD–CIBC, the credit unions did exactly that. "All these mergers do is they serve as a catalyst to increase our awareness of the need for change," explained Robert Quart, chief executive of Vancouver City Savings Credit Union, during an interview in his office, with its panoramic view of downtown Vancouver. "It's already there in a very major way," said the dapper, bespectacled Quart. "Branchless banking is an example" of the changing nature of the competition the credit unions face, he added. Then there are the "new players that are coming into the field that are category killers – they're out all over the place. They're out there on the mortgage side; they're out there in terms of wealth management, whether it's mutual funds or whatever. You've got a category killer in just about every business that we're in. And for most credit unions, the core business is the residential mortgage, and more and more, the viability of financial institutions is not around that particular offering but more around the wealth-management products. And while we're doing well on the mutual-fund side, credit unions by and large are lagging in terms of their ability to provide brokerage services and alternative investment options to consumers and our members. So the need for change is very much there."

In early 1998, the credit unions began looking seriously at ways to expand their competitive edge, and by summer plans were well-advanced for the creation of a new, coast-to-coast co-operative that would feature identical services at about 145 branches across the country. At that time, the new network envisioned by Quart and others was to include twelve credit unions. Among them would be VanCity, the country's largest credit union, and the Civil Service Co-operative, Ontario's biggest. "This bank would be a community bank, but [it] would allow existing credit unions from coast to coast to pool their assets and create virtually instantly a coast-to-coast financial institution that offers the same slate of products regardless of where one is," Quart said in a later interview. Creating competitive alternatives to the big banks was one of the key recommendations of the September 1998 MacKay report, and Quart and other credit union leaders were afforded a warm reception by parliamentarians when they went to Ottawa that fall to talk about giving their movement more national cohesiveness. "We think that if Canada is serious about having a second tier of financial-services delivery, credit unions are ideally positioned to make that happen very quickly," Quart stated.

It was clear that the Liberal government agreed. A revamping of existing laws to enable credit unions to create a federally regulated national co-operative bank – a move that would allow member unions to maximize their financial capabilities by pooling their assets – was expected to be a key element of the legislative reforms the federal government was planning to introduce for financial services in 1999. Under the scheme favoured by Quart, each credit union would keep its own name but would also be a division of the new national co-operative. The credit unions would cut their costs by sharing back-room administration, marketing, and other functions across a wider business base – exactly as the big banks have been doing.

The idea made sense, but it remained to be seen how it would work in practice. For one thing, going national would be a tricky balancing act for organizations whose primary appeal is their ability to offer local, personalized service. "Where we think we have an advantage is that we feel that we're closer to the consumer," Quart said. "And so as we try to restructure ourselves, we've got to make sure that we don't lose that which is our differentiating advantage." It was also unclear how many of the 870 credit unions outside Quebec would go for a new, federally created, national network. The whole idea was contrary to the independent spirit and operational traditions of these institutions. "Suppose you are the CEO of a credit union in one of forty locations in B.C., where you're the only game in town," said Richmond Savings' Jansson. "You're in charge of a credit union in Timbercut, B.C., with a population of two thousand. There is no bank. So why would you be interested in merging with somebody else?" Of the ninety-five credit unions in B.C., Jansson estimated, there would probably be forty that would say, "What's the big deal? My world hasn't changed."

This, then, was the challenge that lay ahead for the credit unions as they tried to adjust to a future that would see them up against fiercely aggressive new competitors whether the major banks were allowed to merge or not.

Ten

Can a Bank Change?

"Until this past Saturday," Ruth Chernia wrote in a letter to the president of the Toronto Dominion Bank, "I had thought that the basis for the bank's relationship with clients was still on an individual basis – but no more, I see." Chernia, a Toronto woman with a forty-year tie, both as a client and briefly as a teller, to TD Bank, explained how she had tried to introduce her eleven-year-old daughter, who earned money walking dogs, to banking. Because the daughter was paid by cheque and was too young to go to the bank herself, and because both parents worked full time, the family was in the habit of going to the bank to cash her cheque once a month on a Saturday. "I had noticed the recent signs that teller services would no longer be available on Saturday but hadn't really understood what that meant to us, a busy family," Chernia wrote.

She soon learned that the word "service" as defined by today's banks can often take on unexpected meaning. When she arrived at the bank one Saturday, Chernia recalls in her letter, "it was explained to me that there was no cash in the bank and the closest TD that was open with cash was at Victoria Park and Brimley – hardly in the neighbourhood. I asked how [my daughter] would get the cheque cashed. They said come back during the week. Not a real option . . . [and] besides, she wanted the money on Saturday to do a bit of shopping. I also said I didn't want to give her a Green card because of her age. While she is responsible and would treat it with respect, what if it were stolen or if she were faced with a bully?

"And so I'm writing to you," Chernia continued in her letter to TD's top executive, "because I asked to whom I could write and complain and was handed a brochure entitled 'TD's Commitment to Independent Business.' So I see very clearly that you are abandoning the family, the small saver, and especially the children who are the future of your business. My daughter has seen clearly that you are not interested in her little account."

While not by a long shot the most egregious incident suffered by bank customers at the mercy of tellers, managers, and unseen phone operators, Chernia's experience seemed to capture the frustration that many consumers feel towards the banks. More than anything else, customers are driven to distraction by the difficulties of coping with a business so large, impersonal, and labyrinthine that their needs hardly seem to register at all – even when the problem they want addressed has been expressly created by the bank itself.

The extent of this aggravation seems almost immeasurable. Every day, judging from the complaints that pour into the media, thousands of people across Canada are out there fuming, stewing, and plotting ways to get their bank's attention to a problem. They write letters, burn up the phone lines, overload fax machines, start court cases, send secret notes to the media from "inside" a bank, pester MPs, join interest groups, and forage through databases for old statistics with which to prove their cases. In Canada, and even more so in the United States, dealing with the banks and trying to overcome their perceived shortfalls has grown into a mini-industry, with legislative committees, bank-paid ombudsmen, court actions, and pressure groups galore trying to ride herd on these financial institutions.

Many Canadians do still respect their banks, but they seem vastly outnumbered by the detractors, who can be found at every level of society and business. "Bank bashing is the favourite sport of some Canadians," laments Gordon Feeney, the avuncular chairman of the Canadian Bankers Association. People resent the huge size and power that the banks have been allowed to amass, with government help, over the course of a century. They resent the profits and the obscene earnings that the bank bosses and their senior deputies in the bank-owned brokerage houses have run up. But even beyond the personal riches of the banks and their high rollers, many Canadians seem galled most of all by the control that bank managers exert over their everyday lives, whether they are looking to the banks for a mortgage, financing for a car purchase, help in avoiding going broke, or a loan to expand a business. As for small business, it has long been said that Canada's conservative-minded, risk-averse, and stodgy bankers would loan money only to an entrepreneur who was so well off that he or she really did not need it.

There was also the vexing matter of ever-increasing costs. In 1997, service charges paid to financial institutions by small- and medium-sized firms rose on average by 12 percent, according to a survey by the Canadian Federation of Independent Business. "This is quite worrisome," said federation president Catherine Swift. "Service charges are out of control, and more than ever are the cash cow for banks and other financial institutions when it comes to dealing with their small business customers." MPs, regularly besieged by small business people with bank horror stories, have tried for years to pressure the banks to expand their loans to small business, with limited success.

Then there is the deep-set anger over the usurious interest charges banks slap on the people they call revolvers, customers who do not pay off their credit-card bills at the end of each month. These charges run from 16 to 18 percent a year, and no amount of public outrage has forced the banks to bring these rates down across the board. There is also the spread between interest rates and the interest banks pay on their customers' deposits. By mid-1997, a customer could have a loan from the bank for 7 percent annual interest. But the same customer was probably receiving only 0.5 percent a year on the money he or she kept in the bank.

Many customers also feel they are being unfairly nickeled and dimed on service charges. Reacting to the banks' announcement of their record 1997 profits, federal New Democrats called for a public inquiry into service charges paid by consumers. "A growing portion of bank revenues from service charges originate from automated-teller machine transactions," said NDP MP Lorne Nystrom. "As the banks move to reduce the numbers of personal tellers and as our economy becomes ever more reliant on a 'cashless' or electronic environment, consumers are increasingly susceptible to unfair price gouging on a range of basic financial transactions. This sort of automated pick-pocketing has got to stop."

And because of the banks' size and the number of customers and transactions they're dealing with, the potential for mistakes and damaging foul-ups seems almost infinite – as does the reservoir of complaints from consumers. Some are shocked when their bank branch disappears while they are away on holiday, others discover mistakes in their accounts, and still more are outraged by the indignities created by uncaring, know-nothing clerks at the other end of the line in the vaunted new telephone-banking systems. (How hopeless can the treatment by phone attendants get? One woman rose before the thousands of people at a packed Royal Bank annual meeting to tell her story. With the Royal chairman looking on from the podium, the woman recounted how, after a series of frustrating inquiries, she had become fed up and told the telephone clerk that she was going to take her problem directly to the office of John Cleghorn. "Who's that?" the telephone clerk had responded blithely.) Here is a sampling of Canadians talking about their banking experiences in their own words.

Voices

Danny Vesperini, on the *Toronto Star*'s "Speak Out" Web site:

> Banks stink . . . period. In a time when many are struggling to make ends meet, it is sad that we sit here and watch the banks reap enormous profits each year. And to make matters worse, they insist on charging the lowly bank account holder for every possible reason, including depositing money. What is especially disgusting is when they have a service charge for those account holders that carry such a low balance. [They] are the ones that DON'T have the money . . . and therefore should get a break from a bank that makes billions of dollars. It is just sick. . . .

Surendra Jeyarajan, in a letter to Finance Minister Paul Martin:

> I received a notice recently from Bank of Montreal that it would increase its interest rate on credit card lending. Bank continues to charge unfair interest on my MasterCard. Canadians like me have no choice. Thank you for letting foreign banks operate and to allow them to lend to Canadians. I asked Bank of Montreal to give me the reason for the increase in the rate and I am told that there is no need for them to do so. Bank informed me that it has an absolute right to charge me any rate at its own discretion. . . . It is unfair for the banks (5 banks that control the market) to have absolute financial rights and controls over Canadians and to move the interest rate in any direction. Canadian consumers have no choice but have to pay the rate demanded. There is no actual

competition among the big 5 banks and all have similar rates.

Maybe the banks operate an undetectable "price fixing" operation? If Canadian consumers like me have no right to challenge their demands then Canadian banks become the 4th level of government, collecting revenue by way of service charge and interest charge. . . . This absolute power over Canadians enables bank executives to easily earn for themselves millions of dollars' worth executive compensation and to achieve their profit targets. . . .

George Muenz, of Vancouver, writing to *Canadian Business* magazine:

I was with TD for eight years, and it seems that, other than ATM transactions, the people there could get almost nothing right. Even more bothersome was their cavalier attitude about their deplorable service. Funny, they seem to claim that merging into ever-larger institutions will make them more efficient. And pigs will fly, right? Some examples:

I transferred my account from one TD branch to another in the same town. I had to talk to five different people, and kept getting different answers about the status of my accounts and ATM cards. I had a monthly deposit going to RRSP mutual funds and wanted to discuss my account with a live person. No one could tell me where to find the office for this. I finally located it – and they were shocked to see an actual customer show up. It's a good thing I did, because they had not registered a $3,000 transfer I had made. . . .

A letter to the media:

IT'S TRUE! – IT HAPPENED TO ME AND TO MY FRIENDS!

I went to the Royal Bank for a loan.

They wanted me to open an account, but were vague about the loan.

At first they said no. I persisted and finally
they said o.k.
BUT
Only if I would switch our investments form my broker to another broker – of course owned by the Royal Bank.

So I switched. It cost me several hundred dollars in "transfer fees" from the other broker!
Part of this was paid by the Royal, later on, when I complained.

Other banks do the same, and many of my friends have been caught up as I was.

Unfortunately few if any bank customers care to complain, as we are up against the big guys, who of course deny!

Media exposure surely helps, and hopefully the banks will back off! But we know they won't , as nobody can really prove anything. Sorry I can't sign my name, my accountant strongly advised me not to!

Lorne V. Phillips, of Toronto, in a letter to the editor of the *Toronto Star*:

It is May 15 at 10:15 a.m. and I am furious! I have just returned from the Toronto Dominion Bank branch at Morningside Mall in West Hill. I wanted to open an account and the conversation went like this:

"I wish to open an account."

"I'm sorry there is no one here to help you."

"Pardon?"

"The person who would assist you has called in sick." (A Friday of a holiday weekend – does that surprise anyone?) "Would you like to come back later?"

"Not really."

"We might have someone at 12:30 if you care to come back."

I thanked the young lady and left. I can't imagine what the service will be like when we get down to two or three banks.

An unsigned letter to the media, purportedly from someone working for the Toronto Dominion Bank:

FROM INSIDE T-DERS

PLEASE PRINT THIS LETTER

So much has been said about the mergers, I certainly agree with Friday's news from trust chief that Canadian banks do not need to merge to compete globally [this reference is to a statement by a well-known trust company figure, probably former Ontario lieutenant-governor Hal Jackman], we have shown it with the billions, not millions, of dollars that the banks have made.

It is greed that bank are merging and the global issue is just an excuse. Bank have made so much million even in time of bad year and they should be more supportive to our Canadian economy than laying off. It's a shame that despite the making of billion last year TD still lays off so many staff and cutting services.

We used to have full time tellers, now we do not have them any more, we have a bunch of ad hoc teller that the bank would call in when they need. Worse still now they have even start with investment Saturday strategy, with no teller on Saturday. How do you expect someone who work and finish work at 5 and by the time they drove to the bank, the bank is closed at 6 p.m. The only day they could do their banking now is Saturday and now with investment day on Saturday, you can't visit any more unless you want to do investment or credit. So you don't have a choice they want you to use the machine and telephone banking – it's all right if you are literate what about those who are illiterate??? The telephone banking is so frustrating, you could be holding the phone for half an hour and still get no answer. Most of the time the staff who handle the telephone banking are not versed in knowledge and keep putting you on hold.

You would think that it's a joke if I will tell you that last year I have to pay $30.00 for my Christmas dinner as head office could only pay $10.00. It's a shame to know that the TD Bank could not even buy their staff a $40.00 plate dinner despite the billion they claimed to make last year. Someone in head office certainly forget that the billions were made not by itself but all the people who have work so hard for TD.

Now with the TD personal banking concept, you have the personal banker looking after only the 20 per cent high value customer whom the branch make money on, so what happen to the 80 per cent customer – you and me???

Thank you for listening.

A letter to the media from Maggi Ansell of Fanny Bay, B.C.:

Life threw a few curve-balls at us last year, and the Royal Bank Bungle has still not been cleared up to my satisfaction.

On 9th March, 1997 we were rescued from our sinking yacht in 30 metre seas in Cyclone Justin off the Queensland coast of Australia, carrying only passports and credit cards. We lost our 50-foot home of seven years, and our belongings.

But we felt lucky. We not only had our lives, we also had many good friends in Canada, and were immediately offered homes until we could pull our lives together.

We used a credit card to secure the cheapest possible fare home, to stay with family and friends across Canada. Japan Air Lines waived the cheap fare pre-booking time-constraint. Thanks also to frequent flyer air miles accumulated over the past few years, we had enough to purchase a cross-Canada ticket with Canadian Airlines. However, when we got to Canada we would need cash for food and day-to-day living expenses.

For the past 10 years, we have had a Royal Certified Service chequing account at the Bloor and Yonge Branch of the Royal Bank of Canada. At the beginning of each year we deposited enough money to cover direct debit payments. However, when we returned to Canada, the money in our account soon dwindled.

On 9th April, US $7000 was sent by Telegraphic Transfer (TT) to our Bloor and Yonge branch of the Royal Bank. An electronic transaction which theoretically is immediate, but in fact usually takes three working days before it is deposited in the account. We have been carrying out transfers like this for the past 10 years.

On 7th May, all is not well. Our account is now $1800 overdrawn, and another monthly direct debit is imminent. Daily for 6 days we telephoned the issuing bank for possible news, and daily we visited the Royal Bank ATM for a mini-statement. No money. In desperation, on the 13th May we fax the issuing bank to urgently transfer our last $5000.

On 14th May the issuing bank informs me that the tracer has got as far as the Royal Bank of Canada who were looking into it.

On 14th May I call the Royal Bank of Canada once more to see if there is news of the missing TT and to see if the new TT has arrived. Customer Service inform us that there has been no TT, and as for the new one sent on 13th May, not to bother inquiring about it until "next week," i.e., Tuesday 20th, after the long weekend. Once again we leave a telephone number hoping for a return call with good news.

By this time we have had the embarrassment of borrowing money from friends to cover current food bills, and to pay into the overdrawn account before the next direct debit is due.

Eventually, on 15th May, I have a call from Suzette Gumbs-Thomas of the Royal Bank of Canada Bloor/Yonge Branch. She has the new TT for US $5000 and will transfer it into our account at the current day's rate of $1.34. Overjoyed that we are no longer destitute, we tentatively ask if there is any possible news of the previous TT for US $7000 sent 5 weeks ago.

"Oh, yes," says Suzette. "I have it here, waiting."

Barely able to contain our dismay, we ask, "Waiting for what?"

"When we get a Telegraphic Transfer," Suzette explained, "It is our policy to telephone the account holder to see to which account they want the money credited. We get into a lot of trouble if we credit it straight away, in case it is in the wrong account."

OK – the transfer was in US dollars, but we only have ONE account, which, if they had taken the trouble to look into, they would see has been getting more and more overdrawn during the past FIVE WEEKS. Previously, they have changed transfers into Canadian dollars at the current day's rate, and credited our only account.

We are aghast, the number they have been telephoning was from 10 years back when I was a mature student at U of Toronto. Notwithstanding that, why was she telephoning? I was overseas, and must admit I have never felt any obligation, when travelling, to call the Royal Bank to let them know my itinerary and where I can be contacted by telephone daily. I pointed out to Suzette, however, that, conversely, I felt the Royal Bank WAS under an obligation to follow instructions given by another bank to transfer funds received, directly into my account without delay. Anyway, when unable to contact me by phone, why had she not sent a letter to my mailing address which has been used for many years? And furthermore, why had they never written to inform us of this "new" policy of holding onto the money until they could speak in person to the account holder? Had this been the case, we would have tried to issue special instructions regarding our transfers.

I tried to explain the trouble I have been in for the past five weeks. The overdraft, the borrowing, the costly telephone calls, but she is unmoved. Suzette says she will credit the 5-week-old transfer today. She confides that I am getting a better rate today than five weeks ago. I point out that there is a fundamental flaw in her logic. Five weeks ago, the exchange rate was higher, in my favour, a difference of about $280. I insist the money be credited at the exchange rate of the day it was received. But no, she has no authority to do this. After some pressure, she reluctantly agrees to check with Treasury, and will call me back.

She does not call back. I telephone again. I reach Suzette and she graciously tells me they will "waive" the overdraft charges incurred so far – some $8.94. Incurred because of their error – Big Deal. No news about the $280 they have. She will call back about that.

But she doesn't call. I telephone her once more on her direct line, but she immediately passes me to Leonie Vernon. Suzette doesn't want to talk to me again. Leonie repeats the information previously given by Suzette. I am chastised for not calling to check. She doesn't listen when I tell her I repeatedly called the Royal Bank Customer Services to check if a TT had arrived for my account, that's how they were able to call me on the 15th about the new $5000 TT.

I can hardly believe how calm I have remained. I ask to be put through to the manager, someone who has the authority to deal with my grievance. Someone who can give me back the $280 I am missing, and reimburse me for my lost interest, the erroneously charged overdraft interest, and the costly telephone calls. I eventually speak to Angie Girardo, assistant manager, who, to give her credit, sounds apologetic and puts the matter "under investigation."

I am staggered by their ineptitude. In summary:

We have only one account at the Royal Bank.

For 10 years, we have made many similar TTs, and this has never occurred before. Transfers received in US$ have automatically been changed into CDN$ and credited to our account.

The bank sat on our money for 5 WEEKS, meanwhile our ONLY account was drifting further into overdraft.

They never thought to write to our mailing address.

We lost 5 weeks' interest on this money. Who has been gleaning the interest, the Royal Bank of Canada?

Although Ms. Girardo promised to "waive" the overdraft accrued because of their error, unfortunately they couldn't even carry that through. It appeared on my next bank statement as a debit.

I have never received a reply [to a letter of complaint to the bank] and certainly not been reimbursed for my costs in trying to trace their error.

Robert Sargent of Toronto, in a letter to the Toronto Dominion Bank:

Please be referred to your statement covering March 30/98 to July 29/98. You have given me interest credit of .23 (March 31), .04 (April 30), .20 (May 29), and .17 (June 30). The total interest I have "earned" on my deposits during this four-month period amounts to sixty-four cents (.64).

It seems to me that in light of the humoungas [sic] profits you have been showing, sixty-four cents is hardly worthwhile. Do you really believe sixty-four cents is a fair return to a faithful and loyal depositor? Obviously not.

I am herewith enclosing my cheque in the amount of sixty-four cents, since it is abundantly apparent to me that you need it more than I do!

These were the words of just a few angry people caught up in the maw of Canada's banks. Their stories touch on some of the common problems customers encounter at their financial institutions. But there are many more sore points. One that seems to irk a great many Canadians is tied selling. Douglas Clark, a businessman who lives outside Toronto, says it was the last thing he expected to run into when he went to see his Royal Bank of Canada account manager about increasing his line of credit.

Clark, a long-time Royal client, says he was told he wouldn't be getting any more credit unless he sold his Fidelity mutual funds and bought Royal mutual funds instead. Clark, an accountant, says he was fuming mad. "I was angry because this was RRSP money," he explained. "If I was to make my investment decisions based on what my account manager told me I had to do to get more credit, I'd have substantially less money to retire on, and that's not right."

Clark received an apology after complaining in writing to Royal chairman John Cleghorn. But tied selling is an irritant that has sparked a small uproar in the financial community and among MPs in Ottawa. Although Clark's experience involved an RRSP being linked to a line of credit, it is considered to be tied selling whenever a client is asked to buy one financial product in order to obtain a loan, a certain rate of interest, or other service. The banks deny it is happening, but complaints from customers, investment dealers, and even former bank employees are widespread enough to convince many people that it is common practice.

In a letter to Finance Minister Paul Martin, Toronto investment dealer Thomas Caldwell said the practice of tied selling by banks has "become abusive to Canadians on a wide scale. Bank staff are actively encouraged to market all bank products under the guise of cross-selling. As a result, cross-selling often degenerates into tied selling."

Michael Lauber, the Canadian banking ombudsman, insisted there was little evidence of tied selling based on the complaints he'd heard. But the banks' critics said that was meaningless. "People will not complain [about] their bank; half of them don't even know what the

Toronto Dominion Bank chairman Charles Baillie and CIBC chairman Al Flood seal their proposed consolidation with a handshake, April 17, 1998.

Garth Whyte, vice-president, national affairs, of the Canadian Federation of Independent Business, and CFIB president Catherine Swift meet with Finance Minister Paul Martin. (*Courtesy CFIB; photo by PHOTO FEATURES*)

Bank of Nova Scotia chairman Peter Godsoe at the podium during the merger debate, in March 1998.

Banking in one of its many new permutations: Bank of Montreal chairman Matthew Barrett and Bill McEwan, president of Dominion/ A & P, officially open new in-store bank branches. *(Courtesy Bank of Montreal)*

The café that ING Direct, the telephone bank owned by a Netherlands-based conglomerate, set up for its customers north of Toronto.

Talking mergers: Al Flood, CIBC chairman (left); MP Andrew Telegdi, a member of the Liberal task force on financial services; CIBC president Holger Kluge; and task force chair Tony Ianno.

Catherine Swift, president of the Canadian Federation of Independent Business, speaks during the merger debate. *(Courtesy CFIB; photo by PHOTO FEATURES)*

The two-headed pig: On September 15, 1998, when the MacKay task force delivered its report, a Council of Canadians activist in Ottawa protests against the bank mergers by wearing the two-headed pig mask the council made especially for the occasion.

Toronto MP Tony Ianno, who chaired the Liberal caucus task force on the financial-services industry.

Humungous Bank's website.

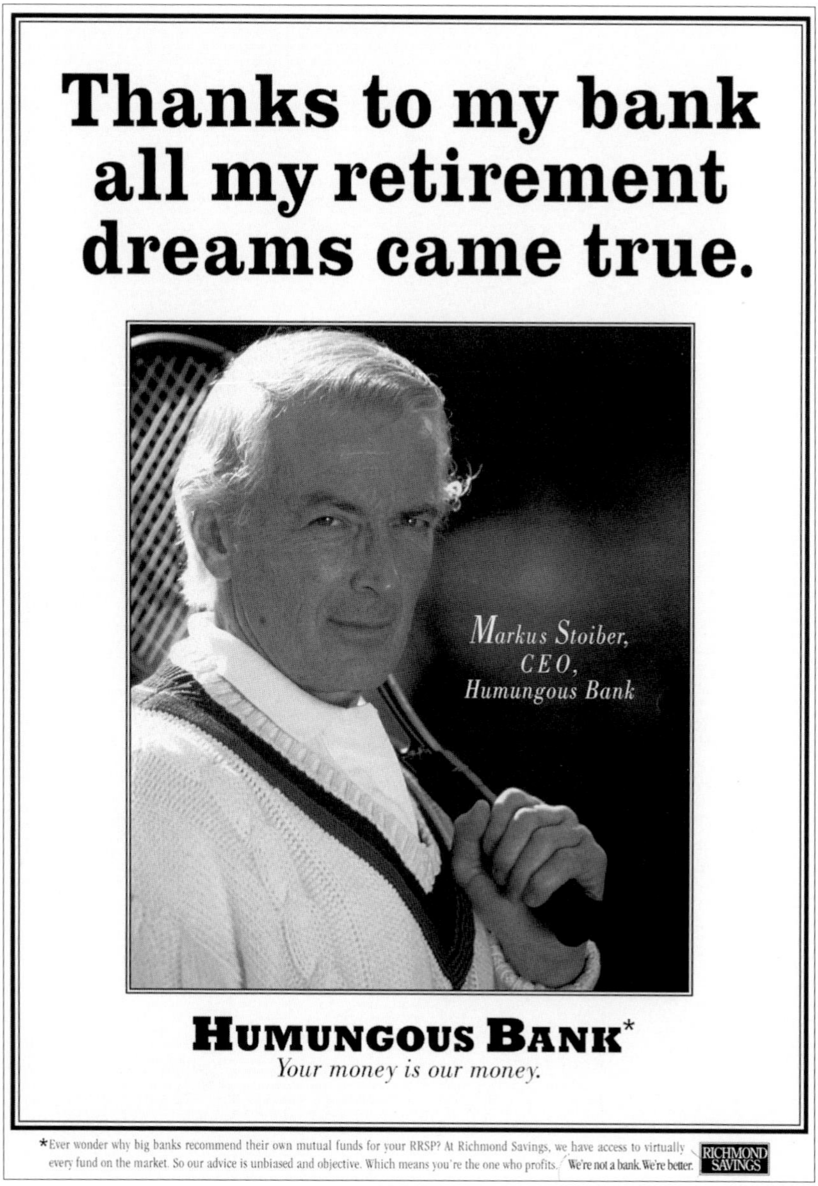

Richmond Savings' satirical ad campaign for Humungous Bank featured imperious-looking Markus Stoiber.

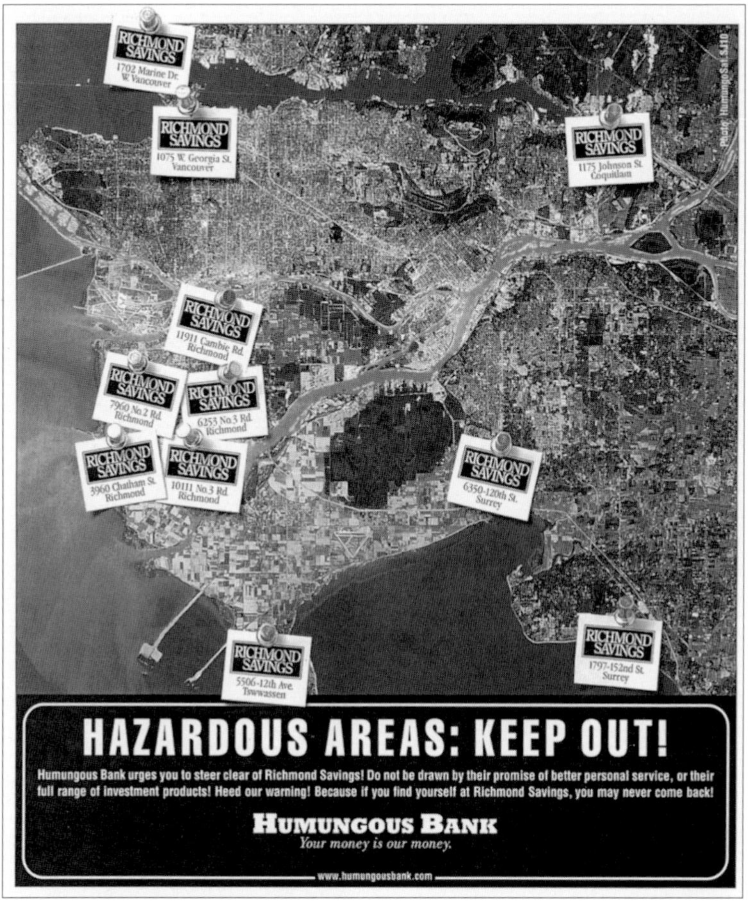

Another ad from the Humungous Bank campaign.

Konrad von Finckenstein, director of investigations, federal Competition Bureau, conducted a landmark study of the bank mergers.

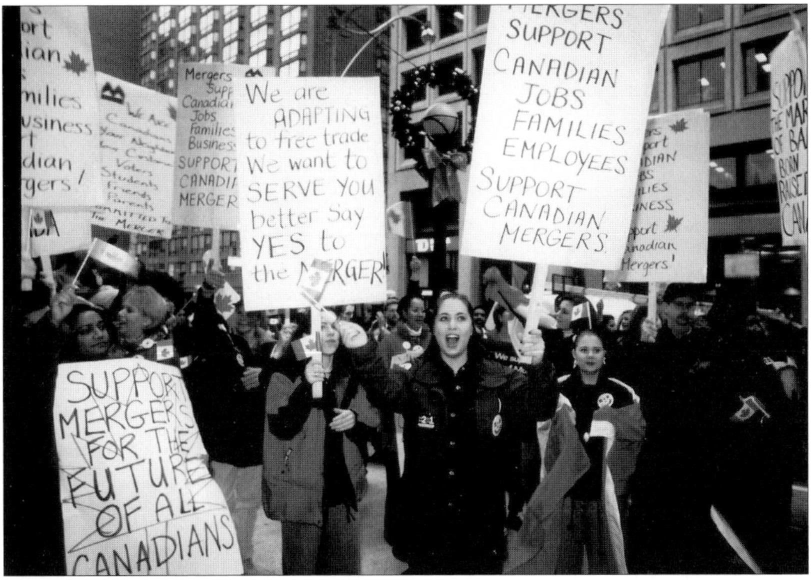

Bank of Montreal employees demonstrate in favour of the mergers in Toronto.

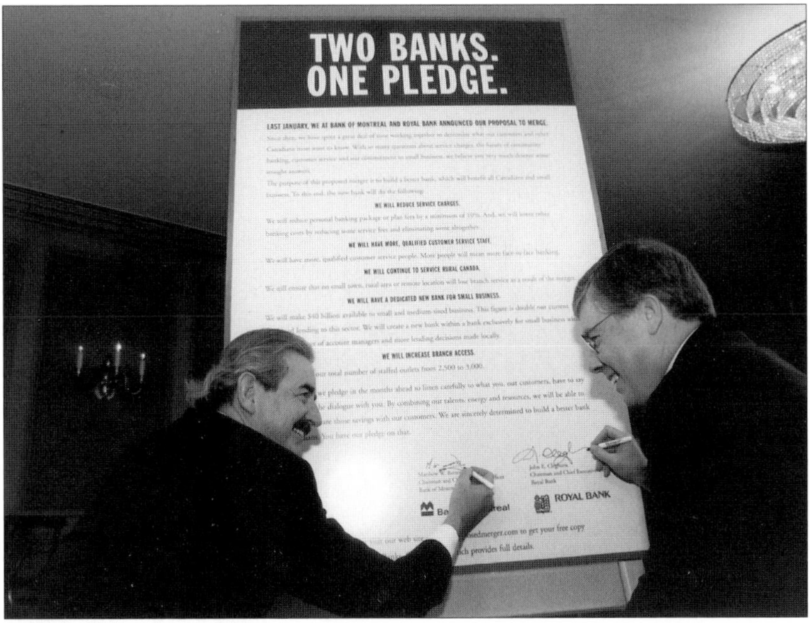

Bank of Montreal chairman Matthew Barrett and his Royal counterpart, John Cleghorn, at a ceremonial signing of their announced promise to improve service and reduce costs if mergers were allowed, November 17, 1998.

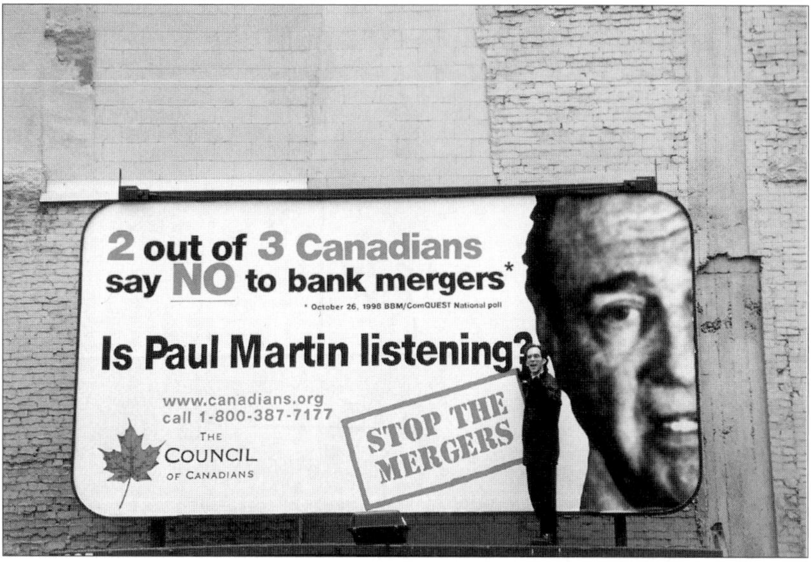

Peter Bleyer, executive director of the Council of Canadians, stands in front of the billboard the council put up just below Finance Minister Paul Martin's office in Ottawa on December 2, 1998.

No to mergers: Finance Minister Paul Martin makes his fateful announcement, December 14, 1998. *(Canapress Photo)*

word 'ombudsman' means, let alone that there is one within a bank," stated Caldwell. "Most people don't want to pursue it that far. Plus there's always the fear of some kind of credit constraint or retaliation."

After dithering over how to distinguish illegal tied selling from legitimate cross-selling, which simply involves offering customers a range of services, the federal government decided in 1998 to toughen the rules. It brought forward a new law that would prohibit the use of undue or coercive pressure by a bank in linking the sales of any product or financial service to any other products or services. "It's important for consumers to know the law is clearly on their side," Maurizio Bevilacqua, chairman of the House of Commons finance committee, said after the committee recommended tightening the rules. But there were widespread doubts that the measures brought in by the Liberals would be tough enough to solve the problem.

Of course, tied selling isn't the only unpleasant reality of banking in the 1990s. Equally annoying is the weekly barrage of marketing material consumers receive from the banks. Although it is always a nuisance, it isn't usually as unsettling as the letter William Balfour received from CIBC's insurance arm. Before thousands of the bank's shareholders at the annual meeting in Toronto, Balfour read the text of a note he received from CIBC congratulating him on his seventy-fifth birthday and offering to help him plan for his funeral. He called the pitch "undignified" and "contemptible." CIBC chairman Al Flood promised to investigate.

The banks have also incurred criticism for limiting low-income Canadians' access to banking services. Surveys suggest that more than 3 percent of adult Canadians, including 8 percent of people with an annual income of less than $25,000, do not have bank accounts. This translates into many thousands of Canadians. It is a demoralizing and unacceptable situation, as is indicated by the following eyewitness account from an unnamed Vancouver social worker in *Banking and Poor People: Talk Is Cheap*, a 1998 report by the National Council of

Welfare. The social worker is describing accompanying a colleague and a welfare mother on what is called Welfare Wednesday.

> We started out first thing in the morning: myself, a line worker, a client and her two pre-school children. The woman picked up her cheque from the welfare office, a process that took about 30 minutes, and we went to a local branch of the Canadian Imperial Bank of Commerce. They had security guards at the door, and we were told they were not cashing welfare cheques on that particular day. However, they said the Bank of Montreal across the street had agreed to cash welfare cheques that month.
>
> We walked across the street. There were security guards at the door. They made everybody who didn't have an account at the bank line up on the street, and they allowed them into the bank one at a time – one at a time on a rainy, cold, miserable day. The bank had a large lobby area inside that was virtually empty. We waited on the street for about 60 minutes.
>
> I was outraged at the way this woman was treated, but she was not overly concerned herself. She said this is what she was used to and what her friends were used to. She said she would not waste her time getting upset, because it was too frustrating to get upset every time she had to cash a cheque.
>
> I have never been treated this way in a bank, and I wonder why the banks feel it is OK to treat poor people like criminals. This is a side to banking that I have not seen depicted in banking commercials.
>
> The experience got me thinking about an earlier visit I had made to the Four Corners Community Savings bank nearby. Four Corners deals almost exclusively with poor people from the [Vancouver] Downtown Eastside. They never had security guards, and they never had any real trouble. People waited inside. There was coffee. There was a bathroom for people to use. And there

> were chairs and low counters so that people could sit down while they did their banking. Needless to say, it was worlds away from the treatment provided by the two chartered banks.

Hounded by the media and anti-poverty groups over their treatment of low-income people, the major banks agreed to address this problem along with the federal government. Since the poor generally carry fewer credit cards and other pieces of identification than those who are better off financially, the lack of adequate ID ranks as one of the main barriers for those who wish to open a bank account. The banks have now agreed to ask for only two pieces of ID (and not to ask for photo ID) from those wishing to open an account or cash a cheque. And a number of other improvements were promised, including a commitment to no longer use employment as a condition of opening a bank account and a program to educate staff to be more sensitive to low-income Canadians.

Progress has been slow, however. Six months after the February 1997 agreement, a survey by the Ottawa-based Canadian Community Reinvestment Coalition found that bank tellers were still asking for too many pieces of ID, and that they were incorrectly telling people they needed a minimum of one hundred dollars to open an account.

Reports from the coalition and the media prompted a sharp letter demanding action from Jim Peterson, the federal secretary of state for financial institutions. In a November 13, 1997 note that has not been made public before, Peterson told Canadian Bankers Association president Ray Protti that the government might be compelled to step in with new rules if the banks' voluntary approach to solving the problem did not soon produce results. "You pointed out in your letter that, notwithstanding the banks' efforts, it is a serious challenge to ensure that all staff have heard the message [to improve service for low-income Canadians]," Peterson wrote. "I believe that for the voluntary approach to be effective, there must be a demonstration that it is working. Otherwise, given that access remains an important concern for many low-income Canadians, there will be pressure on the government to try other measures."

By mid-1998, the banks were engaged in a variety of efforts to improve their performance on this issue. These included training sessions for bank staff, seminars about personal finance for new Canadians at the community level, and extensive surveys of bank performance. These surveys, called mystery shops, were carried out by the Nielsen Media Research Group, which hired people to go into banks pretending to be low-income earners with federal government cheques to cash. To enhance the program, Nielsen and the banks brought anti-poverty groups into the planning of the mystery shops. One of those who was involved was Mike Farrell, assistant director of the National Anti-Poverty Organization. When asked how the mystery shoppers were supposed to know how to act like poor people, Farrell laughed. He said he had asked the same question of the Nielsen representative at one of the planning sessions. "The irony, which I thought was lost on Nielsen, was the guy said, 'They are part-time employees of Nielsen, so they know what it's like to be poor.' " The federal government, which is planning a major package of consumer-protection measures for the financial-services industry in 1999, seems almost certain to increase pressure on the banks to improve service for low-income customers.

Overall, the public's attitude towards the banks was bad. It ranged from grudging tolerance to outright hostility. In late 1997, the National Quality Institute, a Toronto-based, not-for-profit organization, surveyed Canadian consumers on the quality of service offered by a range of public and private institutions. Banks ranked seventeenth out of twenty-one, ahead of only large retail outlets, the postal service, cable operators, and the government. This disenchantment had been on the rise for years, fed by the notorious farm foreclosures of the 1980s, the careless and costly lending spree to developing countries shortly thereafter, and the upsurge of bank profits in the 1990s.

By 1997, the industry was well aware that it needed to mend its image. Many bankers put the problem down to a failure on the banks' part to communicate with the public. "In survey after survey, Canadians have told us, 'I like the security and stability of Canadian banks, but I'm not sure that you really care about me as an individual and my well-being,'" observed Holger Kluge, the intensely serious president of personal and commercial banking at the Canadian Imperial Bank of Commerce. To address this situation, the banks hired former Tory pollster Allan Gregg to initiate extensive opinion testing of Canadians' attitudes towards their financial institutions. After analysing the results, the CBA in late 1997 commissioned a $20-million information campaign meant to improve the banks' tarnished reputation. But the campaign steered clear of the more controversial issues surrounding the banks and concentrated instead on providing educational material on financial services. Could it work? Barry McLoughlin, an Ottawa consultant who counsels bank executives on media matters, was sceptical, saying the banks have a "huge, huge problem" with the public. "People have a perception that they are raking in a lot of money and that they're doing it off the backs of average depositors by nickel and diming them."

The information campaign kicked off on January 13, 1998, with a national TV ad that ran in the prime 10 p.m. news slot. It was an upbeat, modern bit of promotional fluff featuring young women and a romantic couple out on the town. The message seemed designed to show young, hip, urban Canadians that banks are a convenient part of their modern lifestyle. But the campaign got off to a curious start. Only ten days after the ads reached the airwaves, the landscape shifted radically when the Royal and the Bank of Montreal unveiled their merger plan.

An official of the CBA recalled sitting in front of the TV the Friday night of the merger announcement. The newscast featured a flurry of alarmed, sceptical reports about how two of the country's already huge banks had decided it was imperative to get even larger through a merger of unprecedented size. In the middle of these items about gargantuan banks and their expansionist agenda appeared the advertising spot the CBA had put together in hopes of improving the public's perception. "I stared at that ad and all those news items," the CBA executive said, "and I couldn't believe it. I thought, 'What in the hell am I smoking?' "

ELEVEN

OPENING GAMBIT

OR A JOURNEY OF A THOUSAND MILES BEGINS WITH A SINGLE MISSTEP

On the morning of January 23, 1998, Michael Wilson sat in his seat amid the constant drone of the engines of the chartered Boeing 747 ferrying Prime Minister Jean Chrétien's trade mission back from South America. Wilson, a former Progressive Conservative finance minister, was part of one of the federal government's export promotion ventures, the so-called Team Canada trips that bring business people and federal officials together to pursue sales abroad. But as a vice-chairman of RBC Dominion Securities, the Royal Bank's investment arm, Wilson knew something that none of the other passengers was aware of. He knew that in Toronto at about 9 a.m. that day, the Royal and the Bank of Montreal would shock Canada by unveiling plans for the biggest corporate merger in the country's history. In fact, Wilson had been asked to give Chrétien a private heads-up so the prime minister would not be caught completely off guard by the stunning announcement.

Meanwhile, in the early winter darkness thousands of kilometres to the north, the telephone rang at 7:02 a.m. in the Ottawa townhouse occupied by Jim Peterson, the federal minister of financial institutions, and his wife, Heather. "My wife answered the phone and a person whose name I can't reveal said, 'Did you know two banks are going to merge?' " Peterson disclosed months later. "So Heather was the first person in Ottawa to find out about it," he recalled. "I phoned Paul [Martin] at home and told him."

Armed with this as-yet-unconfirmed information, the two ministers with the most important financial portfolios in the Liberal Cabinet got ready to go to work. Apparently unaware that someone had passed the word unofficially to Peterson and Martin, four people from the two banks were gathered in an office in Ottawa urgently trying to alert the government to the upcoming announcement. The group included Anne Lamont, a Royal Bank government-relations specialist; Steven Bright, who held a similar job at the Bank of Montreal; Bryan Davies, senior vice-president, corporate affairs, at the Royal; and Tim O'Neill, the Bank of Montreal's chief economist. At 7:30, before Peterson had left home, Davies reached the minister by phone. "He said John [Cleghorn] might be trying to get a hold of me later and asked where I would be," Peterson recalled. The four bank representatives also left a message for Terrie O'Leary, Martin's trusted chief of staff, and tried to get through to Martin himself. But according to one of the bank participants, they were unable to contact either the finance minister or his aide. Michael Wilson was similarly unable to alert the prime minister on the Team Canada aircraft. Wilson approached Eddie Goldenberg, the prime minister's long-time aide, on the aircraft and said he needed to talk to Chrétien. "They said he was asleep or something," Wilson recalled recently. After telling Wilson that the prime minister was not available, Goldenberg asked the RBC vice-chairman what he wanted to talk to him about. But Wilson would not say, and Chrétien was thus not informed.

Back in Ottawa, the merger plan had yet to be publicly released when Peter Donolo, the prime minister's press secretary, received a phone call from O'Leary alerting the Prime Minister's Office to the upcoming news. Through the PMO switchboard, Donolo reached Goldenberg by radio phone on Chrétien's aircraft. Shouting over the static, Donolo explained what was happening, and Goldenberg passed the information on to the prime minister.

Martin himself, of course, was in a meeting in his Ottawa office just before the proposed deal became public knowledge and declined to take a phone call from Cleghorn, spawning the myth that the Royal–BMO group had insulted Martin by not giving him any advance warning of its plans. Based on what Peterson said, though, it seems that Martin may have already been tipped off unofficially about the merger even before he got the message that Cleghorn was trying to contact him. In subsequent interviews, Martin played down the importance of this alleged snub. Whatever actually happened in that confused, hectic two hours, the notion that the arrogant bankers had slighted the government by springing the deal on finance officials without the least warning became firmly entrenched on Parliament Hill and far beyond. "We didn't know about the damn thing until the world knew about the thing," a finance department official was quoted as saying in an article that ran on the front page of the *Globe and Mail* under the headline "Martin Steaming After Ambush." The description of the finance minister's mood was indeed accurate, those who met with Martin early that day reported.

Right after the banks' announcement, Martin had a ten-minute talk with Cleghorn and Barrett. Then, in a discussion between the prime minister's plane and Donolo in Ottawa, Chrétien signed off on the response Martin was planning to the merger announcement. Following that, Martin issued a statement saying that the Liberals would take their time making a decision on the Royal–BMO proposal. "The government will not be in a position to rule on any such mergers until after the [MacKay] task force has issued its report." The government, the statement continued, would also require "adequate time for consultation and consideration" of the task force's recommendations for changes in the industry. At a press conference, an obviously furious Martin labelled the merger plan "somewhat premature."

The damage, in fact, was worse than anyone at the banks or in the media knew. A senior Liberal source said it turned out that Wilson had had extensive information about the merger, including documentation, to present to Chrétien on the plane that morning. The prime minister and Goldenberg were annoyed, the source said, when they learned that the banks had been able to provide Wilson with all that information in faraway South America, especially given that everyone had been told the merger announcement had been rushed out in such a hurry. "Both the PM and Eddie were pissed off about that," the source said. It was not an auspicious beginning.

Actually, few were aware just how rushed the whole announcement was. It had been scheduled for a week later, during the last week in January. However, in mid-January, senior officials at the Bank of Montreal became concerned that too many people had been brought into the merger-planning process to keep word of the deal bottled up until the end of the month. Thus the decision was made to move it up a week.

Despite the snags that accompanied the hurried announcement, Cleghorn and Barrett were still afloat on their own exuberance as they contemplated the prospect of creating a bank that, when measured by asset size, would have been the second biggest on the continent. Asked about Martin's non-committal response, Barrett told reporters, "We expected that. There's no point setting up a task force and then not asking for [its] opinion."

In those first days, the Royal and the Bank of Montreal viewed Ottawa's approval of the deal as almost a fait accompli. Both banks said they hoped to obtain the official go-ahead from Martin by the following November so that they could close the merger by the end of 1998. Barrett observed blithely in *Maclean's*: "Our attitude is, why wouldn't you want to approve the creation of an international financial player à la Alcan, or the Bombardiers, or the Nortels? Why wouldn't you want to have one of your banks in that league?" The two banks even bought full-page advertisements in major newspapers the day after the merger announcement. Headlined "This Is Important," a title that in itself was revealing of the banks' grandiose view of the event, the statement by the Bank of Montreal and the Royal began, "It's important to Canada. It's important to Canada's future. It's important to you." The lengthy message, unrelieved by any visuals save for two small corporate logos at the bottom, went on to list the purported benefits to Canadians of the planned deal. In the face of increasingly aggressive competition from foreign banks, the ad said, the merger would allow the Royal and the Bank of Montreal to remain competitive. It "will help see to it that Canadians retain a strong stake within our own market and that Canadians will always have a homegrown option to meet their financial needs." The ad went on to say, "Just as important, this merger will allow a Canadian bank to be a major force on the world banking stage. As Canadian businesses take on the world, we will be with them to meet their needs." The banks also told readers that joining forces would give the two companies the resources to survive in the vital race for new technologies and "allow us to reduce our costs and provide you with greater options and better choice."

The banks' confident tone was a reflection of their optimistic view of the prospects for mergers in what was then virgin political territory. No merger of this kind had taken place in Canada for nearly forty years, and there was a widespread perception that the federal government would ultimately step aside and let these two giant corporations do what their head honchos thought was best for business. For one thing, despite the Liberal party's socially active heritage, its stance on free trade and the federal budgetary deficit had given it the image of being in step with big business. Martin, after all, is a former business magnate himself and was the architect of the Liberals' campaign to curb the deficit by slashing cherished government programs. But that perception, though prevalent, is misleading. For Martin is also the inheritor, through his father, former Cabinet minister Paul Martin Sr., of his party's progressive tradition. And the younger Martin, by all accounts, views deficit-fighting as a necessary evil, not as the end in itself championed by Bay Street's fiscal purists. Indeed, in his opinion of the banks, Martin shares the entrepreneur's perspective. In the early 1980s, during his risky but ultimately successful venture to build up Canada Steamship Lines, Martin was dependent on the banks for $180 million in loans. When he was asked a few months after the Royal–BMO deal broke to describe his experience with banks, Martin hesitated a moment and then replied, "Mixed. When I first started out in business, I had no money. And I borrowed a lot of money. And the question I always ask myself is: 'That was twenty-five years ago. Would that opportunity be available today?' "

Martin, a gutsy, no-nonsense politician who likes to cut to the heart of a discussion, did not appear to be the least bit awed by the banks' clout and imposing establishment mantle. In discussing the banks' demands for expanded business powers in an interview in 1995 with a *Toronto Star* reporter, Martin said, "The banks already own almost everything. . . . Is that a good thing?" It is also well known that the finance minister does not like being cornered, and he took great exception to the way the Royal and the Bank of Montreal put him on the spot with their merger bombshell. In the wake of the banks' joint announcement, it took only a few days for Martin to begin to raise the bar for approving their plans. Speaking with a *Globe and Mail* reporter, he challenged the would-be merger partners "to lower consumer charges, to guarantee that there will be no job loss, to guarantee that small- and medium-sized business and that smaller towns in the country will benefit from this." And not long after that, he said forcefully that he was not about to be "stampeded" into approving a merger before the government was ready. "My timetable is not going to be dictated by their timetable," he told the *Toronto Star*.

By the late 1990s, no one in the private sector could touch the banks when it came to spending on government relations, lobbying, and image-pruning. For all that, however, it soon became clear that the distance separating the chairmen's offices in Toronto from the government in Ottawa was a lot greater than the one-hour flight time would indicate. Through much of Canadian banking history, the big financial institutions had enjoyed cosy relations with the men and, to a lesser extent, women who ran the country. The bank barons were used to getting their way by going directly to the top in Ottawa. "Ten years ago, the chairman of the bank called the minister of finance, and they talked and that was that," said a public-relations chief at one of the major banks. "And that," he added, mimicking someone dusting off his hands, "was government relations." Almost everyone involved with the industry, from Canadian Bankers Association president Ray Protti – a former senior federal bureaucrat – on down, admitted that the big banks had for years done a poor job of building bridges to members of Parliament and the public. Prime Minister Jean Chrétien was no exception. In his memoir, *Straight From the Heart*, Chrétien is openly disdainful of the attitudes and motivations of the bankers he came to know as minister of industry, trade, and commerce. Referring to the famous 10 percent ownership rule, he writes: "The Canadian bankers used that limit to avoid being taken over or challenged by Canadians, too, and the result was a small clique of extremely powerful banks whose officers were more or less entrenched regardless of what they did or didn't do. Yet bankers continued to go to their clubs and rant against government intervention over expensive lunches. Eventually the Canadian government had to open up the system to foreign banks to some degree in order to foster a competitive spirit." The book confirmed what Ed Lumley, a former parliamentary secretary to Chrétien and one-time Liberal Cabinet minister, maintained: Chrétien never forgot being snubbed by the banks in his earlier years in Ottawa. In *Straight From the Heart*, he also recalls how, in 1983 as minister of energy, he had, against his own instincts, negotiated a deal to save Dome Petroleum from bankruptcy. He did so, he wrote, because Dome's collapse would have hurt hundreds of subcontractors and created "serious consequences for the financial institutions that had lent billions of dollars to the company." The deal he negotiated averted bankruptcy and, in effect, bailed out the banks. However, he wrote, "[the banks] never gave us much credit for that." He continued: "One of the bankers I had to negotiate with was Russell Harrison, chairman of the Canadian Imperial Bank of Commerce. He could hardly be called a Liberal sympathizer. I had had a couple of arguments with him when I was Minister of Finance [in the late 1970s], and when I went into opposition during the Joe Clark government, he didn't even return my phone calls. When we signed the Dome deal, I said, 'Now that we are partners, I hope you will return my calls.' "

Chrétien's words are indicative of the general attitude towards the banks of the 101-member Liberal caucus that held forth in Ottawa in early 1998. Spearheaded by Toronto MP Tony Ianno, Liberal back-benchers had been using every power at their disposal to wring concessions from the banks, especially on the issue of improving the availability of credit for Canada's job-creating small businesses. Ianno never seemed to get over an insulting remark Barrett had made in 1996. Photocopies of his reported comment about "ill-informed" back-benchers were passed around among Liberal members of Parliament. At a party that year, the spunky, dark-haired MP had gone out of his way to introduce himself to Barrett, saying, as he stuck out his hand, "Hi, I'm an ill-informed Liberal back-bencher."

Ianno also seemed to see plots and counterplots lurking in every shadow. "Tony was born on the grassy knoll," joked one bank lobbyist, in an allusion to the Kennedy assassination conspiracy theorists. Even before the January 23 merger announcement, Ianno and his fellow Liberals had established a caucus task force to probe the banking industry. It was a response to complaints from their constituents about the performance of financial institutions generally and the major banks, in particular, Ianno said. In the months following the announcement, the Liberal back-benchers would prove to be an important conduit of grass-roots sentiment about would-be mergers.

There was no mystery about the emotions the surprise merger proposal stirred among Liberal members of Parliament. "The reaction [among the caucus] was one of incredulity: Why would these people have jumped the gun on a process that was set up to determine this very issue?" asked Peterson in an interview with a *Toronto Star* reporter. "I don't understand why the banks did it, and neither does the caucus," he said during at a two-day Liberal retreat in Collingwood, Ontario, a week after the merger revelation. At the same meeting, Chrétien expressed doubts about it all. "Big to be big? You know for me, even if I were 350 pounds, it will not make a better prime minister," he told journalists. Chrétien didn't sound at all convinced by the two banks' argument that they needed to bulk up to protect themselves from foreign competitors and enhance their standing as global corporate players. "I don't know if they are suffering a lot from the competition in Canada at this time," he said. "What is their competition in Canada at this time from the foreign banks? I don't know. They said they will become the twenty-fifth biggest bank in the world. But you know, the top of the list is all Japanese banks, who are asking help from their government at this time. So we have to look at all the elements of this situation before we make a decision." (According to the banks, the new, merged entity would have ranked twenty-second, not twenty-fifth, in the world, measured by world capitalization.)

Despite the Liberals' lack of enthusiasm for the merger idea, few people seemed to think, in that January-to-March period, that Martin would ultimately rule against it. The prevailing sentiment on Bay Street and in the national press gallery in Ottawa was that the big financial institutions would eventually win out. Private opinion polling by the banks also indicated that Canadians were, for the most part, convinced that the merger would happen – or had already happened. Discoveries of this kind about the grass-roots attitude influenced the banks' early thoughts about how to sell the proposed deal publicly and contributed to decisions that irrevocably shaped the merger debate for months to come.

As part of its merger sales push, the Bank of Montreal and the Royal Bank brought aboard David MacNaughton, a sometimes gruff but collegial communications specialist who had once run the North American operations of public-relations giant Hill & Knowlton. A former unsuccessful Liberal candidate, he was well-connected in the party, having been its co-chair in Ontario when David Peterson was premier. He had also run the unsuccessful leadership bid of former federal Cabinet minister Donald Johnston. Allan Gregg, the pollster whose name seemed forever linked in the public memory to Brian Mulroney's government, was also called in to assess Canadians' attitudes towards the proposed consolidations.

MacNaughton often chaired the 8:30 a.m. daily joint communications meetings – called "jock" sessions, after an acronym one banker invented for the phrase "joint communications committee" – in a Bank of Montreal conference room where, over juice and chocolate chip cookies, the two banks' media directors plotted strategy. Based on early poll results, Gregg and MacNaughton looked at the options for promoting the merger and recommended that the Royal–BMO team steer clear of a high-profile, out-on-the-hustings attempt to win over the Canadian people. The thinking was that Canadians were not paying much attention to the issue, were unlikely to believe the banks' arguments, and would in any case be interested only in what was in it for them as customers – a question the two banks were either unwilling or unable to answer in great detail at the time. In other words, why disturb the sleeping giant of public opinion unnecessarily? As an alternative, MacNaughton and Gregg suggested that the bankers should work behind the scenes to convince the country's elite power-brokers – the politicians, business leaders, editors, and others who might control the banks' fate. "We told them there are five thousand people who will make the decision," MacNaughton later explained over lunch in a trendy Toronto restaurant that looked out across the leaden waters of Lake Ontario.

In the early months of 1998, this was the position adopted by Matthew Barrett's handlers. But Cleghorn, supported by his bank's public-relations team, chose an entirely different tack. He was determined from the beginning of the merger debate to take the argument to the people. And he seemed wholly convinced that his boundless enthusiasm would prove infectious. Within two weeks of the merger announcement, Cleghorn was at the podium at Memorial University in St. John's, Newfoundland, where he trumpeted the proposed amalgamation as "a made-in-Canada response to globalization that will strengthen Canada's means to compete even more aggressively in the major economic leagues." In view of the fact that months later the big banks were accused of failing to address Canadians' concerns about mergers, it is worth noting that even then, on February 9, the Royal chairman sought to speak to these issues. He said a combined Royal–BMO conglomerate would allow cost savings that could be shared with consumers, ensure that small communities were not left without a Royal–BMO branch, add new client services, expand small business lending, and keep lay-offs to the bare minimum. In a remark that was to assume ironic overtones in the months ahead, when Scotiabank challenged the merger, Cleghorn also said, "Here in Newfoundland and Labrador, a merged Royal Bank and Bank of

Montreal would still rank second in market share to Bank of Nova Scotia, with fewer branches between the two of us. Together, we will be stronger and more competitive in this province, because our networks complement each other nicely. So our Scotiabank competitors should stay tuned. You'll be hearing our footsteps – and loudly. And that's good for Newfoundlanders, who will benefit from the increased competition."

In the early months of the merger debate, Barrett spent a fair bit of time in Europe trying to drum up support for the deal. But although the European Commission came out in favour of the Canadian bank merger, the backing from international business and international organizations that the Bank of Montreal sought never materialized in a concerted way.

Why did Barrett and Cleghorn press the detonator on the explosive merger plan in January rather than waiting another year? Both men said repeatedly it was because they were afraid to wait any longer – afraid that if they delayed, the merger partner they most wanted would no longer be available, and afraid that the longer they waited, the more disadvantaged they would become in relation to the increasingly large, aggressive competitors who were rapidly changing the profit-and-loss formulas in the banking industry everywhere. "People say why now," Cleghorn told Peter Newman for an article in *Maclean's*. "I tell them, listen, we've been sitting on our hands since 1925 [Royal's last merger, with Union Bank of Canada], and we didn't know what the value of acquiring another bank was going to be, except that it would probably be too expensive. So the only hope we had of building a serious global presence was this merger."

There was, however, another important factor. This was a statement by the federal government's anti-trust watchdog agency, the Competition Bureau, that it intended to carry out its required analysis of any bank mergers in the order in which they were initiated. "It is the bureau's intention to assess each merger on its own merits and proceed on a first-in/first-out basis," Competition Bureau director Konrad von Finckenstein said in a submission to the MacKay task force. Von Finckenstein's announced game plan for investigating the anti-competitive effects of proposed bank mergers would have handed a tremendous advantage to whichever two banks got in line first. The process favoured by the bureau had been revealed only a month before Barrett and Cleghorn started talking seriously about joining forces, and it was a significant factor in their fateful decision to take action immediately. But as we shall see, this perceived advantage would soon disappear.

On the very day that Barrett and Cleghorn went public with their proposed deal, CIBC chairman Al Flood picked up the telephone and called the chairmen of the remaining major banks – Toronto Dominion's Charles Baillie and Scotiabank's Peter Godsoe. Thus was set in motion a remarkable secret drama that would stretch over the next couple of months. CIBC's assets fit unusually well with those of TD, and the former had long ago identified Baillie's company as its best possible partner. Behind the scenes, Baillie and Flood soon began kicking around the idea of a merger of their own. Accord-ing to bank sources, they were actually already doing so in late January, when Baillie delivered his Calgary speech about TD's lack of interest in a merger. In addition, Baillie was also engaged in merger talks with Godsoe.

TD officials have admitted publicly that discussions with Scotiabank took place, but they have declined to say how far the talks went, referring questions to Godsoe. However, one bank chairman said Baillie had personally told him that the Scotiabank–TD talks were quite serious. Baillie and Godsoe reportedly got as far as talking about what official colour a new TD–Scotiabank conglomerate would sport and who would be its chairman. It was that issue that held up the merger, according to various accounts.

Later in the year, when TD had aligned itself with CIBC and left Scotiabank on its own, Baillie was under pressure to go public about his dealings with Scotiabank. The idea was for Baillie to let it be known how close the Scotiabank chairman had been to signing a merger of his own before he metamorphosed into the foremost anti-merger spokesman. While Baillie never commented on this matter publicly, a top TD executive informed the federal finance department of the TD–Scotiabank negotiations in hopes of blunting the impact of Godsoe's outspoken public opposition. When Paul Martin was asked months later if TD had in fact delivered such a message to his officials, the minister nodded in the affirmative, but then said, "I don't know if that's true. I mean, they all – what the hell, most of these guys – they're all liars, you know. So I took it all with a grain of salt." Asked in December if Godsoe would like to set the record straight, Sandra Stewart, Scotiabank's vice-president of public affairs, said the chairman was not answering media questions at the time. "He talked to many people in the industry about various options [in the weeks after the Royal–BMO announcement]," was all Stewart would say.

Baillie said later that he agreed on February 17 to do a deal with Flood. As all this was happening, Baillie astounded his would-be partners at CIBC by telling the world, via the *Financial Post*, that contrary to what he said in January, he might have seen the light on the benefits of mergers. This fed a speculative frenzy concerning TD and CIBC that peaked on Bay Street in early April. But by then, no one had long to wait. On April 17, a Friday, the news broke. In contrast to the unexpected Royal–BMO deal, this had been one of the worst kept of Bay Street's modern-day secrets.

Measured by assets, CIBC had recently become the country's largest financial institution, surpassing the Royal, so the deal meant a marriage of the biggest and fifth-biggest banks in Canada. Valued at $43 billion, the transaction was labelled the second-largest corporate merger in Canadian history. "In a world of increasing consolidation, size can arguably be an important defence," said Baillie in his low-key, scholarly way at a late-morning press conference at Toronto's Sky-Dome hotel. "It may well be that the smaller players will excel, but there is no guarantee." Baillie and Flood sounded upbeat as they left the press conference to begin what they knew would be a long period of waiting to find out the fate of their proposed link-up. In the first few months after the Royal–BMO announcement, CIBC had watched for a signal from Martin and his officials that mergers were a non-starter. But this had never come. In fact, the indications CIBC had picked up from finance department officials left the bank with the impression that the Liberal government, while not encouraging a second merger proposal, would "understand" if one was made.

Be that as it may, the second mega-deal cast the whole merger issue in a glaring new light. "CIBC–TD Merger Sets Off Alarms," bellowed the headline across the front page of the normally conservative, business-friendly *Globe and Mail* the next day. Barrett and his colleagues watched the announcement on television and agreed that it would be either very good or, alternatively, very bad for the first merger plan. And the reaction from the federal government to a deal that would, along with the Royal–BMO scheme, give four banks control of 70 percent of the country's banking assets was decidedly chilly. Prime Minister Chrétien, back in South America for a Summit of the Americas meeting, told reporters, "It's natural, if the Royal Bank and the Bank of Montreal propose a marriage, two others will propose a marriage and maybe later there will be another. But me, I'm not sure that's the solution." In one fell swoop, TD and CIBC had raised the stakes enormously for the government. The Competition Bureau quickly put an end to the plan to review one merger before the other. Both would be examined simultaneously.

As for Martin, it could be said that if the finance minister was on the spot before, he was doubly so now because of the potentially huge impact of two mergers on the country's financial apparatus. Also, it was widely believed that Martin's ability to stickhandle the merger debate could prove a deciding factor in his bid to take over the leadership of the Liberal party. Because of this, Martin badly needed to shore up his appeal in the Liberal caucus and balance his image as a conservative deficit hawk with populist actions that would find favour with voters. Anyone could see that rubber-stamping the bank deals was not the way to accomplish those goals.

Yet in April, Martin was having to chip away at the widespread impression that the mergers were "done deals" that the government would not block. This was true even though the two mergers flew in the face of the "big shall not buy big" stipulation, a long-standing unwritten law which holds that the finance minister does not allow mergers or acquisitions among the big banks. Giving voice to the view common at the time, New Democratic House leader Nelson Riis said, "Any one who thinks Paul Martin is going to stand in the way of his banking buddies also believes in pink elephants." From Washington, where he was attending a meeting on international financial matters, Martin protested that the latest merger "is by no means a fait accompli." The bank deals, he said, represent "the most fundamental restructuring of the Canadian financial-services sector that we have ever seen, and the Canadian people expect their government to bring down a sound decision." In an interview with a *Toronto Star* reporter, he asserted that the need to protect consumers must be balanced against the need to foster banks "that can compete on a global basis."

In public Martin might have sounded a bit equivocal on the issue, but in private he was not hiding his annoyance over the way the banks had ramrodded their agenda onto the national stage at the expense of his own carefully orchestrated policy-making strategy. In fact, Martin had set the tone for the whole political battle back on April 29, when he and his aide, Terrie O'Leary, dropped into the

Bank of Canada offices for lunch with the chairmen of the major banks during one of their regular meetings with Gordon Thiessen, the governor of the Bank of Canada. In the ensuing conversation, Scotiabank's Godsoe and National Bank president Leon Courville were paired against the other chairmen in a heated debate over the merits of mergers, according to Godsoe's recollection. When Martin joined the discussion, he said, "This is about core banking and nothing else," Godsoe recalled, a reference to the consumer banking that is at the centre of the banks' operations. But Royal chairman John Cleghorn argued that the traditional view of core banking was too narrow given today's more competitive financial-services landscape. Many of the services consumers get from banks can also be obtained from mutual fund companies, credit unions, and other non-bank institutions, Cleghorn said. Thus, when calculating concentration of assets in banking, one has to look at the whole range of financial-services companies. By that measure, the merged banks would only control about 30 percent of financial-services assets, not the 70 percent they would control if only bank assets per se were counted, Cleghorn maintained. Martin, however, wasn't buying the argument. and, as reports of the secret meeting trickled out, it became clear that the finance minister had put the banks on notice that it was up to them – not him – to sell the deals to the public if they wanted Ottawa's approval.

Some months later, Martin addressed in an interview the Bank of Canada lunch and the message he gave the banks. Wearing a long-sleeved royal blue sports shirt and fidgeting with a ball-point pen, Martin said, "I have learned something [about Canadians]. The whole national consensus that was built up on [reducing] the deficit is, I think, incredibly instructive. If you explain to people the situation [on a major issue], and you give them the time to have the national debate, the common sense of the Canadian people comes through in spades. People understand the need for change. They understand evolution. It is not true that people resist change. And I'm going to tell you that you are able to build up a national understanding of very complex issues."

Twisting a bit in the desk chair he had chosen because his back was bothering him on the day of the interview, Martin noted that he felt he had previously reached an understanding with the banks that there would be no mergers until after the MacKay report. "By the banks' attempting to pre-empt MacKay, they were pre-empting the national debate," he said, driving home each word. "That national debate following MacKay may or may not have allowed the mergers. . . . But the fact is that what you would have had, as was the case with the deficit, was a great national debate about the evolution of a very important sector of the economy. What happened when the banks attempted to merge is that they became the prime spokespeople in that debate.

"So my perspective was, 'Okay, guys, you've bought yourself that role. Let's see how you can discharge it.' " Martin paused. "The point that I made to them [during the Bank of Canada meeting] was twofold: number one, you're going to have to convince them [the Canadian public], but you're also going to have to convince me, and I'm telling you that the arguments that I'd been hearing, and [that] I'd heard around the table at the luncheon and elsewhere – I told them, you're not convincing me. You got one Canadian here sitting across the table – you've got all your people sitting there opposite – and I'm hearing your arguments and I'm not convinced. I'm not quite sure how you are going to convince thirty million Canadians."

TWELVE

WITH ENEMIES LIKE THESE . . .

"Some people believe the earth is flat, and some people believe Elvis is still alive," Matthew Barrett mused as a dozen members of Canada's Senate stared at him from their seats around a long, horseshoe-shaped conference table covered with briefing books, water glasses, photocopied speech notes, and empty coffee cups. Barrett, in an appearance before the Senate banking committee in Ottawa, was not poking fun at the zealous left-wingers and consumer advocates who continuously hound the banks. Barrett's sarcasm was actually directed at one of his own – another respectable, million-dollar-a-year bank chairman: Scotiabank boss Peter Godsoe. And Barrett's crack was only one shot in a long, bitter war. Godsoe had emerged during the course of the year as what business columnist Terence Corcoran called the poster boy of the bank-bashers, and the pro-merger banks were beside themselves with frustration and anger as they tried to blunt Scotiabank's highly effective campaign to block the Royal–BMO and TD–CIBC mergers.

In the course of this rearguard action against Godsoe, Barrett joked that the Scotiabank chairman was going to merge with the Maytag repairman, accused Godsoe of blatant hypocrisy, and said his rival's bank was misleading Canadians. The ensuing public spat between Godsoe and the pro-merger banks was as unseemly and embarrassing a spectacle as anyone is ever likely to see from the country's top bankers. They are, after all, members of a subdued, tradition-bound fraternity who would seem more at home trading golf jokes over drinks at the country club than carrying on a nasty, heated feud in front of the entire nation. What drove this long-running soap opera bouffe was, of course, Godsoe's decision to hold out against the multi-billion-dollar mergers sought by his compatriots at the helms of the other major banks.

The merger proponents at the Bank of Montreal and the Royal Bank, in particular, were almost obsessed with Godsoe's philosophical stance. They believed what a Scotiabank official admitted over lunch one day in mid-1998: that Godsoe's team was not against mergers per se; it was just opposed to these two specific mergers. What's more, the other bankers knew that Godsoe had been involved in the flurry of merger discussions and jockeying that went on among the big banks as far back as the 1996–97 period. And on top of everything else, they knew that Godsoe had tried but failed to land a merger partner of his own shortly after the proposed Royal–BMO amalgamation was revealed. This was the basis of Barrett's jibe that Godsoe was going to do a merger with the Maytag repairman – in other words, with another member of a sort of lonely hearts club. "I have had extensive discussions with Peter over the years, and I have never once heard a philosophical aversion to mergers mentioned," Barrett told the members of Sen. Michael Kirby's banking committee. He gave members of Parliament the same message.

Speaking to the House of Commons finance committee, Barrett remarked, "I believe Mr. Godsoe would have merged with another institution if that's how the chips fell, but they didn't."

Godsoe began staking out his anti-merger position almost from the moment the Royal–BMO betrothal was made known. Within days of that announcement, he told shareholders at the bank's annual meeting in Ottawa that he was not in favour of getting in bed with another bank. "I'm not here to announce the merger of Scotiabank with the rest of the world," he declared. "We think – we know – we are big enough right now. We do have the necessary resources to invest in technology and to give our customers the products and services they demand." As the debate unfurled over the following months, Godsoe embellished his anti-merger arguments and had ample opportunity to explain his motivation.

As a dyed-in-the-wool member of Canada's establishment, he was clearly uncomfortable with his new-found exposure and was vulnerable to personal attack by his fellow bank bosses. In conversation, he seemed genuinely distressed about being singled out as the wallflower at the merger ball. But that did nothing to forestall his energetic, determined fight. In reference to the proposed megadeals, he said, "I think it's very wrong-minded public policy, and on behalf both of our employees and [of] our shareholders, it would be silly not to state that fact. I know of no country that would allow one-third of its banking system to disappear on some future threat that hasn't been proven." This was an allusion to the pro-merger banks' contention that they had to get bigger to survive against mounting competition from foreign financial institutions. Of that notion, he said, "I think they decided to merge and then made the threat up." Godsoe explained that he had to go public because other corporate leaders were unwilling to express their objections out of fear of possible repercussions in their dealings with the banks. "This is pretty serious for these big companies, and I think some of the thinking ones are really quite concerned about [the mergers]," he remarked. "[But] there's a reluctance to speak out because these two groups [TD–CIBC and Royal–BMO] will be so powerful if approved. But underlying it, anecdotally, from our customers and people we see, they don't really like what they see – this concentration of power and awful loss of competition."

For more than six months, the Scotiabank chairman orchestrated a full-scale public campaign against his competitors' plans. Working with at least some advice from former prime minister and anti-free-trade campaigner John Turner, Godsoe left few stones unturned as the bank rolled out a program of speeches, economic analysis, political influence, and media promotion. He and his lieutenants took the anti-merger message across the country. In Regina, Scotiabank vice-president Robert Chisholm predicted widespread branch closures and jobs cuts, prompting a Canadian Press reporter to send out a story that began, "Two proposed bank mega-mergers would sweep through Saskatchewan like a Prairie brush fire . . ." Speaking in Calgary, Godsoe declared, "We should not even consider the proposed mergers until we think through the overall direction of the sector and get a clear sense of where we want to go as a country." Citing the severe problems bedevilling Japan's big banks, he went on to say that maintaining a smooth-functioning financial system is crucial to economic stability. "Think of what would happen to the Canadian oil industry if the banking industry was unable to lend to it, or what would happen to our agriculture industry. That is why more competition – not less – and credit access and credit granting are critical to our economy." He added, "Long-term consumer benefits will not come from mega-mergers. Access and choice will be reduced. Lower income and older Canadians, small business, as well as people in smaller, rural communities, would be hardest hit."

As the debate intensified, the Bank of Nova Scotia, once known as "the bank of no comment" because of its low public profile, cranked up its communications strategy. Besides giving speeches, Godsoe appeared before parliamentary committees, met newspaper and magazine editors, and ordered up economic studies. Scotiabank's public-relations staff even arranged interviews in Toronto for Montreal-based National Bank president and fellow merger opponent Leon Courville. A participant in a public debate on mergers in Toronto recalls noticing, partway through the evening, that "the place was filled with Bank of Nova Scotia employees who were all cheering the Scotiabank speaker and booing the speakers favouring mergers." Later at the debate, a local CIBC bank manager bumped into a Scotiabank manager from another part of the city in the hall where the public meeting was taking place. "What are you doing on my turf?" the first manager was said to have asked jokingly. "We got a message from head office," the Scotiabank executive is said to have replied. "It said, 'Get out to the meeting, or explain why not.' "

Godsoe and his chief economist, Warren Jestin, sparked crisis-tinged headlines by releasing a study suggesting that in the Toronto region alone, the two proposed bank mergers would mean the loss of twelve thousand direct jobs (and double that if indirect job losses were counted) and the closure of 360 branches. Based on his own experience cutting jobs post-acquisition, Godsoe told the *Toronto Star*, he knew that financial institutions could not hope to amalgamate without significant reductions in employment. Scotiabank also said that the proposed Royal–BMO and TD–CIBC marriages would give the two banks control over 66 percent of the country's domestic-banking assets – a percentage far in excess of the level of concentration seen in Switzerland and the Netherlands, two countries often cited as having the world's most concentrated domestic-banking markets.

Godsoe's offensive prompted a fierce counterattack from the Royal–BMO group. In the opening round of a verbal sparring match on the op-ed page of the *Globe and Mail*, Godsoe argued in detail that "overall, there's no case for mergers." His views were paired with an article on the same page by Barrett, who went after Godsoe personally. "Life is full of surprises," Barrett wrote in a reference to Godsoe's opposition to mergers. "I'm puzzled because Mr. Godsoe's recent statements fly in the face of his long-held public position on the subject." Barrett went on to quote from Scotiabank's 1997 submission to the MacKay task force, which said that "in principle, we favour eliminating the 10 percent rule and encouraging mergers between large institutions to help create strong, internationally competitive companies." Barrett also contrasted Godsoe's earlier public comments about the threat of foreign-bank competition with the Scotiabank chairman's more recent assertions that the foreign threat was being exaggerated. "How do we reconcile these contradictory statements?" Barrett asked. "Either there has been a startling reversal of affairs in the financial-services industry, or something has occurred to make Mr. Godsoe see the world in a very different light. If the latter, one might ask what is behind his sudden conversion. And it is hard not to suspect that it owes something to the fact that, this time around, no bank has asked his to merge." Barrett also took issue with Godsoe's predictions on job losses and branch shut-downs as a result of mergers. Scotiabank's forecast was "in direct contradiction" to the public promises made by the Royal and the Bank of Montreal to preserve jobs and branches, Barrett said, adding that Godsoe should provide some evidence of why he chose to ignore his fellow bankers' personal pledges.

A few days later, John Cleghorn also used a *Globe* op-ed page to accuse Godsoe of flip-flopping on the merger issue. This prompted a letter to the editor written by Jestin, Scotiabank's chief economist, in which he maintained that the pro-merger bank chairmen were taking Godsoe's position on mergers out of context. While he had indeed told the MacKay task force that he favoured consolidation between large financial institutions, Godsoe also said that the benefits of such mergers needed to be "weighed very carefully" against the possible negative public-policy impact. Scotiabank supports the creation of strong, globally competitive financial institutions, Jestin added. But the proposed bank mergers, he said in the conclusion to the letter, "are not about global competition at all. They are in-Canada mergers designed to achieve dominant domestic market share. They are about eliminating competition."

The Royal–BMO group was particularly incensed that Godsoe was telling people the two post-merger conglomerates would control 66 percent of banking assets. Analysts, Royal–BMO officials said, should look at assets in the entire financial sector, including mutual funds, life insurance, and pension funds. When all financial assets were considered, the two merged bank groups would hold a total of 31 percent, Bank of Montreal deputy chief economist Rick Egelton maintained. Referring to the larger number put forward by Godsoe, Egelton said, "This figure is completely meaningless and misleading, and therefore any analysis based on it is equally misleading. It's like saying that two newspapers control 66 percent of the news market and ignoring that there are thousands of other sources of news, including radio, television, and magazines." John McCallum, the Royal's chief economist, also waded in, accusing Godsoe of spreading "distortions" and "myths." In one of the stranger moments of the entire merger drama, McCallum raised the spectre of duelling economists by challenging Scotiabank's number-crunchers to stand up and debate him face to face.

As they viewed this somewhat unedifying spectacle, senior executives at CIBC and TD could only shake their heads. For the most part, they agreed with the initial position taken by the David MacNaughton–Allan Gregg faction at Royal–BMO – they believed that trying to mount a massive public-education campaign to sell mergers was not only a waste of time but also possibly counterproductive. "There was a philosophical difference between the two different mergers," said one TD executive. "Their view was 'Let's debate it'; our view was, 'Let's get it done.'" From the TD–CIBC point of view, it made even less sense to openly engage in messy, high-profile public spats with other bankers, members of Parliament, or the media. "Getting into a pissing match [with Godsoe]," as one member of the TD–CIBC team put it, was a ludicrous, no-win tactic that could only damage all the banks' aspirations.

In the end, of course, the banks knew it would all come down to how Finance Minister Paul Martin assessed the merger proposals. By the summer, Martin had let it be known that he had no intention of holding any private chats with Baillie, Flood, Cleghorn, or Barrett while the national debate was in full swing. But he did agree to see Godsoe at his office in the finance department on September 16. Martin made it clear in an interview some months later that Godsoe had indeed made an impression. "Peter simply made the points to me privately that he was making in his speeches," he said. Looking back over the whole affair, Martin commented: "I think that Peter did play an important role in the public debate, because he clearly gave the other side of the argument a degree of credibility that it might not have had."

While the government did not need Godsoe's input to understand the concerns about bank concentration in the domestic market, Martin explained, the Scotiabank chairman had provided valuable insight on the international aspect of the debate. "Where Peter gave this thing a lot of relevance was on the globalization side," Martin said. By reminding Canadians that Scotiabank had been able to expand its international operations without having to merge with another bank, Godsoe showed "that there is more than one way to skin a cat," Martin remarked. Scotiabank's success in international banking, in fact, dovetailed with the government's position that rather than putting all their eggs in the merger basket, the major banks should be expanding their business activities abroad through other strategies. This was what Martin meant when he said, "We want them [the banks] to go global, [but] it's not up to me to tell them how to go global." Martin concluded, "So, yes, in the public debate, Peter gave a lot of credibility" to the argument that banks could grow in the world market without having to merge.

But Godsoe's role was not by any means the only source of tension and frustration on the merger battlefront. At the highest levels of the Royal–BMO team, there was continuing angst over the lukewarm attitude towards corporate consolidation that was being expressed by TD chairman Charles Baillie and Al Flood, his CIBC counterpart. Senior executives of the Royal–BMO group were wondering aloud if Baillie and Flood were really out to sink the whole merger project with their public mutterings that they sought to merge only to protect themselves from the Royal–BMO colossus.

Then, in early June, Baillie got on the telephone for a routine conference call with the bank analysts at the major brokerage houses. These discussions are usually assumed to be private, but this time a reporter had managed to get in on the call. Baillie told the analysts that there was a "high probability" that Martin would eventually approve the two planned bank consolidations. "I don't think the government wants to turn this down," Baillie said. In a reference to the liberalization of banking regulations taking place in most industrialized countries around the world, the TD chairman added, "I think we would look Neanderthal." Unbeknownst to Baillie, the comment was destined to make headlines the next day. From a strategic communications point of view, it was one of the single most damaging events in the entire year-long controversy. Even within the TD–CIBC team, the outspoken, unpredictable Baillie was a source of regular anxiety. "We never knew what Charlie was going to do next," said one executive. By the same token, considerable second-guessing took place when Flood made headlines by saying that CIBC would have to weigh any merger-related concessions to federal authorities against the demands of its shareholders.

While Royal and Bank of Montreal officials stewed over the ill winds whipped up by Baillie and Flood, their counterparts at TD–CIBC grew increasingly convinced that the whole enterprise might never overcome Cleghorn and Barrett's original decision to push ahead with mergers before Martin was ready. From time to time, each group quietly went out of its way to make sure that outsiders understood the shortcomings and quirks of their rival merger group. While Royal–BMO executives chuckled about Baillie's coup in arranging to get the top job at the merged TD–CIBC, officials at TD–CIBC were more than a little tickled by the way things went with the federal Competition Bureau.

The bureau was charged with investigating the two proposed corporate deals to see if they would result in undue restrictions in the banking choices available to consumers and businesses in any specific areas of the country. It had launched an initial investigation into the Royal–BMO merger shortly after it was proposed in January. But when Konrad von Finckenstein's officials received merger-related documents from TD–CIBC after the second deal was unveiled, they went back to Royal–BMO and hit them with a subpoena requiring further disclosure. Von Finckenstein explained in an interview, "We felt they weren't forthcoming in the way that merger parties are normally forthcoming, and we felt that there was no way we could meet our [deadline without issuing the subpoena]." In the case of TD–CIBC, Competition Bureau officials said they turned over enough documents to make a subpoena unnecessary. However, Royal–BMO officials disputed any suggestion that they did not cooperate as fully as TD–CIBC. "As they [the Competition Bureau investigators] got into it, they may have felt they wanted a lot more detail than we would have automatically provided," Royal vice-chairman Bruce Galloway told the *Globe and Mail.* "If they asked for it without a subpoena, we would have given it to them. The subpoena to me is simply part of the process." Executives with CIBC–TD also quietly let it be known as the bureau's investigation progressed that their merger, which promised to have less overlap in products and services than their rivals', was presenting fewer anti-competitive red flags.

The inter-bank squabbling, both publicly and behind the scenes, added a fractious note to an overall picture that, if anything, seemed to be deteriorating for the pro-merger institutions as the year went along. But the bank chieftains did not give up easily. In the spring, both Barrett and Flood journeyed to London to attend the opening of a refurbished Canada House. The ceremonial dinner to mark the occasion was paid for by the Business Council on National Issues, and Flood, as chairman of the council, was seated with a dozen or so others at Prime Minister Chrétien's table during the gala dinner. Later, reporters covering Chrétien's visit to Britain went after the prime minister for having dinner with a Canadian banker whose company was seeking government approval for a merger. But Chrétien brushed aside the accusation. "We did not really discuss that [the merger] at the dinner," the prime minister commented. "I've been able to resist some lobbies all my life." For his part, Barrett tried to use a brief receiving-line chat with Chrétien at Canada House to work a little pro-merger magic. According to a report in the *Globe and Mail,* as Barrett gripped the prime minister's hand, the banker implored: "Please say yes."

By late summer, the publicity battle pitting Godsoe against the would-be merger partners at the other big banks had become intense and unforgiving. "The Royal public-relations machine is just absolutely awesome," Godsoe told the *Financial Post.* "I don't know how many people they have, but it is awesome. They have advance parties out to set up these town meetings. This thing makes presidential campaigns look amateurish." He went on to say, "If there's a negative story anywhere in the country, there is a letter to the editor from Royal or there's a phone call to the publisher in some cases. I don't think that's happening because they think they've won the battle. They sense they're losing."

THIRTEEN

OPENING THE FLOODGATES

Matthew Barrett flew into Manitoba on a perfect sunny day in July 1998 to meet Liberal MP David Iftody. The Bank of Montreal chairman had personally asked to pay a visit to Iftody's sprawling rural riding of Provencher after the two men had clashed on banking issues during the hearings on financial services set up by Liberal back-benchers. Iftody was typical of those Liberal members of Parliament who were deeply distrustful of the banks, and he openly worried about the effects of mergers on consumers, rural Canada, and small business people. Two years earlier, with the M-word being heard more frequently from bankers, Iftody had even taken the unusual step of trying, unsuccessfully, to pass a private member's bill in Parliament that would have blocked bank consolidations.

Barrett met Iftody at the MP's office in Steinbach, an Eastern Manitoba Mennonite farming centre where that day the women donned their bonnets, the locals built colourful floats, and the farmers revved up their huge tractors for an agricultural parade. After a glimpse of that spectacle, Barrett was invited to a lunch Iftody had laid on with influential business people involved in trucking, lumber, construction, and other enterprises. Over borscht, Barrett extolled the merits of his bank's planned marriage with the Royal. The business people listened politely throughout the lunch, Iftody said. But he added, "At the end of it, one of the fellas said, 'Look, I've been doing business with one of the banks that wants to merge for forty years and I do $200 million a year in revenues, and I feel things are quite satisfactory as they are.' "

All day long, Barrett and Iftody bounced around the riding by plane or in the MP's four-by-four truck. In Pinawa, a small town dependent on the increasingly unviable atomic-energy industry for its economic well-being, Barrett spoke with local authorities who were worried about the likelihood that the Bank of Montreal would cut back service or close its local bank branch because of the lack of business. Barrett promised the Pinawa town fathers that the branch would not close because of the planned merger, but he said the Bank of Montreal, nonetheless, had to apply a business yardstick to any decisions about the local office. Because of insufficient demand at the Pinawa branch, the company had two choices: close the branch or reduce its size, said Barrett, according to the *Paper*, the local weekly. "In retrospect, we could have been more sensitive, more creative and explored more opportunities [in deciding what to do with the local branch]," the newspaper quoted Barrett as saying.

When he was asked how the bank chairman went over in Pinawa, Iftody said it was "pretty well the same thing there [as in Steinbach]; they were very distrustful of the mergers." Still, whether meeting local authorities or wide-eyed students, the Bank of Montreal boss was at his charming best that day, Iftody admitted. "I was struck by the fact that he's a great guy. He was a lot of fun, he joked, it was an entertaining day. The constituents liked him." Later, Iftody enjoyed telling a story about how, when it was all over and the sun was setting, he drove Barrett to his plane. As the bank chairman climbed aboard, the MP said he told him, "You're the kind of guy I'd want to have as a best friend." And then, as Iftody told it, he went on to say, "But you've got a bad idea at the wrong time." That wasn't the way it really happened, however, according to someone else who was there. By that witness's account, Barrett simply asked Iftody to keep an open mind about mergers, and the MP replied politely that he would. What actually took place is incidental, however. Iftody was no doubt correct when, some months later in answer to a question about whether Barrett had managed to persuade people in Provencher riding that mergers were a good thing, the MP replied, without hesitation, "Absolutely not."

Barrett's Manitoba public-relations foray, just one of hundreds undertaken by the senior executives of the four pro-merger banks, underscored the deep-set alienation many Canadians felt towards the country's largest and richest financial institutions. This attitude was fertile ground for those who opposed the bank consolidations. In the hours after the first merger announcement in January, the media, as is its habit, turned to the "usual suspects" among the left-wing nationalists and the bank watchdog lobby, and they, as expected, rang the alarm bells. But that was just the initial clamour. Within days, various interest groups were beginning to think seriously about launching major publicity campaigns intended to rally national concern and action against the banks' plans to expand.

In time, this movement would grow into a vast menagerie of anti-merger opponents of every stripe, from the august chairman of the country's fourth-largest bank to a group known as the Raging Grannies. The festival of protest came to include write-in campaigns, billboards, public-speaking tours, town-hall meetings, satirical ads, TV send-ups, and thousands of individual expressions of concern by e-mail, letter, fax, and phone. The struggle for public opinion, which some compared with the 1988 debate over Canada-U.S. free trade, had by the end enveloped almost everyone in the financial-services industry in one way or another. As well, it brought together people and groups who would usually find themselves far apart on most political and economic issues. And it was notable because of the absence of many of the corporate wagon masters of opinion-making, the same business leaders who had been so instrumental in clearing the way for the Mulroney government's free-trade initiative.

One of the most effective organizations to join the fray was the 89,000-member Canadian Federation of Independent Business, which gave notice shortly after the January Royal–BMO announcement that it intended to pull out all the stops to halt the banks' consolidation plans. "The message from small business," said Catherine Swift, the CFIB's personable and articulate spokeswoman, "is bigger is not better, and that more concentration within the banking industry will mean fewer financial options for small business." And, she added, it was the smallest firms, those with four employees or less, who were most worried. These little companies were the most active job-creators in the economy. Swift went on to say that in meetings with the CFIB, senior bankers had been unable to convince the organization that mergers would be positive for small business, or for the country overall. "Our members have consistently told us they want more and relevant competition in banking services. What we see is a reduction in competition, especially in the smaller communities, along with no improvement in those areas which have been traditionally troublesome for smaller firms, such as high service fees, excessive collateral demands, lack of adequate financing, and revolving-door managers, to mention just a few." The CFIB sent a questionnaire on mergers to its membership in June and July of 1998. Among the eleven thousand who took the trouble to respond, the reaction to the mergers, perhaps not surprisingly, was decidedly negative. Some 68 percent said they opposed the banks' plans, while only 20 percent came out in support. Opposition was most pronounced among small business people in Newfoundland, New Brunswick, Alberta, and Manitoba. The reaction convinced Swift's organization to step up its campaign against the bank consolidations.

As a business group that favoured leaner government in general, and hard-nosed deficit-reduction in particular, the CFIB did not, as a general rule, find itself on the same side of issues as the Council of Canadians, the 100,000-member, "non-partisan" group known for its support of nationalist economic and cultural issues – usually in opposition to corporate Canada. But fighting the big banks was turning out to be something nearly everyone could come together on. Maude Barlow, the council's national chairperson, explained that her organization, which was probably best known for its fervent but ultimately fruitless stand against the Mulroney government's push for liberalized continental trade in 1988, saw fighting the mergers as part of the same, long campaign against corporate globalization. In Barlow's eyes, the trend towards mega-banks, both in Canada and elsewhere, was just one aspect of the ongoing attempts by big business, both globally and nationally, to free itself from the constraints of government policy, regulation, and restrictions. Barlow and her compatriots were more determined than ever to challenge this strategy, which they saw as harmful to the long-term interests of Canadian consumers and workers, not to mention what the council saw as the country's economic and cultural interests. In the same vein, Barlow believed that public opposition to the mergers was emblematic of a wider unease on the part of Canadians about the growing power of corporate forces, whether that power was manifested in U.S. cultural hegemony or the unpredictable, menacing effects of global capital markets.

As 1998 wore on, the council enthusiastically rolled out an attack plan against the mega-banks that employed thousands of petitions, blitzes by council supporters of MP's constituency offices, and street protests. One day in September, the council staged a series of actions. A demonstration at a Royal Bank branch in Vancouver featured a group of elderly women activists known as the Raging Grannies. Another demonstration was held in Toronto, and in Ottawa the council brought out its mascot, a person in a specially made two-headed pig costume, to protest outside a Bank of Montreal office. "The big banks routinely behave as though they are above the public will and beyond the control of elected officials," said Peter Bleyer, the council's executive director. "This has never been more in evidence than in their current, singled-minded drive to grow bigger at the expense of Canadian jobs, communities, and the national economy." He went on to say that the merger moves by the major banks showed, if anything, that the banking industry "needs urgently to be re-regulated in the public interest – before it is too late." And in a remark that underlined the dilemma faced by the federal government on this issue, Bleyer said, "Canadians are waiting to see where Paul Martin's sympathies lie – with the big hugely profitable banks or with them."

Another force to be reckoned with, as far as the banks were concerned, was Duff Conacher, an Ottawa consumer advocate who wanted to be to Canadian banks what Ralph Nader was to the American auto industry. Although his obsession with the banks gave Conacher the aura of being a one-issue campaigner, he did know a great deal about the industry and its activities. On behalf of the Canadian Community Reinvestment Coalition, an umbrella group for seventy-seven labour, left-wing, poverty, women's, and other organizations, Conacher embarked on a cross-country speaking tour to stimulate resistance to the plans of Cleghorn, Barrett, Baillie, and Flood. His assessment of the public mood reinforced the findings of pollsters – namely, that Canadians doubted that Martin and the Liberals would stand up to the banks. "People are just looking at the record of the government, which talks the talk but hasn't walked the walk," he remarked.

Conacher also had ties to another group that saw the banks as a prime target – the New Democratic Party. Shortly after the proposed Royal–BMO deal was announced, the federal NDP decided to put the issue high on its agenda for 1998. Typical of the campaign they mounted was a letter to constituents sent out by Pat Martin, the NDP member of Parliament for Winnipeg Centre. The mailing listed twenty Winnipeg bank branches owned by the Royal and the Bank of Montreal that Pat Martin considered at risk of being shut down in the event the two banks merged. It said, in part:

> Two years ago, the Bank of Montreal ran an advertising campaign which asked, "Can a bank change?" Well, the answer is in. The merger of the Royal Bank and the Bank of Montreal makes it very clear the only thing a bank can change is its name.
>
> For the last 10 years the big banks have been enjoying record-breaking profits and at the same time have been gouging customers and abandoning inner cities. There are empty bank buildings throughout our community. In 1997 alone, the banks closed 12 branches in inner-city Winnipeg. Can a bank change? Many Winnipeggers already know that it is hard to find a bank that will even make change. At the same time that the banks were announcing that their senior officials were making as much as $10 million a year, Winnipeg banks were seriously cutting back on the hours that they gave to part-time and casual staff. . . . The NDP believes that the giant mergers that have taken place since the Free Trade Agreement came into place have created unemployment and reduced competition. The government has to step in and ensure that bank employees and bank customers have their interests protected.

The anti-merger campaign gave the NDP considerable media attention, but it was impossible to tell how much it helped the national party in its efforts to reinvigorate its lacklustre public support. NDP leader Alexa McDonough appeared to find the bedfellows adopted by her party in the anti-bank crusade odd enough to merit a humorous reference before the assembly of media and parliamentarians at the 1998 press gallery dinner. Entering into the satiric, self-deprecating spirit of the annual party in the dome-ceilinged parliamentary dining room, McDonough said the NDP was against the greedy banks, but "we're now okay with greedy small business and greedy trust companies."

Ian Waddell, the small business minister in the NDP government of British Columbia, tapped a deep reservoir of anti-bank spirit with the roving consultative task force he organized in mid-1998. The task force came to Kelowna, a bursting-at-the-seams city in the heart of the Okanagan Valley, on a scorching July day to measure opinion on mergers. It went away with an earful. "In our communities, there are a lot of retired people who don't like bank machines – they want to talk to tellers," John Colbourne, head of the South Okanagan Labour Council, told the provincial task force. There were complaints about the Bank of Montreal's decision to close its branch in nearby Peachland after fifty-one years of operation. "The Bank of Montreal placed full-page advertisements in local papers around the time it closed the Peachland branch," said Robert Harriman, who headed a banking committee for the Peachland area. "These advertisements stated they were closing the branch to increase or improve service to their Peachland clients. What a joke!"

Another unique voice in the national debate was that of Lillian Morgenthau, the energetic, feisty president of the Canadian Association of Retired Persons. The nationwide non-profit organization speaks for 370,000 retirees and others above the age of fifty. Addressing Liberal members of Parliament at public hearings among the stone archways and leaded windows of the University of Toronto's Hart House in June 1998, Morgenthau said, "We are concerned that choice of banks will be lessened, especially in small towns, and will eventually be curtailed to the point of no choice at all, resulting in the end of competition. We know that the heads of the two banks planning to merge have said that they would guarantee maintenance of their respective branches in small towns where branches of both banks existed. However, we are concerned about how long this policy would be in effect and how meaningful it would really be for consumers even when it is in effect, since both branches would be part of the same conglomerate."

Morgenthau also talked about how uneasy many consumers, especially older people, felt about the new banking technologies. As the merger debate evolved, it became clear that this unquantifiable, often inarticulate, but nonetheless potent resistance to change underlay a lot of the merger discussion and may have played a much more important part in forming the public and political mood than many had originally suspected. "Although the current trend in financial institutions is to reduce the number of tellers, replacing them with ATMs, many of our members still prefer to do their financial transactions with a real, live human being," Morgenthau told members of the federal Liberal task force headed by Tony Ianno. "Customer service and jobs are being sacrificed to profits, which in the last quarter have been very high for banks."

Looking back on it, one might have thought that Canadians had been challenged to show how many different, original ways could be found to express their resentment, concern, and scepticism about the banking industry. In August, the city of Yellowknife, in the Northwest Territories, claimed the distinction of being the first jurisdiction to officially tell Paul Martin to reject the mergers. "I think the message we're giving is that Canadians are concerned about the banking situation," Ben McDonald, a councillor in the city, told a reporter writing for the *Toronto Star*. "Mergers are not necessarily good for Canadians, and we want to have a look at it before our politicians endorse it." With intriguing accuracy, McDonald went on to predict, "I think we're potentially on the crest of a wave."

The chorus of opposition grew to include consumer groups, anti-poverty organizations, individuals, labour unions, economists, and much of the media. The *Montreal Gazette*, for example, published an editorial in September that sharply criticized the pro-merger banks. The newspaper took issue with the banks for saying that the promised benefits – specifically, lower service charges and no lay-offs – might be jeopardized if the banks' plans were rejected or if Ottawa imposed onerous regulatory conditions on the banks as the price for allowing the mergers. "Canada's merger-minded bankers only harm their prospects for public approval of their wedding plans when they stoop to the kind of bullying tactics they are now using," the *Gazette* said. Of the promised reductions in service fees, the newspaper remarked, "Canadians will be forgiven for saying they will believe in price cuts when they actually happen." In a satirical gesture, the *Ottawa Citizen* asked two advertising firms to design tongue-in-cheek ads promoting bank consolidations. The paper then ran a page of these fake notices, including ones that read "One Less Bank to Refuse Your Loan" and "Half As Many Bank Commercials."

From the East Coast, the Atlantic Canada Opportunities Agency, a federal organization dedicated to regional economic improvement, expressed doubts about the wisdom of bank mergers. "From an Atlantic region perspective, it is important that some level of competition or choice be maintained in sources of banking services available to clients," the agency said in a brief to the federal Competition Bureau. "Given the small size of many Atlantic communities, any reduction in the number of participants in the banking sector may be cause for concern." The agency noted that 50 percent of the population in Atlantic Canada resides in rural areas, and that studies have found that a limited physical bank presence in such areas tends to result in a number of problems, including higher interest rates owing to a lack of competition, unavailability of small business loans as a result of the high cost of vetting such loans, few options if a borrower is turned down by one bank, and possible delays in the handling of loan applications because local bank managers lack authority to grant loans.

On the political level, the provincial premiers let it be known that they had serious doubts about bigger banks. Ontario Premier Mike Harris and Finance Minister Ernie Eves shared the view of others from small towns about the potential for lost jobs and fewer bank branches as a result of mergers. "If you have a small community, in like a Collingwood [Ontario] or a Huntsville [Ontario], and you have a Royal Bank, a Bank of Montreal, a CIBC, and a TD, how many are going to be left after the banks merge?" asked Eves in an interview with a *Toronto Star* reporter. "Are they still going to keep four branches open on the four corners? Highly unlikely, I would think." Harris and Eves quietly exerted their influence behind the scenes to forestall the mergers, business sources said. Nova Scotia Finance Minister Don Downe and his Manitoba counterpart Eric Stefanson also said bank consolidations raised serious public-interest questions. The cascade of complaints and outrage took every form. But the prize for rhetorical overreach perhaps belonged to Sarkis Assadourian, a Liberal MP from Brampton, who sent out a public letter raising the possibility of job losses from bank consolidations and noting that his constituents were overwhelmingly opposed. For the kicker at the bottom of the letter, he wrote, "The banks say larger is better but we must remember the same thing was said about the Titanic and we know how ill-prepared the world's largest passenger liner was when disaster struck."

The major banks, of course, had for years been engaged in a power struggle with other players in the financial-services industry. And two simultaneous developments – the bank mergers and the federal government's planned overhaul of regulations governing the financial sector – brought out the banks' competitors in full force. During the course of 1997 and 1998, in fact, the effort to influence the government's decisions became a mini-industry, with a half-dozen federal task forces, regulatory bodies, and parliamentary committees putting out the call for written submissions and personal testimony. The resulting stacks of briefs, graphics presentation decks, and speeches could be measured by the yard as the studies progressed and the public hearings droned on hour after hour in House of Commons meeting rooms, school auditoriums, and dreary hotel ballrooms across the country.

Among the banks' foremost opponents were the insurance companies. Both segments of the business – life on the one hand and property and casualty insurance on the other – had been fighting an intense and, as of 1998, successful rearguard action to keep the banks from encroaching further on what they considered their business turf. Since 1992, banks had been permitted to sell insurance through subsidiary insurance companies. However, in a crucial stipulation, they were barred from hawking insurance through their extensive branch networks and from using information from their banking operations to target potential customers.

Throughout most of the 1990s, the insurers had mounted a very effective lobby to keep the banks at bay. And to the extent that this was a political issue – as opposed to an economic one – the insurance industry was well-positioned to do battle. Its army of tens of thousands of agents and salespeople, with their strong connections to the communities in which they worked, constituted a ready-made grassroots lobby of undeniable power. Insurers had deployed these people to lobby their local members of Parliament before, and they clearly would do so again. "I do not believe that a merger is necessary for these banks to remain globally competitive or to withstand the so-called assault on their domestic franchises by aggressive foreign competitors," Dominic D'Alessandro, president of Manulife Financial, said at the company's 1998 annual meeting. "The facts are that foreign financial institutions have been allowed to operate in Canada for many years. Despite this substantially unrestricted access, they had made few inroads. Unlike other industries, our banks have shown that in Canada they can hold their own with anybody."

The focus of the insurance representatives who came before the various parliamentary committees studying these issues was how to maintain a healthy, vibrant industry that would not be dominated by aggressively expanding banks. George Anderson, president of the Insurance Bureau of Canada (which represents 230 companies selling auto and home policies), took issue with the concept, promoted by the MacKay report, of a liberalized, more competitive financial-services landscape. MacKay favoured allowing bank mergers under certain circumstances, as well as giving banks the right to sell insurance through their branches. "The task force has given you its vision," Anderson, referring to MacKay's work, said to members of Parliament. "Of course, political decisions have to be inspired by some kind of informed vision. But every vision has its dark side." Calling MacKay's blueprint for change impractical, Anderson added, "The task force sees a future where smaller financial institutions will thrive and provide new competition to the major banks. But how long will this take? And how successful will it be if, in the meantime, two or three Canadian mega-banks develop?" Then, noting that some small Canadian banks had said they might be tempted to enter into mergers if the MacKay recommendations were implemented, Anderson remarked, "The danger is that things could just as easily unfold in the opposite direction. Rather than a more competitive financial-services sector, the task force's vision could leave us with significantly fewer financial institutions."

Michael Toole, who spoke for sixty thousand brokers who sell car and house insurance, delivered a similar message – but in a more angry tone. He told members of Parliament that the wide-open regulatory regime envisioned by MacKay will "reduce competition, not increase it." Furthermore, he commented bitterly, "There is no evidence that consumers are promoting this debate" over changing the rules governing banks. "They certainly are not clamouring for bigger, more powerful banks." He said the issue before Canadians was not the competitiveness of the property- and casualty-insurance sectors. "The real issue is about a lack of competition in Canada's banking sector." And he predicted that regardless of Ottawa's merger policy, thousands of independent brokers would find themselves out of work if banks were given the right to sell insurance through their branches.

Power Corp. of Canada also weighed in. The Montreal-based giant owned Winnipeg's Investors Group, the largest provider of mutual funds in the country, and two of the major insurers, Great-West Life of Winnipeg and London Life of London, Ontario. No other company in Canada had the political clout of this conglomerate, which was created by entrepreneur Paul Desmarais. Paul Martin had worked at Power Corp. for many years and, more than that, one of Desmarais's sons was married to Prime Minister Chrétien's daughter. In an appearance before the Commons finance committee, Power Corp. delivered a brief that was a clear warning to legislators:

> Today, Canada stands at a crossroads. For decades, an ongoing process has been underway; there has been a steady whittling-away of the other pillars and competitors by the leading chartered banks. With the disappearance of independent trust companies and investment dealers, the banks have come to dominate all major lines of business except life insurance.
>
> Some examples of growing bank dominance are as follows:

	1986	1996
a) in the brokerage field		
discount brokerage	0%	95%
full-service brokerage	0%	76%
b) in the trust and loan field		
personal trust services	0%	93%
term deposits/GICs	40%	68%
residential mortgages	31%	60%
c) in investment products		
mutual fund distribution	5%	61%
RRSPs	37%	68%
independently managed pension funds	0%	12%

Canadian financial-service policy should allow for and encourage: diversity of choices, diversity of distribution modes and diversity of ownership structures.

And the company went on to say that the MacKay task-force recommendations, by dismantling existing bank regulations, might ironically have an opposite effect to what MacKay intended. "Canada might well end up with a small number of very large banks controlling all of the facets of the financial industry, resulting in less, not more, competition, and these financial institutions could be principally owned by foreigners, not Canadians."

Power Corp. also joined the chorus of insurance interests arguing against any expansion of bank powers into their field. Specifically, the company was opposed to any change in the existing rules barring banks from using data on their existing customers to sell these same people insurance. Dropping this regulation would confer a tremendous marketing advantage on the banks, argued James W. Burns,

Power Corp.'s tall, patrician deputy chairman, during a break in the House of Commons proceedings. "Only Revenue Canada has that kind of information on people," he remarked.

If insurance companies were determined to keep the banks from being allowed to sell insurance through their branches, auto dealers were no less keen to prevent the banks from expanding into vehicle leasing. Gerald Drolet, president of the Quebec Automobile Dealers Association and an executive of the Canadian Automobile Dealers, angrily told Canadians such a move would threaten the livelihood of 3,700 dealers employing 115,000 employees in communities across the country. Speaking to the Commons finance committee, Drolet asserted that the MacKay task force had been established on behalf of the banks and focused throughout on the needs of the banks. "In sum, MacKay is all about a vision of what is good for the banks. It is not about what is good for small business, not about what is good for the small communities, not about what is good for the auto industry and not about what is good for consumers in the long run," Drolet said heatedly. "Let me ask all members of Parliament around the table," he went on. "How many of you have been approached by your constituents demanding that banks lease cars? Have you felt any public pressure to let banks expand their powers?"

A similar pitch was heard from General Motors of Canada Ltd. president Maureen Kempston Darkes. In a talk with the Senate banking committee, she warned that allowing banks to lease cars would lead to a long-term reduction in competition, rising leasing costs, and a more difficult environment for auto dealers across the country. "Due to their dominant position in the financial-services industry, banks have a history of capturing market share and driving out competitors in new markets through the use of loss leaders," the no-nonsense Kempston Darkes remarked. "Such a policy is not conducive to long-term support for the auto-leasing industry, and would be followed by reduced competition and hence higher prices for consumers."

Ed Clark, president of Canada Trust, the country's largest trust company, also joined the debate. Appearing before the Senate banking committee, he said that Canada Trust was not against bank mergers as long as the government acted to preserve competition in the financial sector. "One condition should be that the merged banks divest a significant portion of their customers and their related assets and liabilities so neither of [the newly merged bank partners] will have excessive market dominance in any of their main products." Clark told the senators that his and other companies would be keen to acquire the divested assets, as long as they were high-quality assets. Later, appearing before the same committee, Matthew Barrett said he favoured that idea, but only up to a point. "You can have a few toenails, but if you want my heart, the operation ain't on," he quipped.

In his testimony before the Senate committee, Clark, who became known in the business community as "Red Ed" when he helped create the National Energy Program twenty years earlier, urged the government not to saddle financial companies with a host of new regulations that would be a quid pro quo for bank mergers. Bank executives – hearing this from the man who was the architect of the Trudeau Liberals' heavy-handed program to exert control over the oil industry, perhaps the most extreme attempt by a government to regulate business in modern Canadian history – could only shake their heads in disbelief.

Montreal's National Bank, the country's sixth largest, relayed its doubts about bank mergers in no uncertain terms to both the public and the legislators. "If mergers are to occur in Canada, concentration will increase, the [newly merged banks'] market power will be sizeable, and therefore this will create either market problems or will lead to more regulation of the banks, which we don't favour," explained Leon Courville, the bank's president, in an interview. "In our own particular situation, we are in an environment in the province of Quebec, especially, where there is a fair amount of competition, not only from banks but also the caisses populaire, which have 40 percent of the market. And constraints that are imposed on banks, whether they merge or not, will be imposed on us, and that will again limit our ability to compete with the cooperative movement, which has a much greater range of powers than we do."

Like others in the anti-merger camp, Courville dismissed the threat of foreign competition often raised by the banks as a justification for increased concentration. Referring to the Canadian banks' loss of credit-card and mutual-fund business to U.S. companies, he said, "I think this is competition at work. Are they trying to protect themselves from the competition? You cannot compete efficiently and win all the deals, you know." A certain amount of competition from abroad is good for the Canadian financial system, he asserted. "It keeps us on our toes. Foreign competition should not be limited by market concentration in Canada."

Courville said there is no easy way for Canadian authorities to create meaningful competition for the existing big banks. More competition is "a good idea if you can achieve it," he commented. "We've had a long history in Canada [of] trying to promote competition against the banks. The trust industry was viewed at one point [as an alternative to banks]. But there's no more trusts now. They were constrained by regulation. They grew too fast. CCB and Northland [two western Canadian banks that failed in the mid-1980s] are good examples of that." Pursuing the point, Courville added, "And credit unions are not there, except in two provinces, in a sizeable fashion. In banking, you cannot grow very fast and be good at what you do. So I don't see that, either from inside the country or outside the country, you are going to see major competitors that have the stature similar to what the banks in Canada already have. . . . From the retail and commercial banking point of view, the infrastructure is too costly. I mean, we've cornered the market. I hate to say this, but in a way, we've had our consolidation, say, fifty years ago and . . . you may not like the pun, but, as I say, banks in Canada are not too small, it's the country that's small." So while there is some increase in competition here from foreign banks, Courville concluded, there is no evidence yet to explain the nationalist threat expressed by the pro-merger banks. "They raise the flag even before the battle has started."

As the months passed in the wake of the banks' merger announcements, the Liberals in Ottawa were listening closely to the rising flood of opposition to the deals – indeed, they were courting it through their consultations and committee hearings. And if for some reason Finance Minister Martin had failed to notice, the mail pouring into his office on Laurier Street in downtown Ottawa would in itself have been enough to remind him that large numbers of Canadians were strongly opposed to the banks' expansionary plans. Insiders said the overwhelming majority of letter-writers were dead-set against the mergers.

FOURTEEN

HEARTS AND MINDS

Looking tired but relaxed in an open-necked golf shirt, Paul Martin was finally getting a few minutes to let his hair down at a noisy cocktail party. It came at the end of an evening of speeches and debate during the annual three-day talk-fest at Lake Couchiching, in cottage country near Orillia, Ontario. Earlier, Martin had been pressured into holding a media scrum, during which he had to fend off charges that the Chrétien government was insensitive to the state of the then-plummeting loonie and its negative impact on Canadians. That summer should have been an easy one for Martin, who just a few months before had become the first finance minister in decades to declare a balanced federal budget. But the weakness of the dollar, the spreading world economic crisis, and the bank merger controversy had all conspired to deprive Martin of what might have been a period for resting on his laurels and consolidating his personal political gains. Nonetheless, the warm August evening offered an opportunity to chat with old friends, fellow Liberals, and reporters over beers by Lake Couchiching. Before long, someone asked Martin about the implications of the proposed bank mega-mergers. What about the brokerage houses that were owned separately by the banks? the finance minister was asked. Wouldn't mergers mean that shareholders would see a lot of their investment options disappear as competing brokerages became one? Martin thought for a second, then spoke. "People here in Orillia, they're not thinking about the combination of the banks' investment houses because of the mergers, they're thinking about the closure of the local bank branch," he said, his voice rising over the din of the cocktail party. "But believe me, we are!"

While the unguarded remark illustrated Martin's personal awareness of the troublesome questions raised by the amalgamation plans of the big four banks, the finance minister was for the most part keeping his feelings about the proposed deals to himself at that time. The publicity battle over the mergers was hitting full stride by summer, but most of the participants still had little idea what Martin and the rest of the Chrétien Cabinet were really thinking, or what the outcome of the whole endeavour would be. Despite enlisting the help of some of the best-connected – not to mention expensive – lobbyists in the country, the banks had been unable to get a reading on the finance minister. "Martin refuses to say how he's approaching it; he only says, 'I'm going to go through the review process, and then I'll give you an answer,'" complained one experienced consultant with high-level connections in Ottawa.

By mid-1998, the banks had shed the early cockiness they exhibited about their merger plans, and had begun to realize that rather than being engaged in a sprint to win public and government approval, they were caught up, as one banker put it, in a marathon. Most journalists and Bay Street business people still seemed to believe that Martin would ultimately say yes to the merger-prone banks. But some of the more experienced public-relations hands at the banks were beginning to sound worried. Before Martin would decide whether to allow the mega-deals, all involved would have wait out the preparation of a host of reports slated to be delivered between September and December. The study groups included the federally initiated MacKay task force; an ad hoc committee of federal Liberal members of Parliament, headed by Tony Ianno; the House of Commons finance committee; the Senate banking committee; the Office of the Superintendent of Financial Institutions; and the federal anti-combines watchdogs at the Competition Bureau.

While everyone knew by summer that the process would be exhaustive, it was still unclear how long the unprecedented policy review would ultimately take, or what the crucial deciding factors would be. From the point of view of policy design, the government was placing great stock in the MacKay task force, which Martin had always viewed as a means to establish a road map for the future of Canada's financial services. But from a technical perspective, it was equally clear that the key report would be that of the Competition Bureau, the quasi-independent investigation agency directed by senior bureaucrat Konrad von Finckenstein. His task was to spell out in detail just how the two planned mergers would affect the competitive banking options available to consumers and business people. Martin, under his authority as finance minister, would give the final thumbs-up or thumbs-down to the banks' plans, regardless of what the Competition Bureau advised. But the finance minister had already said, in no uncertain terms, that he would not reverse a negative report from von Finckenstein. "It would be a frosty Friday before the government would overrule the Competition Bureau finding that there was an undue concentration of banking power," Martin had said when von Finckenstein released his guidelines for assessing the proposed bank deals. In that mid-July press conference, however, Martin had reminded everyone that the bureau's technical analysis was not his only criterion. "I have the final say, and I will certainly exercise my judgement based on what I deem, and the government deems, to be in the national interest," he remarked. "The interests of the Canadian public are obviously paramount. We are not going to allow rural Canada to find itself without a reasonable level of service."

By then, as well, the tone of the grass-roots debate was already much in evidence. Between February and June, the task force of Liberal members of Parliament directed by Ianno had heard from 136 witnesses in thirty-seven meetings in every major city in the country. In keeping with the Liberal committee members' view of the banking community, the hearings became a sounding board for the public's dissatisfaction with the way big banks operate, and of the distrust of the proposed mergers and the motivation behind them. Among those who raised questions about the banks' plans in appearances before the Ianno committee were representatives of the Retail Council of Canada and the Consumers Association of Canada, former Conservative Cabinet minister Sinclair Stevens, former trust company owner Hal Jackman, well-known businessman Adam Zimmerman, and mercurial University of Toronto economist John Crispo. Raymond Garneau, president of the Quebec insurance company Industrielle-Alliance, told the Liberal MPs that "banking is a privilege, not a right. Banks have a social responsibility." André Bérard, chairman of the National Bank, said at the hearings that the probable motivation of the pro-merger banks was to eliminate competition to gain the freedom to raise prices. "Let's be frank," he said. "If you have no competition, why would you drive prices down?"

The committee was by all accounts also impressed by the issues raised by Peter Godsoe in his appearance. Conversely, several members of Parliament reported that they were less than pleased with the appearances of John Cleghorn and Matthew Barrett. "I don't think they took our committee seriously," Nick Discepola, a Quebec MP and bitter critic of the banks who was vice-chairman of the task force, told the *Toronto Star*. "To the point where they were almost laughing us off." But the mood of the whole exercise might have best been epitomized by Crispo, usually known as a staunch opponent of governments telling business what to do. "Our own banks," he told the members of Parliament, "have put a gun to our heads." He suggested that the Liberals should bring the bank chairmen before their committee and grill them on how much money they stood to make from the mergers as a result of inflated stock options. As to how to handle the questioning, Crispo barked: "Put a lie detector on 'em." When Ianno was asked in the early summer about the testimony that was presented to the task force by the pro-merger bank chairmen, he summed it up: "They just haven't got a case."

To some extent, the members of the Ianno committee were right about the banks' view of them. Bankers were aware that the results of the Liberal back-benchers' hearings reflected the anti-merger opinion that was building like summer storm clouds across the country. But in the minds of some bankers, the Ianno task force was little more than a political sideshow – and one whose ultimate influence on Martin's decision-making process might prove negligible.

In mid-1998, according to senior bankers who dealt with federal officials in Martin's department, the Royal, the Bank of Montreal, TD, and CIBC were still being given to understand that approval of the mergers, while difficult for Ottawa, remained a serious possibility – even if the banks were eventually required to modify the details of their marriage arrangements. A report dated August 5 by stock analysts at the Royal Bank's investment unit, RBC Dominion Securities, gave the mergers a 65 percent chance of approval. But the analysis said Martin would force concessions from the banks that would be more onerous than initially expected, including limiting job losses, forced divestiture of some bank branches, and capping service fees.

As the banks stepped up their promotional campaign, John

Cleghorn obtained a meeting with Prime Minister Chrétien. In a chat in Chrétien's Langevin Block office in July, Cleghorn laid out the case for bank consolidations. Chrétien listened noncommittally, then recounted his involvement with the financial-services industry as a Cabinet minister and MP going back to 1963, when the Liberals changed the Bank Act to block an American takeover of a Canadian bank. Then, in September, the prime minister, who had been a member of the TD board from 1987 to 1990, met with Charles Baillie at the Toronto airport. In the course of their discussion, Baillie suggested to Chrétien that blocking the banks' mergers would lead in time to the demise of Canada's banking sector, and with it, loss of Canada's standing in international circles. If they were having this conversation ten years hence, Baillie theorized, he might not be talking to a G-7 prime minister. That would be a serious loss, Baillie told the prime minister, because membership in the prestigious G-7 had been of great benefit to Canada. But Chrétien was unfazed, replying (according to what Baillie later told others) that it hardly mattered, since Canada didn't deserve to be in the G-7 anyway. According to Baillie's version of events, the prime minister went on to say that Canada was brought in only because the U.S. wanted an ally at the table to even the score with France, which had insisted on including Italy to offset the influence of Britain. The most memorable aspect of the Chrétien-Baillie chat was Baillie's request that the federal government come to a decision as quickly as possible on the merger proposals. Chrétien told the TD chairman not to worry, that it wouldn't be long before the Liberal government would be ruling on the matter.

Meetings with the prime minister were just one of a great many ways in which representatives of the four would-be merger partners tried to influence the government's thinking. In all, the four banks spent untold millions of dollars in their eleven-month campaign to win Martin's approval. The outlays ranged from huge legal fees to advertising charges to payments made to outside economic thinkers to extensive travel bills for the executives who criss-crossed the country extolling the deals. Not least among the costs were the retainers for lobbyists, pollsters, communications experts, consultants, and other assorted spin doctors, whose fees started at an estimated $15,000 a month even before the operating expenses were added on. As might be expected for the biggest corporate gamble ever undertaken in Canada, the supporting cast was a kind of influence-peddling all-star team. It included some of the most experienced, well-known practitioners of the art: Bill Neville, the grainy Tory operative, one-time aide to former prime minister Joe Clark, and ultimate Ottawa insider, was brought in by TD; Rick Anderson, a former Liberal and public-relations powerhouse who went over to Reform as a key adviser a few years ago, assisted the Royal–BMO group; David MacNaughton, the erstwhile organizer for Paul Martin and a former Hill & Knowlton PR executive, was also in the Royal–BMO line-up; and Bank of Montreal chairman Matthew Barrett relied on Patrick Gossage, the ebullient former press secretary to Pierre Trudeau. The on-the-ground work in Ottawa was carried out by the likes of Herb Metcalfe, whose well-connected Capital Hill Group lobbying firm assisted CIBC, and by Larry Mohr, another CIBC operative. The stylish James Lorimer, of Humphreys Public Affairs Group, toiled for the Royal–BMO contingent, as did Rick Kuwayti, Steven Bright, and former MP David Walker. The Bank of Montreal could also call for advice from Dick O'Hagan, the dean of the country's image-makers. Unfortunately, many said later, O'Hagan, a former aide to Pierre Trudeau and Lester Pearson, had retired and was out of the country – and therefore was not consulted – when Barrett and Cleghorn hurriedly rolled the dice on their planned merger in January 1998.

Made conspicuous by their absence from this array of lobbying firepower were principals of the Earnscliffe Strategy Group, one of the most influential consulting operations in the capital. But as senior partner Mike Robinson explained, there was ample reason for the firm to stay well away from the banks' campaign. First, through an associated company, Earnscliffe Research & Communications, the group was very closely involved in Paul Martin's efforts to manage Canadian public opinion. In this case, Earnscliffe was handling the private polling on mergers for the finance department. And Robinson himself, who had run Martin's unsuccessful 1990 Liberal leadership campaign, was worried that conflict-of-interest accusations might have arisen had he helped the pro-merger banks. "Given both my personal views and the fact that my working for a bank could possibly become an issue, I decided I didn't want to be within one hundred miles of this issue," Robinson told the *Globe and Mail.*

The Bank of Nova Scotia was not without resources of its own as it went about trying to scupper its competitors' plans. In fact, Godsoe was part of a group of people who formed a natural support and advisory group for Martin. This group included John Turner, the former prime minister; Liberal fund-raiser Gerry Schwartz; Barry Campbell, the former Liberal MP who was once parliamentary secretary to Martin; and John Webster, another Liberal, who was expected to help organize the finance minister's next leadership bid. And then there was Kaz Flinn, the head of Scotiabank's government-affairs operation. A Maritimer who worked as an organizer for Turner in Atlantic Canada, as well as for former Nova Scotia premier John Savage, Flinn was said to be as capable of influencing the debate in Parliament as anyone in the game. "Kaz Flinn knows every executive assistant [to a Cabinet minister] in Ottawa," said an official at one of the rival banks.

With the help of its phalanx of lobbyists, the pro-merger banks unleashed an extensive campaign to influence members of Parliament, and some believe it backfired. "The MPs were telling us, 'We're happy to hear from you but don't send us too much information – we're overwhelmed by the banks,'" one lobbyist who worked against the mergers recalled.

While the power struggle went on in the corridors, bars, and restaurants of Ottawa, the banks continued to try to lay the groundwork for merger approval with Canadians at the grass-roots level. The evidence suggested, however, that all the speeches, question-and-answer sessions with members of Parliament, and chats with business and community leaders were going for naught. Word leaked out that polls being done privately for the various banks and others detected that public backing for the mergers, while never strong, appeared to be weakening. To the extent that people were thinking about banks and potential mergers at all, they were thinking negatively – and often in fairly acrimonious terms. Insiders at the banks agonized over Canadians' lack of understanding of their own stake in the continued fiscal health of their big financial institutions. One official revealed, for instance, that when the banks hired consultants to set up focus groups to measure public attitudes, the bankers couldn't get over how hard it was for the participants to accept the fact that half of all Canadians hold bank stocks through shares, mutual funds, or pension funds. "That just doesn't seem to register," the bank official recounted in bewildered tones.

With the months slipping away, the pro-merger banks were being hurt not only by their critics and opponents, but also by a lack of support from their natural allies. The Canadian Bankers Association, the major industry group, was rendered silent by the split within its ranks created by Scotiabank's stand against the deals. Other big business associations, such as the Business Council on National Issues and the Canadian Chamber of Commerce, stayed on the sidelines for similar reasons. Godsoe said big business did not support the mergers but did not want to offend the banks by going public. "I'm reminded of that Voltaire quote on his deathbed when he was asked by his priest to renounce the devil and he said, 'Is this any time to be making new enemies?' " Godsoe remarked in the *Financial Post.*

That's not to say there was no support for the four banks' proposals during the course of the national debate. The conservative, Vancouver-based Fraser Institute produced a study that supported the mergers and said the deals would lead to improved efficiencies that would benefit Canadians in general and bank employees in particular. "The bank mergers make sound economic sense," said the report, entitled *Bank Mergers: The Rational Consolidation of Banking in Canada.* Walter Robinson, federal director of the Canadian Taxpayers Federation, warned the government against second-guessing the strategies of private business and said "governments need to concentrate on the future, not the past." David Banks, chairman of fast-expanding New-court Credit Group, threw his company's support behind the pro-merger forces. "We support them because we believe in free markets and we believe that size is important in today's global financial markets," Banks told members of Parliament. And the C. D. Howe Institute, the Toronto-based economic think-tank, put out an analysis praising the efficiencies that can be realized through corporate consolidations.

But overall, it was clear that the tide of public opinion was moving against the banks. As the summer drew to a close, bankers acknowledged that convincing Canadians of the wisdom of the bigger-is-better strategy was proving to be very tough. With this in mind, executives at TD, CIBC, the Royal, and the Bank of Montreal increasingly pinned their hopes on the release of the MacKay task force report in September. The study, meant to be an in-depth and forward-looking examination of the financial-services business, had been set in motion by the Liberal government twenty months before. Its original chairman, prominent Bay Street lawyer James Baillie, had been forced to quit in mid-1997 amid questions about a possible conflict of interest when it was reported that he had been involved in the Bank of Nova Scotia's takeover of National Trust. His replacement, Harold MacKay, was a Regina lawyer known for his even-handedness and his connections to the Liberal party. MacKay, fifty-seven, was a slight man with a supple mind, a refreshing way of looking beyond vested business and political interests, and a wry sense of humour. "I'm from Saskatchewan, so I know what a level playing field looks like," he used to say. When he was asked how the proposed bank mergers had affected the work of his task force, MacKay said it "would have been boring" without them.

On the morning of September 15, the green-and-white bound documents that were the end result of the task force's nearly two years' worth of work were stacked high outside the National Press Theatre in Ottawa. In all, the cornucopia of information officially entitled the *Report of the Task Force on the Future of the Canadian Financial Services Sector* included a 258-page summary of recommendations, five lengthy background papers, and eighteen detailed research studies. The thrust of the report was indeed innovative, if not downright revolutionary. Its 124 recommendations were a recipe for widespread change that would lead to a new era of more open competition among banks, insurance companies, and other financial providers. Most important, MacKay said the government should scrap its long-standing rule that "big shall not buy big" in the financial-services industry. "There should be no absolute ban on mergers among large banks, insurance companies or other financial institutions," the report stated. But it went on to say that "no such merger should take place if it is not consistent with the public interest." Explaining the gist of the task force's conclusions, MacKay told reporters, "We have not put up a red stoplight, nor have we issued a green light [to bank consolidations]. What we have done is put up a flashing yellow light."

The task force's call to throw off the regulatory strictures governing financial services was balanced with recommendations for a tough new strategy to enhance consumer protection. MacKay also presented extensive suggestions for creating more competition in the sector. These included allowing life-insurance companies, mutual-fund companies, and investment brokers access to the national system used by the banks to process financial transactions; making it easier to start new banks; encouraging more activity in Canada by foreign banks; and streamlining regulations to create national credit-union networks that could better compete with big banks. Another recommendation was that the federal government require merger participants to undergo a detailed Public Interest Review Process, which would examine the implications for employment, costs and benefits to consumers, and other factors.

MacKay's recommendations were not binding on the federal government. And the position taken by the task force on mergers was in many ways ambiguous. Nonetheless, the pro-merger banks seized on the task force's recognition that corporate marriages may be a viable business strategy in today's changing environment. "We agree with the report that the industry is being rapidly transformed by powerful worldwide forces that are radically changing the Canadian competitive landscape and making the status quo in financial services unsustainable," John Cleghorn announced. In a media briefing, Matthew Barrett declared, "I would argue that many of the forces the MacKay task force outlines have been raging for five, six, or seven years, so the quicker we can get about restructuring the Canadian financial-services industry, the better." But Martin responded by tossing the whole issue back into the court of public opinion. He latched onto MacKay's suggestion of public-interest hearings for mergers, saying they would be mandatory. "This government wants to make clear that no major bank merger would be allowed to proceed without public hearings on that specific merger proposal," Martin said in a statement. "This will guarantee that the people of Canada will have every chance to be heard, because it is the interests of all Canadians that will determine the final decision." The implication was that even if the proposed deals were not sunk as a result of the slew of public consultations and regulatory studies already planned by Ottawa, the banks would face yet another round of public hearings in 1999 before Martin would consider going ahead.

Despite that daunting prospect, the four pro-merger banks were buoyed by MacKay's report. To their way of thinking, it provided a solid body of objective analysis that could be used as a basis for further debate in the House of Commons finance committee and the Senate banking committee, both of which were preparing to hold public hearings on the task force's recommendations. Also, MacKay had sought to dispel some of the emotion surrounding the taboo of big bank mergers – an effort that could not help benefiting the banks. So with the long-awaited task-force study now completed, the banks took up the battle for Canadians' hearts and minds again with a renewed sense of anticipation and a feeling that, after months of spinning their wheels, they now had a somewhat better chance of persuading the public and the government to go along with their proposals.

FIFTEEN

RUDE AWAKENING

In the last week of October, Tony Ianno never seemed to sleep. Unlike the directors of most of the well-funded committees and blue-ribbon task forces studying the bank mergers, the member of Parliament from the Trinity-Spadina riding in Toronto was operating on a shoestring. Ianno, the forty-two-year-old son of Italian immigrants, has a reputation as one of the best on-the-ground organizers in the party. A supporter of Paul Martin in the jockeying to be the next leader of the party, he is said to be harbouring ambitions to be, as one Liberal put it, "the Sergio Marchi" of a Martin government. It is also said that Ianno, who has made a career of trying to improve bank lending to entrepreneurs, has hopes of eventually becoming the first minister in a new Cabinet portfolio for small business. But in late 1998, he was the chairman of the committee of Liberal backbenchers who had been running their own investigation of banks during the previous ten months.

With the debate over the proposed mergers nearing a climax, the Liberal members of Parliament were ready to present their findings. To write the report, Ianno had earlier enlisted the help of Toronto consultant George Radwanski, a former journalist closely connected to the Prime Minister's Office. But it was Ianno who flew down to Toronto from Ottawa to handle the final editing and to oversee the printing of the 237-page document. His goal was to have it ready in time for the weekly Liberal caucus meeting on Wednesday, November 4. If he missed that window, it meant waiting another two weeks, because Parliament wasn't sitting from November 9 to 13. But computer glitches held up production and left Ianno wondering until almost the final moment if he would make the Wednesday deadline. The last of the reports didn't roll off the press in Toronto until 7 p.m. that Tuesday evening. "My staff rented a van and drove the report to Ottawa themselves," Ianno recounted. Before noon the next day, seven hundred copies of the blue-jacketed document were ready to be handed out to members of Parliament and the media. In the hours that followed, the report resonated across the country with more force than Ianno could possibly have anticipated.

Although it was titled *A Balance of Interests*, the report was actually a broad indictment of big banks, their record, and their merger predilections. "There is persuasive evidence that the proposed mergers would be likely to have very adverse consequences for the Canadian public interest," the report stated bluntly. Fifty Liberal members of Parliament – out of a total of 156 – and four senators put their signatures on the study, which gave it unusual weight. The report went on to recommend that Finance Minister Paul Martin turn down the planned corporate marriages, saying that the bankers had utterly failed to justify their need to reduce the number of big banks from five to three.

The proposed mergers, the report stated, would lead to large-scale job loss, reduce consumer choice, and concentrate too much political and economic power in the hands of the two post-merger conglomerates. The task force also warned of reduced availability of small business loans and widespread closures of bank branches. Ianno and his colleagues said as well that they did not buy the argument that the banks needed to merge to be more competitive in the global market and fend off foreign competitors. And they dismissed the banks' claim that mergers would create cost-saving efficiencies that could be passed on to customers in the form of savings. On another contentious issue, the task force said the government should turn down the banks' requests to be allowed to expand their operations by selling insurance and leasing automobiles through their branches. Instead, the caucus produced a grab-bag of recommendations for improvements in the way banks operate. These ranged from requiring financial institutions to educate rural Canadians on the use of automated-banking systems to encouraging more lending for small business to stipulating that bank branches should all have waiting areas with chairs.

Martin reacted with circumspection, telling reporters, "This is an important report; it's good work." He added, "It's part of a series of reports which the government is going to take into consideration when we make a final decision." But opponents of mergers saw it as a crushing blow to the four big banks' political hopes. "The mergers are dead," declared New Democratic Party finance critic Lorne Nystrom. Within the TD–CIBC group, there was a discernible attempt not to overreact. CIBC president Holger Kluge noted that while Ianno had come out against mergers, the MacKay task force had been more open to the idea. With the new report from the Liberals, then, "the score is 1-1," Kluge concluded. At Royal–BMO, the mood was more combative, with spokesmen suggesting the Ianno report would prompt celebrations in U.S. banking circles because it would tie Canadian bankers' hands while inviting foreign firms to expand their operations.

But there was no doubt that in a battle where image was everything, the banks had suffered a major setback. "Scathing Liberal Report Dims Bank Merger Hopes," read the huge front-page headline blaring out from *Globe and Mail* newspaper boxes across Canada the next day. Inside the paper, Michael Ancell, an analyst with St. Louis–based investment dealer Edward Jones & Co., suggested that now "it will be tough for Martin to approve this politically."

The Ianno report crystallized the debate over the banks and marked the beginning of a period of more bitter, acrimonious activity. Auto dealers, insurance brokers, and nationalists applauded, but the business community was discomfited by the Liberals' heavy-handed approach. Greg MacDonald, director of public affairs at the Alliance of Manufacturers and Exporters Canada, labelled the Ianno study "very strident" and said the alliance's members, while not in favour of bank mergers, disagreed with the dire impact foreseen by Ianno. The chasm between Ottawa and Bay Street was reflected in the reaction of Hugh Brown, the respected bank analyst at Nesbitt Burns. In a response that probably articulated the feelings of a lot of people in the investment community, Brown wrote in a report to clients:

> Essentially, the Ianno Task Force appears to believe banks are social institutions or public utilities that should be used to subsidize perceived disadvantaged groups such as small business, rural Canada, auto dealers, insurance brokers, etc. Nowhere in this report is there discussion of the role of, and need for, adequate profits and capital to sustain a viable banking system. The report makes no reference to the roughly 7.5 million Canadians (and voters) that directly or indirectly have $75 billion of their life savings invested in bank shares.
>
> To carry the Ianno report to its ultimate conclusion, and to be fair, if Canadian banks are really public utilities, then nationalization makes sense. Of course we all know the disastrous

> worldwide performance of government-owned or directed financial institutions. . . . We doubt if Canadians want another post office.

But all evidence suggested that average Canadians were thinking along very different lines. Around the time of the Ianno report, various interest groups released polls indicating that national opinion was indeed stiffening against the banks. A Decima Research survey for the Insurance Brokers Association of Canada found that 59 percent of respondents opposed or strongly opposed mergers. The Canadian Federation of Independent Business said its small business members opposed the bank deals by a similar majority. And the Council of Canadians reported that two-thirds of Canadians surveyed in a BBM/Comquest poll said bank consolidations would be bad for them personally. "Our data show that the banks have little credibility, and that the majority of the public is against these mergers," Peter Bleyer, the council's executive director, told the Senate banking committee.

In the days after the Ianno report, representatives of the banks in Ottawa and senior executives in Toronto began to admit more readily in private conversations that their amalgamation plans as originally conceived had little chance of approval. Dozens of variations on what became known as the "No, but . . ." scenario were spun by the bankers. What all this speculation had in common was the notion that Martin, after initially saying no to the four banks, would give them a chance to reapply for permission to merge. The idea was that the banks would have an opportunity to do so after overhauling their merger proposals to address the concerns raised by the Competition Bureau.

Even before the scathing Liberal report, Cleghorn and Barrett had been telling parliamentarians that they were quite willing to put in writing their commitments not to slash jobs or wipe out existing bank branches. Furthermore, they had said, they would agree to subject their companies to full government scrutiny to ensure that they'd complied. Now, in a last-ditch effort to reverse the direction of the debate, the Royal–BMO team launched a massive publicity campaign a few weeks after the Ianno report. It was a response to criticism that the banks had failed to provide enough information to the public on their plans, and it was meant to establish a communication conduit to Main Street. "This is one way of getting the message across," said Matthew Barrett. "It's been hard to get that out, sort of unfiltered, if you like. There's been this committee meeting and that committee meeting and the other committee meetings, and you leave booklets with people and they don't read them."

The new Royal–BMO information blitz, rumoured to cost millions of dollars, included national newspaper ads headlined "Two Banks. One Pledge." If allowed to join forces, the two banks promised, they would reduce service charges, hire more customer-service staff, keep rural branches open, set up a new small business bank to make $40 billion available in loans, and increase staffed bank outlets. The two banks' chequing-account customers were sent a six-page blurb amplifying these promises in their bank statements. And a twenty-four-page booklet covering the same information was made available in Royal and Bank of Montreal branches.

The banks seemed to be admitting that they had neglected to address the old-fashioned, human aspect of the equation. Referring to the customer-friendly promises highlighted in the new promotional material, Barrett explained, "There's a goodly percentage of the population for whom high-touch, personal, face-to-face contact is still the most preferred way as distinct from electronic banking only. What we're responding to is, we will have more walk-in places where you can shake hands with somebody before they reach for your wallet than we've had before." But the public reaction to this latest communications tactic was at best mixed, with some people saying the pledges were too little and too late. "Banks Dangle a Big Carrot; People Figure It Must Be Rotten," shouted a prominent headline in the *National Post.* The article quoted Nick Discepola, a member of the Liberal task force, who said, "Damn it all, when the bank chairmen were before our committee, we asked them what's in this for Canadians. Why didn't they lay this out for us then? What it shows me is that they're desperate because the stakes are so high."

Despite the open, magnanimous tone of the latest Royal–BMO communications initiative, the mood inside the banks was veering from defensiveness to forced optimism and back again to frustration. Charles Baillie appeared to grow tired of tip-toeing around the politics of mergers. In a remarkable speech a few weeks after the Ianno report, he sharply criticized Canadians' tendency to lapse into easy assumptions about the efficacy of government control as a solution to troublesome business issues. Corporations, Baillie asserted, are ill-equipped to deal with social problems, which are the responsibility of government. "That, after all, is why our shareholders and our customers pay taxes to the government," the TD chairman told a business audience. "Surely we have learned enough from the experiments and the errors of the sixties and seventies and early eighties to have a clear understanding of what the respective roles of government and the private sector ought to be. Surely, much as it might be emotionally satisfying to some and politically convenient to others, we don't need a National Energy Policy for the banks," Baillie remarked. He was alluding to the 1980 Liberal government attempt to assert control over the oil industry – an initiative that still raises hackles in Western Canada.

Then, taking direct aim at Ianno, Baillie said banking may be a privilege, but it is also a public right. "I believe it is telling to note that the only countries in which operating a business is considered to be a privilege – and not a right – are, in fact, totalitarian." He went on to say he does not "fall down before the altar of globalization or technological change. But I do accept them for the forces that they are. In an ideal world – in a dream world – we might wish that mergers were not on the agenda." But this, he said, is not the case. "Nostalgia," he concluded, "may be nice. But it's no way to run a bank – or a country." By then, Baillie was obviously tired of the long haul of public speeches and debate over the banks' future. Chatting after the speech, he agreed that the banks' attempt to promote the mergers had forced their chairmen to perform like politicians running for office. Yes, said Baillie wearily, "and by people who are not used to it." Barrett had also begun to publicly express his reservations about the whole process. Speaking to an audience of financial-services colleagues in Vancouver, he said Canadians had been deluged for almost a year with "arguments, predictions, assessments, prognostications, accusations, utterly unsupported assertions, and even the odd fact or two."

Barrett, Baillie, Flood, and Cleghorn had never hidden their conviction that in the choice faced by Canadians, the status quo was not on the table. As the day for Martin's decision neared, they began to increasingly raise the spectre of an alternative strategy that many Canadians would regret. As Barrett put it, cuts in bank jobs and the number of branches were inevitable if Martin blocked the banks' expansionist plans. "It is inescapable that there would be a reduction in employment and branches" unless the mergers were allowed, he told reporters. He said Canada's banks had to use mergers to become more efficient, "or risk withering on the vine." Although he claimed he didn't want to be accused of "scare-mongering," the threat was clearly there. "Something has to give," the Bank of Montreal chairman remarked. For his part, Baillie put it this way: "I do not believe that smaller, separate, and weaker banks would, in the long-term, be a very good guarantee of jobs." This raised a question of some import, because the four pro-merger banks had a combined 170,000 employees.

The banks asserted that without mergers, they would not have the cost efficiencies to compete with aggressive new entrants in financial services. Thus they suggested that to stay profitable, they would have to drop marginal lines of business and concentrate on niche strategies in those operations most likely to turn a profit. This might mean the end of the full-service national bank operations meant to be all things to all people, bank officials suggested. Barrett warned: "The pressure to produce acceptable rates of return means that Canadian banks will have strong incentives to drop lines of business altogether. We would increasingly concentrate on strong, profitable businesses – or in other words, we would not continue to invest in those businesses that were not profitable and not expected to become so." The bankers also pointed out that Canadian banks had, for the most part, already been forced by bigger, lower-cost competitors to pull out of payroll-processing and the custody business of holding clients' investments. Mortgage-processing was cited as another operation where cut-throat competition might cause Canadian banks to shift business operations to big United States firms, meaning the disappearance of jobs in Canada. But this kind of threatening talk did not go down well with members of Parliament. "I think it would be unwise for anyone to speak in those terms," said Ianno in an interview. "I think that a scorched-earth policy is not good for anybody."

Feelings on both sides of the issue became more heated as the end of the year drew nearer. The Bank of Montreal, in particular, was not in any mood to abandon the fight. When the *Toronto Star* reported in early November that bankers were privately expecting Martin to deliver a no – and possibly by as early as Christmas – BMO president Anthony Comper reacted by sending a letter to employees asking them to promote the mergers with their members of Parliament, their families, and their customers. "We have not given up," Comper said in a letter to 10,700 Toronto-area employees. He said the *Star* article underscored how important it was "for all of us [at the Bank of Montreal] to make our views heard."

Even before the *Star* article appeared, John Carver, senior manager of the Bank of Montreal's MasterCard division in Toronto, had led hundreds of employees into the fray. Some people considered credit-card operations to be one of the areas of Canadian financial services vulnerable to foreign competition. So on the day after the Liberal back-benchers released their study rejecting mergers, Carver sent a petition signed by more than five hundred workers to Jean Augustine, the Liberal MP who represented the riding where their office in Toronto was located. The letter said: "I have just finished reading the Ianno report, which you and 53 of your caucus supported. This is the most disappointing document produced to date on the subject of the bank mergers. We, the employees at Bank of Montreal MasterCard, have a significant stake in this process, and do not understand Mr. Ianno's recommendation nor the support it has received."

In the next few weeks, bank workers continued to take a more prominent role in the debate. Hundreds of Bank of Montreal employees waving maple leaf flags and placards and blowing whistles gathered on a frigid noon hour in downtown Toronto one day. "Canadian banks combine / They're yours and mine," chanted the employees in a pep-rally kind of mood. "This is really important to us – this is our jobs," explained Lin Parker, a call-centre manager who sported a red scarf and leather coat. "This is Canadians saying, 'We want the banks to merge.' This is everyday Joes. The Canadian people should see that we're really in support of mergers."

After the Liberal caucus report was released, Ianno went on CHIN radio in Toronto. One caller, a Bank of Montreal employee, said to the MP, "As a Liberal, I'm very disappointed in your task force. Your recommendation is that Martin just say no to the bank mergers, and I think that is a very fearful argument that you've put forth." When Ianno tangled verbally with the caller, Bank of Montreal spokesman Joe Barbera, another guest on the show, intervened. Barbera suggested

Ianno was adopting a "McCarthy" approach that would bar bank personnel from taking part in the discussions. Ianno went on to ask the caller to make sure to write him about her concerns. "We'll gladly read it," he said. "But you know, we had fifty-plus members of Parliament support this. Joe can easily say that we were doing it for political expediency. I don't think members of Parliament have to act that way, especially when another election is not for another four years."

Stepped up efforts by the bank employees sparked more tension between the Liberal members of Parliament and the big financial institutions. Bank of Montreal employees, for example, bombarded Martin's office with pro-merger e-mails and tied up MPs' phone and fax machines with their missives. The Liberals reacted with fear and anger to what appeared to be a blitz of political pressure. MP Sarmite Bulte said $1,500 worth of tickets to her fund-raising dinner were dropped by the Bank of Montreal after she put her initials on the Ianno report. But Bank of Montreal officials said this was simply a misunderstanding caused by a scheduling conflict. Of the fax and phone campaign, she told the *Toronto Star*, "We've been bombarded. . . . They tell us that we're terrible people and wonder how I, as a woman, cannot understand. I've found it personally very upsetting. . . . When you get personal, what do you gain by that? You only gain ill will." Jean Augustine said the phone offensive temporarily halted her office operations.

The gulf between the bank's view of all this and the view of the politicians was pronounced and insurmountable. It was clear that the bank had encouraged its employees to take a hand in the discussion. But Barbera thought those who expressed alarm when Bank of Montreal personnel did so were cheapening democracy. Just because people work for a bank doesn't mean they shouldn't be able to contact a member of Parliament and express an interest in a major decision affecting them, he insisted. Later, when Augustine did hold a meeting with bank employees to discuss the mergers and the Liberal caucus report, Ianno went along with her. At one point, he bluntly told the employees their bank was using them as political pawns.

Sixteen

Baillie-ing Out

During the summer, in the rolling hills of Quebec's Eastern Townships, where both men have country homes, Paul Martin and John Cleghorn would occasionally bump into each other while picking up groceries or running errands around the town of Knowlton, Quebec. But there was never any talk about the mergers. For months, Martin had stuck to his position that he would not hold one-on-one private meetings with the pro-merger bank chairmen while the government and the public were debating their corporate plans. But in late November, with the deadline for a decision looming and the banks clamouring for meetings, the finance minister changed his mind. Why? "Because they're very large institutions and they have to be treated fairly, and at that point I said as a courtesy I would meet with them," Martin explained on December 18, in the first interview he gave on the subject.

Cleghorn was the first pro-merger bank boss to see the finance minister. He arrived at Martin's home in Montreal on Sunday, November 29, at 11 a.m., and Martin's wife, Sheila, made ham sandwiches for them. During the course of what Martin described as two and a half hours "of non-conclusive polite conversation," the Royal chairman laid out the justifications for the proposed merger with the Bank of Montreal. In turn, the finance minister stated the difficulties presented by the planned consolidations. "I listened and basically said, 'No decision has been taken on this, but here are some of the problems,'" the finance minister recounted.

The no-final-decision technicality notwithstanding, there was no mistaking Martin's attitude towards the merger proposal, and Cleghorn left convinced that the negative signals the bank had been receiving from senior officials were no mistake. The Royal chairman's talk with Martin was recounted during the usual early morning Royal–BMO media strategy session the following Monday. The participants in the meeting were stunned. Afterwards, Cleghorn telephoned TD's Charles Baillie to give him the news. Meanwhile, two senior executives from TD and CIBC were scheduled to meet that same day with Scott Clark, the professorial deputy minister of finance. The bankers designated to talk to Clark were CIBC president Holger Kluge and TD vice-chairman Bill Brock, the two men who had been in charge of the planning to mould the two banks into one. Clark gave Kluge and Brock the same impression Martin had given Cleghorn: that a negative decision was likely.

These revelations from Ottawa touched off a frantic three-day scramble as the four banks sought clarification from the highest levels of government. Like all public companies, the banks were under a legal obligation to disclose any information to shareholders that could affect the value of the corporation's shares. But at the same time, they did not want to jump the gun and tell the world that their own merger plans were null and void on the basis of signals received in behind-the-scenes chats with the government. At that point, only

Cleghorn had met one-on-one with Martin. The other pro-merger bank chairmen were scheduled to do so later. Flood, for instance, said he wasn't going to issue a statement that the merger had failed unless he heard it directly from the top.

Baillie and Flood tried to reach Martin on that Tuesday by telephone, but Martin was unavailable. Word came back that he would move up his planned meeting with Baillie and Flood to Thursday of that week. But CIBC was scheduled to release its 1998 results that day, making it impossible for Flood to go to Ottawa. Finally, the deputy minister, Clark, phoned back and told Flood and Baillie that, in fact, no final decision had been made. That was enough to convince Flood to hold off on making a statement, but a day later Baillie decided, over CIBC's objections, to go public and let TD's shareholders know that approval of the mergers was doubtful. A senior banker said the really irritating thing was that because of the joint merger-planning between the two banks, TD officials knew that CIBC would be releasing dismal 1998 financial results on that Thursday. And TD made its statement on the probable collapse of the mergers only moments after CIBC's results were made public.

"Based on conversations with senior folks in Ottawa, it's clear that the likelihood of the mergers being approved is pretty low," Kym Robertson, TD's normally effervescent spokeswoman, told Dow Jones news service. The story moved on the Dow Jones wire at 11:25 a.m. on Thursday, December 3. Divulging the information was a calculated move. There had been newspaper articles going back a few months suggesting that, based on changing share values, some TD shareholders felt they should be getting more shares in the new, proposed bank for every share they owned of TD. Robertson told Dow Jones that because of the negative prognosis for bank consolidations, these on-going questions about the relative share values of the two banks were no longer as germane. With the deals looking iffy, that issue was "less and less relevant," Robertson said. Afterwards,

TD denied it had intended to do anything other than keep its shareholders apprised of information of importance to them. But the whole blow-up represented yet another instance of inter-bank squabbling. Some CIBC officials were angry that Baillie had made the declaration, particularly on the day when CIBC released its poor annual results. One official said TD's objective was really to "delink its share price from ours." To members of the media, who had been waiting almost a year for the denouement of the bank story, the TD statement was a major event. It wound up as the top story for both the *Globe and Mail* and the *National Post* the next day. The *Globe* didn't mince words. "Bank Mergers Are Dead, TD Fears," said the headline dominating its front page.

The explosive disclosure by TD reverberated through the nearby office towers occupied by the Royal–BMO group. That Thursday, according to bank sources, Cleghorn telephoned Martin. Unable to get the finance minister out of a meeting, the Royal chairman told Martin's aide that if he didn't get some reassurance from Martin that the deal was still alive, his bank was going to issue its own press release saying the whole thing was off. As the story is told, the minister was subsequently dragged out of a meeting, at which point he telephoned the Royal chairman and said, "Cleghorn, I haven't made a final decision. You heard me right." With that, Cleghorn decided against a public announcement. In Ottawa, Martin reiterated his position to the media that same day. "I have made clear that there are still reports to come in . . . and it is not until we have received all reports and have had a chance to consider them that we'll be in a position to make a decision." He was referring to the as-yet-unfinished studies from the Senate banking committee, the House of Commons finance committee, the Office of the Superintendent of Financial Institutions (OSFI), and most important, the Competition Bureau. All were expected within the following two weeks.

Two days after the TD bombshell, on Saturday, December 6, Barrett also journeyed to Montreal to enjoy a sandwich and a talk at Martin's house. The two men met for a couple of hours, Martin recalled. Then, on the following Monday, December 8, the finance minister met with Flood and Baillie at his office on Parliament Hill. "The conversation," Martin said in an interview, "went pretty much the same [with all the bank chairman]: 'No decision has been taken, waiting for the Competition Bureau, primarily, and OSFI, but look, there are a lot of problems.'"

Glancing back over the entire affair, it is clear that these secret meetings are crucial to any full understanding of events. Either out of courtesy, as Martin claimed, or for some other reason, the finance minister let the banks know a week before the decision was made public that the mergers were unlikely. Martin described his motivation candidly: "The officials in the department had met with them [the banks' representatives], and the department more or less indicated to them that no decision had been taken, but you guys ought to understand the way it's going. We were leaning one way, and it was really going to come down to whether the Competition Bureau [report] was either going to confirm that decision or effectively throw that decision up in the air."

Martin insisted that he did not know what the Competition Bureau was going to say in advance. That makes his statement to the bankers all the more arresting. He was telling them that the government had pretty much made up its mind against the mergers before it had even seen what the Competition Bureau had to say. Of course, Martin pointed out in his chats with the bankers that no final decision had been taken. But the chairmen were smart enough to read between the lines on that score. One senior banker remarked that the whole process had become "like being strung up with piano wire – a long, slow death." Another executive who worked outside of

Toronto later said, "When Flood got back to Toronto after seeing Martin, his secretary called me and said, 'Mr. Flood is throwing out his merger binders. Do you know anyone who wants them?' "

Publicly, some of the bankers, perhaps hoping for a miracle, continued to put on a brave face. It was not as though they had much to hope for, however, from the upcoming report from Competition Bureau director Konrad von Finckenstein. The bureau's officials had been working closely with the would-be merger banks ever since the fourth week in January, when von Finckenstein got a mysterious telephone call from a lawyer for the Royal Bank. The lawyer asked if the director could meet him and some unnamed clients at 8 a.m. on Friday, January 23, for what was billed as a very important announcement. "I didn't think about the bank merger, frankly," the tall, exacting von Finckenstein recalled in an interview. "I thought it was a gasoline merger and I said, 'Sure, why not?' " Early on that Friday morning, the Royal Bank's lawyer arrived at the Competition Bureau's high-rise office in Hull, Quebec, with his clients in tow. "I shook hands with four people I'd never seen before and they said, 'We're here to announce the merger of the Royal and BMO [pronounced "Bee-Mo"], which will take place in fifteen minutes,' " von Finckenstein remembered with a laugh. The bank representatives were carrying a draft agreement – papers that had been approved by the two organizations' respective boards of directors only hours before. "[It] took us, of course, totally by surprise, like everybody else," said the Competition Bureau director. "And also it was the first time ever somebody has issued the request for an advance ruling – you know, by putting something on the table and saying, 'The cheque will be in the mail.' "

The deals presented an enormous challenge to the Competition Bureau, a quasi-independent agency under the auspices of Industry Canada. In its director, von Finckenstein, the bureau had one of the most experienced and savvy members of the federal bureaucracy. A long-time industry and trade official, von Finckenstein was known as a tough-minded, independent thinker. He was also at home – both socially and professionally – among politicians and ex-politicians with extensive influence in Ottawa. The fifty-three-year-old lawyer was best known for his role as chief legal counsel in Canada's trade negotiations office when former prime minister Brian Mulroney was pursuing the 1988 Free Trade Agreement with the United States. Oddly, von Finckenstein had, in late 1997, raised questions publicly about the finance minister's power to block mergers between large financial institutions. In a brief submitted on behalf of the Competition Bureau to the MacKay task force, von Finckenstein had said the government does not need special rights to curtail bank mergers because the Competition Bureau's authority was enough to quash any anti-competitive behaviour on the banks' part, even after mergers.

The probing of the two planned bank deals was the biggest investigation ever undertaken by the bureau. It was also the only one ever done that involved four corporations at once. Over eleven months, the bureau put together an investigating team that in the end included about one hundred officials, lawyers, economists, and experts. The officials dug up some four hundred thousand pages of documents. In keeping with von Finckenstein's position that his work should be as open and transparent as possible, the bureau's senior people met on a weekly basis with representatives of the banks for much of the year. Thus by the autumn, it was well known that the bureau was likely to find significant anti-competitive problems with some aspects of the proposed deals.

With the decision nearing, Barrett went to Washington, D.C., to talk to senior figures in the Clinton Administration. He said later that these top-level officials could hardly accept the idea that Paul Martin might be getting ready to turn down the Canadian banks' merger plans. "Paul's a smart guy, he'll do the right thing," the U.S. administration figures reportedly told the Bank of Montreal chairman. All through early December, the momentum had been building as legislators and regulatory authorities rushed to complete their reports. On December 2, the Senate banking committee released the results of its hearings on the MacKay recommendations. While not commenting directly on the plans of TD–CIBC and Royal–BMO, the senators said megamergers could make business sense and should not be barred across the board. But it drew the line at allowing large banks and insurance companies to join forces. Then, a little over a week later, the House of Commons finance committee, chaired by MP Maurizio Bevilacqua, released the results of its post-MacKay consultations. Bevilacqua, who had said all through the fall that he was trying to move the debate on the future of the industry beyond the predictable interest-group boilerplate, tabled a document saying that Canadian banks might need to merge. "The government should not block efforts by Canadian institutions to become internationally competitive," wrote Bevilacqua. The report also said would-be merger partners should be given a chance to address any anti-competitive red flags raised by the Competition Bureau.

But Bevilacqua's conclusions were all but lost in the frenzy of media speculation that final week about the federal government's upcoming decision. Word finally came that von Finckenstein would release his long-awaited analysis after the stock markets closed on Friday, December 11, which would give the government the weekend to review it before the markets opened again the following Monday morning.

By then, those following the story in the media could not have expected anything but a no from Martin to the mergers as initially conceived. What remained unclear, however, was what would happen next. In most proposed mergers, the business partners receive the report of the Competition Bureau and are then given a chance to address the bureau's concerns. For instance, companies might agree to divest themselves of certain assets or business operations to eliminate anti-competitive situations identified by von Finckenstein's watchdogs. But in this case, the Bank Act gave Martin the power to bring the deals to a complete halt, which would block any further discussions between the banks and von Finckenstein about making the deals acceptable from an anti-trust standpoint. That kind of final no from Martin was what the banks feared most. Their hope at that point was that the finance minister would come in with a "No, but . . ." scenario that would allow the banks to negotiate with the Competition Bureau, or at least contemplate new applications with revamped blueprints in the first half of 1999.

For some reason, the banks and the government tried to keep it a secret that the four bank chairmen were flying to Ottawa to be briefed by von Finckenstein. But details of their plans trickled out Thursday night. On Friday, however, the first people to go over to the Competition Bureau office in Hull to hear from von Finckenstein were not the chairmen, but Martin, Jim Peterson, and a dozen senior finance department officials. Martin claims that he and the rest of his party had been given no previous details of the bureau's analysis, although some find it hard to imagine the department did not have a pretty good idea what was coming. In any case, von Finckenstein decided that since the session was starting at 3 p.m., while the stock markets were still open, the briefing would be handled like a federal budget lock-up – that is, anyone who was present at the beginning could not leave until it was over. By then, the stock markets would have closed for the weekend. (One of the minor ironies of all this was that Martin was being "locked up" with the same kind of secrecy that surrounds the finance minister's annual budget message to Parliament. At that time, it is Martin who knows every detail of the announcement in advance. Others who need to know a few hours early, mainly those members of the media who have to prepare articles and electronic reports for immediate dissemination, are "locked up" for reasons of confidentiality.) When Martin heard he was going to be confined in this way for almost two hours, he said, "Geez, I'd better get a coffee," and hopped up and went looking for one, a Competition Bureau official said. Von Finckenstein's briefing lasted until 4:45 p.m.

About that time, Barrett, wearing a camel-coloured topcoat, and Cleghorn, in a tweed overcoat, were taking the escalators to the second-floor landing of the building that housed the Competition Bureau. When asked a few days later how the briefing of Barrett and Cleghorn went, von Finckenstein said, "There were basically no surprises for them." This was because the two banks' representatives had been dealing closely with the bureau for months, the director said. Of the two chairmen, von Finckenstein observed, "They were very polite." The director quoted Barrett as saying, "Well, it seems to be a very uncontaminated report. You know, it's based on data, not on anything else."

Barrett and an exhausted-looking Cleghorn, hounded by reporters as they emerged at 6:30 p.m., sought to put the best light possible on what they had heard of the still-secret Competition Bureau findings. Barrett, who had earlier told Liberal members of Parliament that he would cry if the mergers were rejected, asked a *Toronto Star* reporter, "Do I look tearful?" And Cleghorn stressed the same line his bank had taken for weeks. "It was a productive meeting, and the concerns that have been raised and various processes, if we're allowed to continue, we can follow up with [von Finckenstein's] officials," the Royal chairman told reporters. This remark from Cleghorn, which suggested that the banks could, if given a chance, find remedies to the bureau's concerns, was later passed on to the government by reporters seeking comment. It prompted a swift response from finance department officials who were working late that night. No, these officials said pointedly, the bureau had not laid the groundwork for further negotiations between von Finckenstein and the banks. In fact, Martin's officials pointed out in no uncertain terms, the bureau had found too many problems for the minister to let the mergers proceed at all.

The message from the finance department did not go unnoticed. By Saturday, the media was brimming with prominent reports that Martin was poised to turn down the deals outright. This was the atmosphere Baillie and Flood encountered when they arrived in Hull that Saturday morning. Asked if the two chairmen were by then resigned to a negative outcome, von Finckenstein said, "Well, they had all read the papers and, if you believe the papers, they all had met with Mr. Martin, too, so I have no idea what went through their minds." He then went on to say, "They seemed to be generally appreciative that we had tried to come to the best answer that we could on the basis of the facts and the economic experiences and the interviews that we had conducted, and they were very complimentary. And I don't think – I mean, obviously, they may have some questions about our analysis – but neither pair [of the two groups of bank chairmen] suggested in any way there was anything seriously wrong with what we had done."

Both Baillie and Flood looked dejected, however, when they left that Saturday. They told reporters they felt they could address von Finckenstein's concerns if given the chance, but they sounded doubtful that they would get that opportunity. The two had been saying for months that to keep their deal from falling apart, they had to be allowed to proceed quickly. "We did announce it in April. You can keep morale up and handle employee uncertainty for only so long," Baillie, wearing a trench coat and fedora, told the media. "I think the minister will give us some encouragement and say there's something and it wouldn't be too far away, or else he'll say it's going to be a long time, and that would be too long for us." Commented Flood: "We realized these weren't slam dunks from the beginning."

SEVENTEEN

THE LAST ACT

Five days short of a year after the Christmas party in 1998 where Matthew Barrett and John Cleghorn first broached their proposed merger, the national media assembled in Ottawa to hear Paul Martin's verdict on the entire affair. The press conference that Monday, December 14, was held at 8:30 a.m. so that the information would be in the public domain before the stock market opened. Martin strode into the media theatre purposefully, sat down before a backdrop of red-and-white maple leaf flags, and laid out his decision. By then it was well known that the finance minister was likely to turn thumbs-down on the two planned bank consolidations. But the tone and the finality of his statement stunned observers and bankers alike. Reading from the seventh page of the eight-page written announcement, he said flatly, "I am announcing today that the bank mergers will not be allowed to proceed because they are not in the best interests of Canadians."

Martin based his decision on three main points, the same as those specified in the so-called talking points circulated in the Prime Minister's Office that day. First, Martin said the mergers were unacceptable because of the immensity of the two institutions that would be created. Citing the report he had received on December 10 from John Palmer, the federal superintendent of financial institutions, the finance minister suggested the post-merger banks would have been so big that there would have been intractable problems if one of them ever ran into financial trouble. "The sheer size of the institutions that would result from these mergers would constrain the alternatives available to regulators and to government," Martin intoned. Second, the federal Competition Bureau had concluded that the mergers would raise anti-trust issues. The consolidations, Martin said, quoting from the bureau's review, would "lead to a substantial lessening or prevention of competition that would cause higher prices and lower levels of service and choice for several key banking services in Canada." And third, Martin said the mergers opened up another important area of public interest – concentration of power. Noting that Canada already has one of the most concentrated banking systems in the world, he stated that the planned mergers "would mean leaving decisions on credit allocation – which are so crucial to the efficient functioning of the economy – in the hands of even fewer, larger institutions, thereby raising serious concerns that go well beyond the issue of competition." He added, "There is value in having more rather than less choice" in bank financing or credit advice. More choice, he asserted, provides "greater opportunity for more innovative ideas to flourish, for more entrepreneurial risk to be taken, and for more options to be explored in creating a productive economy."

Martin went on to say that the Liberal government would move to put in place a new policy framework for the financial-services sector that would, among other things, better respond to the needs of consumers, promote increased competition by encouraging more new domestic and foreign financial players, and enhance the growth of Canadian financial institutions in the world market. "The government," Martin pronounced, "will not consider any merger among major banks until the new policy framework is in place." And even then, he said as he wrapped up his remarks, the government would not give the go-ahead unless it was sure the mergers would not raise the concerns he had already mentioned – too much concentration of power, the creation of companies so large as to pose regulatory problems, and reduced competition in the industry.

Much as Tony Ianno had done six weeks earlier in the same media theatre, Martin was laying down a marker. In both his words and his blunt, uncompromising tone, the minister was putting the banks and everyone else on notice that it was the government, not the bankers, that would set the agenda for change in the all-important financial-services business. In the press conference, he repeated his often-heard conviction that the banks would have been better off had they refrained from announcing their merger plans until after the government had developed a new regulatory blueprint. Referring to the first merger revelation, in January 1998, Martin said, "We feel – as indeed we felt then – that industry restructuring must be driven by the broader public interest and by the evolution of the overall sector, not by the specific needs of any individual institution." When he was asked if the mergers had, in fact, been dead on arrival, the minister replied that the banks' "proposals as originally set out would have been very difficult to approve." As for the future, Martin said it would take more than a year before the government could complete the planned overhaul of the financial sector that would open the door for possible approval of bank marriages. Prime Minister Chrétien concurred during brief remarks he made on his way into a Cabinet meeting. "They did not make a case," he said of the banks. "It's a major problem from the point of view of competition."

Despite being forewarned that the decision was no, many bank executives were still bitter about the stern, unyielding note struck by the government. "Based on Mr. Martin's statement this morning, it is clear that he has closed the door on any significant consolidation in the Canadian financial-services industry in the foreseeable future," John Cleghorn and Matthew Barrett said in a joint communiqué. In a reference to their earlier warnings that blocking mergers would inevitably lead to a deterioration in the country's banking industry, the statement said, "History will judge if Mr. Martin has made the right decision for Canada." TD chairman Charles Baillie issued a similar statement on Ottawa's decision. "This is disappointing," he said, "given the pace of consolidation among competitors around the world and the intensifying competitive landscape here in Canada." TD and CIBC moved that day to terminate their merger agreement, and the Royal and the Bank of Montreal followed suit in a terse press release the next day. After all the millions of words and thousands of lengthy press releases, the thirty-six-word statement made for a bleak, inexpressive epitaph: "Bank of Montreal and Royal Bank today announced that, effective immediately, they are terminating their agreement to merge in light of the announcement by the Minister of Finance yesterday that the merger will not be allowed."

While suddenly reluctant to speak out in detail, for fear of further alienating Martin, senior bankers privately expressed resentment and dismay about the way it had all gone. In particular, they criticized the government for what they saw as a highly politicized decision-making process. "It's more than just a matter of regulation," said one senior executive. "It's regulation and politics." That banker also said people in the industry felt that the MacKay task force and the House of Commons finance committee had delivered solid reports on the future of financial services. But "it almost seems as if Ianno was given more weight." He added, "One problem with the process was that it was a prototype. The rules were being made up as they [the Liberals] went, and to some extent it was necessary to do this [present the merger proposals] just to find out what the playing field looked like, because we didn't know."

Before December 14, the banks had been wondering how the finance minister might qualify his merger rejection, and what the next step in the process might be as a result. Would the banks get a chance to reapply with new merger proposals, and how long would they have to wait? Three months? Six months? Instead, the government had slammed the door on bank consolidations. What's more, by saying that the banks would have to surmount tough regulatory hurdles to merge even after the government overhauled the sector's regulatory framework in a year or two, Martin was clearly telling Bay Street to forget about it as long as the current group of Liberals was running the country. "Everybody was sort of stunned that there wasn't a notion of a twin-track at all," said James Lorimer, who worked for the Bank of Montreal in Ottawa. By twin-track, he meant an arrangement whereby the revamping of financial-services legislation could take place simultaneous to a continuing review of the TD–CIBC and Royal–BMO deals. "The two things could have been done in tandem," he said. Lorimer also said that Martin, by requiring a lot of new legislation before the mergers would be reconsidered, was not just asking the banks to wait a year or so, as the minister claimed. "This will take three to five years," Lorimer remarked. As for the government's motivation, he said, "Who knows, except for the obvious? It's a short-term political issue." Commenting on the Liberals' approach to the banking sector, he added, "I don't think they know where they are coming from yet. It's a crass political decision. It was short-sighted." Lorimer also believed that the Liberals, by allowing the Ianno task force to come down as hard as it did on the banks, had created a political situation that precluded any serious consideration of mergers. "Martin took a hands-off approach with [the Liberal] caucus and let the government get all wound up. In any case, whoever created the political mood, it happened and they [senior Liberals] couldn't go there."

"It was first and foremost a political decision," agreed Bill Neville, a seasoned and well-connected lobbyist who was on TD's payroll. "And I don't mean that critically – that's these guys' jobs." Of Martin's ruling, Neville said, "It had to do with his leadership aspirations and a disposition not to take on the caucus, and then there was public opinion." Given those factors, he added, "Certainly biggest buying biggest is not on with this government." Neville also said that the kind of arguments the banks used about the future effects of change in the industry did not appeal to the Liberals. "You're trying to make a long-term argument with people who think long term is what happens next Friday." Neville, with his long experience in Ottawa, said it was clear from the beginning that convincing Canadians to applaud bank mergers was almost a non-starter. "I told my client [TD Bank] right off on the very first day [that] if anyone thought they were going to win the public-opinion battle, they must be smoking dope. People think intuitively that mergers lead to consolidation, rationalization, and downsizing – and most of the time they do." As well, he said, there was immediate public resistance because of the dislike of financial institutions in general. "Shakespeare wasn't all wrong when he said money lenders aren't the most popular people," Neville remarked. The two factors – public resentment of banks and suspicion of mergers – amounted to a "lethal combination." On top of that, "Banks have overall done a very lousy job of presenting themselves." The lobbyist noted, for instance, that Canadians feel they are being gouged by service charges, when in fact the costs are average on an international basis. And then there was the issue of the banks' approach: "There's no question they project a kind of arrogance, not a very touchy-feely image."

In private, some bankers were vitriolic, claiming they had been double-crossed by finance officials who hinted that Martin was likely to deliver a no verdict on the mergers, but that he would probably give the banks a chance to keep the process going in 1999. Others were upset at the way senior Liberals seemed to tolerate, or perhaps exploit, Canadians' penchant for bank-bashing. In a private memo that became public, Brian Steck, chief executive officer of Nesbitt Burns and a vice-chairman of the Bank of Montreal, told the investment dealer's 4,300 employees that the government did not deem the proposed bank deals to be "in the public interest." Or, he added, perhaps not "in the best interest of our political icons." The memo from Steck, a stalwart Liberal backer and fund-raiser, continued, "Quite frankly, the disgusting innuendoes repeated by many of our politicians relating to bankers were and remain reprehensible." He said he could only hope that future governments would "create a less confrontational environment." In addition, Steck wrote, "You will excuse me for offering the views of my friends on Wall Street. They wish to applaud our government for its 'internationally surprising stand' and giving them a delightful Christmas present. To Tony Ianno, they wish to collectively thank him for his naiveté and complete lack of comprehension."

On the political front, one of the few critical voices was that of Scott Brison, the Progressive Conservative finance critic, who favoured the mergers. He told the *Toronto Star* that Martin had made "a politically expedient decision . . . [that] obviously put politics ahead of public policy." He also said the move would make Canada look like a "banana republic."

Of course, those on the other side of the merger debate reacted with a mixture of approval and relief. "We very much believe Martin did the right thing, certainly for small business, and I think he did the right thing for the country, too," commented Catherine Swift, president of the Canadian Federation of Independent Business. Duff Conacher, head of the Canadian Community Reinvestment Coalition, lauded the decision as "two steps forward in the public interest." Credit unions approved Martin's call to revamp the financial sector to spur increased competition, and the Council of Canadians said the government's rejection of the banks' plans was "welcome – if overdue – news to the vast majority of Canadians."

The New Democrats also applauded, and called the decision a victory for the public against the power of the banking establishment. The Reform party, which had been caught between its dislike of overweening government and its populist, anti-bank roots, said the government had ended up adopting the Reform position (no to mergers until there is more competition in the banking industry). In making that claim, Reform bank critic Dick Harris was, in fact, correct. But Harris went on to blame the Liberals for the current lack of competition in financial services. "During five years in government, the Liberals have taken no action to open up the financial-services sector, and Canadians, including the banks, are paying the price," he said. For its part, the media had a field day poking fun at the fall of the powerful fat cats of Bay Street. "Bankzilla" is no more, wrote one business columnist. The *Toronto Sun* ran an editorial-page cartoon depicting two chunky men in pinstripes holding hands in front of a preacher. "Sorry, boys," says the preacher, "but the public finds this type of marriage a bit repulsive!"

Looking ahead, as one might be expected to do after perhaps the biggest corporate fiasco ever in Canada, the financial-services landscape was littered with unknowns. Relations between the Liberals and the banks, generally tense in recent times, were probably destined to grow more strained than ever in coming years. And then there was the tension that had been stirred up among the pro-merger banks. That internal friction was not likely to be smoothed by the huge newspaper advertisement the Toronto Dominion Bank took out shortly after Martin's ruling. The headline in the ad, a quote from Baillie, read, "From the Outset, We've Always Respected the Public Process with Regard to the Mergers." It was hard to view that as anything other than a restatement of TD's long-held gripe that the Royal–BMO group had derailed the process of orderly banking reform by moving too quickly with its merger plans. It was not something that the dejected merger proponents at the Royal Bank and the Bank of Montreal wanted to hear just at that moment, and in private they reacted bitterly.

But what of Peter Godsoe, the Scotiabank chairman who had achieved a huge public-relations victory by being the most prominent opponent of bigger banks? Despite having won big, Godsoe decided that silence was the better part of valour and refused immediate public comment just like the four bank chairmen whose plans were crushed by Ottawa. Godsoe instead issued a two-sentence statement: "Scotiabank commends the government for its efforts to thoroughly assess the financial sector and set the future framework for the industry. We fully support the process of review that has taken place and we look forward to playing a constructive role in the formation of revised financial sector policy." Issuing this bit of dry fluff was probably wiser than releasing a statement that might have been construed as gloating. In the aftermath of the merger failures, Scotiabank officials were concerned about how their non-conformist organization would be treated in future by the other big banks – namely, would Godsoe's rivals exercise their frustrations by going out of their way to undercut Scotiabank's competitive position?

Despite the debacle of industry back-biting and government-bank conflict created by the merger wars, some bankers tried to look on the positive side. When he was asked if Canada was better off for having had the merger debate, Cleghorn said, "Sure. I think, obviously, the debate is long overdue. The debate should have been held before." He added that the discussions and policy-making decisions for the industry were still going on even though Martin had said no. If the government "can do this [bring in new legislation] within a year or so, that's reasonable. What would be frustrating is if we got into endless debate [and] nothing happened. We get into another election [and] it's all put off. Then you're looking at ten years before really anything gets done."

In the aftermath of Ottawa's decisive rejection of the banks' merger plans, much speculation was focused on Paul Martin's motivations. In a wide-ranging interview he gave shortly after the announcement, he went into great detail on his thinking about the banks and the issues at stake in the merger debate. He seemed struck by the top bankers' early certainty about their ability to persuade Canadians of the need for bigger firms. "They were absolutely convinced that they could go out and change public opinion. They were so convinced of the rightness of their cause that they felt they were absolute apostles and could convince people of it," the minister said.

However, Martin did not seem impressed by the arguments brought forward to justify the merger strategy. When he was asked about the banks' claim that they needed to grow to stay even with increasingly aggressive foreign competitors, Martin said he understood that the business world is undergoing profound changes. "There's no doubt that the whole question of globalization and technological change, for the banks, opens up great opportunities and great threat and great challenges," he commented. A businessman himself, Martin said that he would not tell anyone else how to run his or her company, and that it was up to the bank executives to decide how best to meet these challenges. Having said that, however, Martin admitted that he did not believe the pro-merger banks' "original story" about the need to merge to become global competitors. "I know a little bit about this," Martin said, "and I'll tell you, the global competitors [are not big banks]." The global competitors, Martin said, are the big investment operations such as Goldman Sachs and Merrill Lynch, and "these [mergers] weren't going to make them a Goldman Sachs or a Merrill Lynch. So my first thought was, 'Wait a minute. Their rationale for doing this, in the sense that they are going to become global, bears no relationship to the other big global players.'" Martin said that reasoning didn't "make any sense" to him. "I've spent twenty-five years in business, and I've dealt with all of these firms all around the world, and I know damn well what the hell a global financial institution does and [it's not what the Canadian banks were talking about]."

The finance minister then went on to say, "Subsequently, the banks changed their story, and it became 'We don't want to be a global player, we want to be a major North American player,' and that made a little more sense." But at the same time, Martin said, the pro-merger banks were warning of "the huge domestic hit" that was coming from foreign financial-services firms active in Canada. "So, again, the same thing happened," Martin explained. "I said, 'Boy, I've taken a look at foreign bank entries around the world, and to the best of my knowledge, in the Swiss equivalent of Red Deer, Alberta, there are not a lot of foreign banks.' " He also said it was clear from the research done by the Competition Bureau that the economic barriers to foreign bank entry in the Canadian market are steep.

In summing up his thoughts about the banks' warnings, Martin admitted that there might have been some truth to them, but he said that the Canadian banks had presented "a lot of confused messaging." And even if the threat was real, Martin added, it still had to be weighed against the public interest. "I have to look at the potential problems caused here. If the way to solve the threats to Canadian banks is to decimate competition within the country by going from five to three big banks, or to create a major concentration of economic power, then the threats to the banks pale against the costs that would be incurred." The resulting reduction in competition would be felt by rural Canadians, small business people, and consumers, and that would be unfair, Martin said.

The finance minister stressed that his decision should not be construed as a reflection of a negative attitude towards banks. "I am not a bank-basher," Martin declared, pointing out that unlike banks in many other countries, Canadian banks are efficient and well-run. But he went on to say, "I wish they were a little more open to small business, I wish they were a little more open to rural Canada, and I wish they were a little more open to some of the high-tech industries." Still, all companies have some shortcomings, he added, and he had respect for the people who run the country's banks. "I think these people do a tremendous job," he said.

When he was asked to assess the months of public debate, Martin said he was surprised by the lack of support for bank mergers from big business. "The big business community remained silent, which I think was a very telling message." Although corporations are more global than they used to be, Martin theorized, "National ties are still very, very important. So while big business can bank around the world, there are still very strong ties to a domestic banking system, and [big business'] views in terms of a reduction in competition [because of mergers] were exactly like [those] voiced by the small business community. The frustrations were exactly the same as [those of] the small business community."

The best way to protect the consumer in this era of change, in Martin's opinion, is to enhance financial-services competition. "Let's face it. We have had a structure in place in this country for the last fifty years that has said, 'We don't want more competition in the banking business.' " He argued that any claims made in the merger debate about the dangers of opening up the system to more competition have to be viewed in light of the fact that the government and the bankers have worked together to prevent competition until the last few years. "Then for the banks to come along and say, 'There is competition coming [from foreign banks], and the way we want to deal with it is to have less competition in this country' – it doesn't make any sense. What we're saying is, 'We believe in competition, we want to have more competition, and if we do, that in turn will increase the flexibility that government can allow our banks to have.' "

Martin stressed that killing the mergers was a policy decision based on the reports of the Competition Bureau and John Palmer, who runs the Office of the Superintendent of Financial Institutions (OSFI). But in the days after the government's ruling, some bankers said privately that the government had used the reports to prop up what was essentially a political decision. Nevertheless, Competition Bureau director Konrad von Finckenstein did find extensive cause for concern about the anti-competitive implications of the mergers. On the Royal–BMO deal, the bureau said competition between bank branches would be hurt in 104 of 224 local markets, many of them in rural areas. Businesses seeking loans of between \$1 million and \$5 million would be hampered by a "substantial lessening" of competition in British Columbia, Manitoba, Saskatchewan, Ontario, and Nova Scotia. And stock buyers would be disadvantaged as competition declined substantially in 39 of 63 markets where the activities of Nesbitt Burns (owned by the Bank of Montreal) and RBC Dominion Securities (owned by the Royal) overlapped. On the CIBC–TD merger, the bureau found it would lead to excessive concentration in 36 of 179 local markets, and would create unacceptably weak competition in mid-market loan business in the Yukon, Prince Edward Island, and the Northwest Territories. The bureau also predicted excessive concentration in one of 22 areas for the two banks' brokerages.

Despite these findings, officials at the highest levels at both the Royal–BMO group and TD–CIBC insisted they would have been able to meet the competitive concerns raised by the bureau had Martin given them a chance to follow up. This claim was expressed with particular vigour by officials at CIBC, which had less overlap with TD than was found in the Royal–BMO group. Some people at the banks also felt that Martin was using Palmer when he cited OSFI's concerns about the banks becoming too big. In his four-page letter to the finance minister, Palmer said OSFI's study did not uncover any reasons why the mergers would undermine the financial viability of either of the two new, combined banks. "OSFI is not able to identify any prudential reasons, in and of the two merger proposals themselves, why you should not consider them," the superintendent wrote. However, as Palmer noted, Martin had also asked OSFI to say whether it would be harder for the government to resolve any financial problems among the big, merged banks than it would be if the banks were smaller. The answer to this tautological question was, of course, obvious. As Palmer dutifully and ploddingly noted in his letter, bigger banks might make for more difficult problems if one of them got into trouble. The banks, who could easily have argued that being bigger would have made them less prone to getting into trouble in the first place, saw Martin's position on that issue as a speculative bit of argumentation they could never win.

Then there was the question of public opinion. In the interview, the finance minister insisted that the banks had "absolutely" misjudged public attitudes. Indeed, there was little doubt where Canadians stood. Prior to releasing its decision, the government had done $200,000 worth of private polling that showed that public attitudes had shifted against the mergers over the course of the year. In a November survey of 1,608 people, Earnscliffe Research found that 61 percent said it would be in the best interests of Canada to reject the deals. In a similar poll in May, 42 percent had been opposed. A similar growth in opposition was seen when Canadians were asked whether the mergers would benefit them personally. In November, 65 percent said blocking the mergers would be in their own best interests. In May, only 47 percent said the best thing for them personally would be the rejection of the mega-deals. One of the curiosities of these polls was that a majority of Canadians, even though they themselves were opposed to mergers, felt the government would approve them. In November, 55 percent of respondents said Ottawa would allow the consolidations. In May, 75 percent of those surveyed had expected a go-ahead from the government.

When CIBC chairman Al Flood finally broke the bank chairmen's self-imposed public silence in late January 1999, he admitted that the four pro-merger banks had made a mistake by pushing forward with their strategy before Martin's policy-review process could unfold. "We got out in front of the government and we got out in front of public opinion," he told reporters after CIBC's annual shareholders' meeting. "Our timing was wrong, we have to work in coordination with government policy," he said. Then, as the CIBC–TD team had often done in 1998, Flood blamed the strategic blunder on Royal and Bank of Montreal, whose merger announcement (which the CIBC chairman labelled a "pre-emptive strike") preceded the CIBC–TD merger plan by three months. "I wouldn't have done it myself," he said of the Royal–Bank of Montreal move. However, Flood added, "Once the cards are dealt, you have to play the game. But I think it would have been better if it had been a more coordinated approach." Nonetheless, Flood said, the year of study and national wrangling over the issue had helped Canadians to grasp the dimensions of change looming in financial services. "I think it is important that we understand the threats that are coming at us, not only as an industry but as a country, and how we will respond to that, and I think there is a much better understanding of that today than there was a year ago."

In the financial-services industry, with a halt brought to what Martin had once labelled the most important structural change ever, the talk turned to where things would go next. No one, not even Martin, expected Canada's financial-services sector to remain static. Elsewhere around the world, in the weeks just prior to Martin's decision, the merger craze had resumed with even greater ferocity than it had in 1997. And the Canadian financial industry was changing too, regardless of the fact that the Liberal government was demanding another few years to start making adjustments. On the very day Martin rejected the banks' merger strategy, as bankers pointed out ironically, the biggest discount brokerage operation in the world,

Charles Schwab Corp. of San Francisco, announced it was moving into Canada by buying an independent investment house.

Among the major Canadian banks, it was widely felt that the next step would have to be a strategic realignment to allow them to concentrate on their most profitable business lines while letting others go. In some cases, this approach was being demanded by large institutional investors. In others, it appeared to the banks' senior managers to be the only effective game plan. Within days of Martin's merger rejection, Standard & Poor's, the New York–based rating agency, raised a warning flag about four of Canada's big banks. It put the Bank of Nova Scotia and the National Bank on credit watch and downgraded its outlook to negative from stable on the Bank of Montreal and CIBC. "Following the Canadian government's veto of the proposed mergers, the banks will have to rethink their strategies in several business areas which may lead to increasing focus on specialized services," said Tanya Azarchs, director of Standard & Poor's financial-institutions ratings group.

Would all this mean that the Canadian banks would cease to be full-service, national operations, shedding branches and jobs as they pursued niche strategies? No one knew. Most people were inclined to believe that the bankers' threats of wholesale closures and job losses – the so-called scorched earth policy – exaggerated. A month after Martin's decision, for instance, Matthew Barrett sent out what was meant to be a comforting letter to Bank of Montreal customers. "Let me assure you that this outcome [the government's anti-merger ruling] will in no way affect the quality of service you have come to expect from your bank," Barrett wrote. But there was no doubt change was coming. At CIBC's annual meeting in January 1999, Al Flood said the bank would continue to shake up its operations in the wake of a year when its profits were drastically hurt by the turmoil on world financial markets. In 1998, CIBC had let go about 500 people as it trimmed its operating cost base by $200 million. Another $100 million in cuts were expected as the bank reduced its presence in risky Asian and European markets and concentrated on its U.S. and Canadian business lines. "Our future strategies will be highly focused and disciplined with appropriate risk/reward benefits directed to our strengths in these markets," Flood told shareholders. He also announced that day that, as planned, he would be retiring in 1999.

Cleghorn agreed with Flood that Martin's decision would not freeze the industry in its current form. "I think, as far as the whole merger experience is concerned, this book is only volume one," he said. "It's like Sherlock Holmes. Don't kill all the players at the end of the last chapter, because you may want to have volume two, or even volume three." He went on to say, "Seriously, it's hard to predict, but there are going to be consolidations of business lines and there will be consolidations of institutions. I mean, if I went back ten years ago, I would have said it would be terrific if Royal Trust and the Royal Bank could get together because there would be some real strengths in combining, but I wouldn't have put a bet on the possibility of that happening. But it happened; it happened rapidly." (The Royal Bank bought the financially crumbling Royal Trust in 1993.) Cleghorn said mergers may not be out of the question forever. But for now, the banks would be looking for new strategies. "We have to spread our capabilities on both sides of the border. I'm not talking about the corporate-lending field or high-risk, high-yield [business]. I'm talking about personal and commercial banking and wealth-management activities." If the Royal Bank was going to expand into the U.S., he said, it would consider "partnerships or acquisitions, provided there are synergies [that bring cost benefits]."

However the new alignments in the financial-services sector take shape, the Royal chairman explained, there is a certain urgency. That's because it takes longer than most people realize to make the changes needed to stand up to new competitors. "Some people think that from the time a merger takes place, everything has changed. But it takes a long time to develop in a competitive way. When you see new forms of competition coming in – companies who are experienced at what they do, and they bring their scale, they bring their market clout – you're probably five or ten years away before meeting them effectively in the marketplace." He added, "It takes a long time to build up skills and get the right people and build up credibility for your product and so on, whereas somebody who has a recognized name, whether Canadian or coming from outside Canada, can start an awful lot faster."

Just as the Royal Bank would continue its efforts to become a North American force in wealth management, the Bank of Montreal was expected to use its beachhead south of the border, the Harris Bank of Chicago, to expand its operations in the U.S. And TD was expected to concentrate on its formidable discount brokerage operations, among other things. If the banks could manage it, this was just the kind of strategy the federal government favoured, according to Martin. "We're not saying that things are frozen in time," he said. "We think it's worthwhile getting the structure [of the industry] in place." The government does not take the position that "Canadian banks shouldn't become major North American banks," Martin revealed. "We want them to be major North American banks. Absolutely. All we're saying is we're not prepared to sacrifice the Canadian consumer for that to happen." As for the challenges of globalization and new technology, "There are many, many ways of meeting them," Martin asserted. "There's niche marketing, forming alliances, and bulking up through mergers. All are valid."

Even with the mergers dead, major battles still loomed. Chief among them was the banks' request that they be allowed to sell insurance and lease automobiles through their branches. Martin still had to come down with a decision on that issue, which was a part of the government's broader overhaul of the legislation governing banks, insurance companies, trust companies, brokerages, and other financial-services operations. In early 1999, indications were that the government would move quickly to bring in a package of consumer-protection measures aimed at these financial institutions. After that, the Liberals would try to develop a comprehensive set of reforms that would be likely to include greater leeway for credit unions to organize national networks, increased access to Canada for foreign banks in certain business areas, measures to spur new entrants in financial services, and rules to allow mutual life insurers to transform themselves into publicly owned companies. By itself, this so-called demutualization movement, which would give nearly two million Canadians a $10-billion windfall, would quickly inject fresh momentum into the upheaval in the country's financial sector. The new public companies would be banned from merger activity for two years, as decreed by Ottawa, to give them time to adjust to their new status. But after that, they would be free to pursue acquisitions of their own, or could become takeover targets themselves.

The struggle for control of Canada's most profitable business was almost certain to go on at a fierce clip. "We expect change in our industry will continue at an accelerated pace," Flood told CIBC shareholders in early 1999. "This will be spurred on by changing demographics; the expanded use of digital technology; faster and more accessible communication systems; continuing growth of the capital markets, both wholesale and retail; new and stronger competitors; and a more sophisticated and independent customer who will have more choice than ever before." Dominic D'Alessandro, the astute president of Manulife Financial, the country's largest mutual insurer, also said Martin's refusal of mergers would not halt the shake-up in financial services. If anything, the upheaval would move faster as the banks looked for other acquisitions and mergers with insurance firms, trusts, or other financial companies. "The thrust of the banking system into related activities such as insurance is going to be more pronounced as a result of their frustration at not being allowed to merge," he predicted in an interview.

As the dust settled after Martin's ruling, the impression that the banks had "blown it" by failing to sell the merger idea gained wide currency. But was that really what had turned this grand corporate adventure into an all-time disaster? Asked shortly after Martin's announcement about Prime Minister Chrétien's view of the banks, a well-placed source in the Liberal government said, "The PM's views may be complex. On the one hand, he served on the board of directors of TD Bank [and so understands the business] . . . [but] I think he resents the role that the Canadian banks have played in the dilution of the dollar." (It was commonly believed in early 1998 that currency traders at the banks were ruthlessly driving down the value of the falling loonie to bolster their companies' trading profits. The banks, of course, denied this.) The source went on to say, "I think that he wishes they were more bullish on Canada [and] on selling Canada abroad. And I know from his members of Parliament, from his caucus – all he ever hears about the banks is grief and complaints, and I think that the whole approach to this merger [by the banks] was one of overweening arrogance and presumptuousness that really turned him off."

In a reference to the opinion prevalent in the Prime Minister's Office during the year-long bank debate, the source said, "There was never a desire to approve the mergers. If the Competition Bureau had been positive, it would have made it more difficult to kill the mergers and we would have had to worry about the 'just-playing-politics' [accusations]." In fact, the source said, there was a strong inclination at the highest levels of the Liberal government to kill the proposed deals right away. As this option was discussed, however, "there were people initially saying, early on, that we should wait to see [the] MacKay [report] before turning down the deals," the source recounted. "And the prime minister wondered aloud whether we should actually do that or whether we should just say no. This was months and months before the Ianno report [in November]." In the end, the prevailing view was that the government should wait until all the reports were completed before taking action. "If we didn't want to be accused of playing games, we had to endorse the process. The prime minister was more inclined to go quickly, but he agreed with that view," the source revealed.

In the days after the government's decision to halt the mergers, Chrétien sat for the usual round of year-end television and print interviews. His handlers kept pushing the prime minister to talk about the government's rejection of bigger banks, but "there was never an opportunity," the source said. Then he added: "That's the problem when it's a good, politically popular decision by the government – it dies pretty quickly."

INDEX

Index